THE IMPACT
INVOLVEMENT O
ACADEMIC AC

NIDHI PANDEY

TABLE OF CONTENTS

CHAPTER 1

INTRODUCTION

"Education is a shared commitment between dedicated teachers, motivated students and enthusiastic parents with high expectations."-Bob Beauprez

1.1 Introduction

Adolescents are the future of the human society. To achieve positive progression and development of the society at large, all round development and mental stability of adults during their adolescence is a quintessential prerequisite and should thus receive utmost priority from the adults (parents, teachers and peers) who may be directly or indirectly related to adolescents parents, educators and members of our society unequivocally acknowledge that adolescence is a critical period for physical, emotional and mental development that will ultimately provide adult life contentment and a sense of achievement. Researchers across the world have reiterated that 13-19 years of age are the most fascinating years of growth when children experience not only physical transformation but also undergo hormonal changes. These changes lead adolescents to adopt both positive and negative outlook / decision making when they come at the crossroads in life.

Parents, educators and psychologists around the world have been found to show keen interest in identifying various factors which might positively affect Adolescents' 'Academic Achievement' and 'Behaviour Adjustment'. This research aims to determine how and to what extent, Parental and Teacher's Involvement influences the achievements and 'Behaviour Adjustment' of teenagers. Comprehensive knowledge of this subject may not only help to recommend 'Parenting Practices' but also 'Policies, Practices and Activities of Educational Institutions', with both working in tandem towards the common goal. It may also facilitate teachers in devising a roadmap for their involvement, while aiming for improved Academic results and 'Behaviour Adjustment' in teenagers. The research may help in designing and developing a concrete plan for Parental and Teacher's Involvement, including constructs that eventually may get identified which have most positive and powerful impact in adolescents. Epstein et al. (2002), through their work, harmonised that "When parents, teachers, students, and others view one another as partners in education, a caring community forms around students and begins its work". The partnership activities ought to facilitate them to guide, connect and motivate adolescents to achieve triumph not just academically but also behaviourally.

1.2 Adolescents and their Characteristics

WHO (2015) defines 'Adolescents' as "Individuals in the 10-19 year age group". In India, Adolescent age is defined as children in the range of 10-19 years. American Psychological Association (APA, 2002) further adds that "During the adolescence period, major changes occur at varying rates in physical characteristics, sexual characteristics and sexual interest, resulting in significant impacts on body image, self-concept and self-esteem. Major cognitive and social developments take place as well".
Kasomo (2006) in his research said "Adolescence is a stage in human life when rapid changes take place during which an individual grows physically, mentally and socially while his personality develops new dimensions".
According to Hall (1904) "Adolescence is a period of 'storm' and 'stress' where major physical changes takes place causing major psychological changes. It is crucial period of life filled with changes, difficulties and special problems, 'turbulent' and 'unstable', a time of self discovery and self assertion". Casey et al.(2008) states that reasons for these are mainly the biological changes which cause mood swings, along with the fact that their minds are however still developing to comprehend the same.

1.3 Need of the Study

The researcher being from the field of education has experienced first-hand the dilemma of parents to get involvement in the adolescents' life. Having travelled the length and breadth of the country in the capacity of an army officer's wife, the researcher has observed the struggle of parents closely. The researcher in her duties as the principal and a teacher in various aided and unaided schools have gained diverse experience on the subject which has been the field of her core competence. Throughout the journey, as a principal and teacher, it has been the researcher's observation that some parents outdo other parents when it comes to involvement in their child's school activities, while in certain other instances parents were observed to be indifferent about their child's activities, whether academically or socially. The researcher observed that some teachers were more forthcoming in helping adolescents in their difficult times, whether emotionally or academically, while few others were complacent with only completing their task. Some teachers took initiative in making their class more interesting through various aids, teaching methodology, etc. and also helped children in coping with their adolescent quandary and stress management.

During the literature review it became evident that one of the most intriguing topics of interest for researchers and educators across the globe has been the relationship of adolescents with parents as well as teachers. Over the years, various researchers from different countries have tried to understand and examine the Impact of Parental' and Teacher's Involvement on Adolescents' life, with focus on their wellbeing, Academic excellence, happiness quotient and motivation to name a few.

Literature review has revealed on the one hand that children's Behaviour, as observed both in and outside school, is closely related to the family dynamics and the home environment, while on the other hand it has also recognised that teacher's role in adolescents' life is multidimensional and has high potential to influence emotional wellbeing and mental health of adolescents.

When all the stakeholders namely parents, teachers, students and others view each other as partners in education, they form a kind community around the students for their synchronised betterment. students were also observed to behave better when they perceived teachers as caring and responsive, along with support and motivation from parents to perform well in school.

The need of this study arises as the researcher found very few studies related to the involvement of both parents and teachers and their individual / combined impact on Adolescents' 'Academic Achievement' as well as 'Behaviour Adjustment' / emotional wellbeing. During the literature review, there were rarely any studies which took into consideration views of all stakeholders, specifically adolescents, parents and teachers and presented results after comparison of data. Some studies just focused on teacher's Involvement and its impact on either Adolescents' 'Academic Achievement' or emotional wellbeing or both while some studied the impact of Parental' involvement on these aspects. There were hardly any research studies which deliberated the impact of both Parental and Teacher's Involvement on Adolescents' 'Academic Achievement' and / or 'Behaviour Adjustment', which gave an impetus to the researcher for choosing this inadequately addressed topic for her study.

In contemporary times, in many cases both parents are working and their busy working schedules might not offer them opportunity to spend adequate time with their children, thus leading to considerable decline in their adolescents' mental wellbeing, loss of focus, inhibited problem solving ability and declining Academic results. On the other hand, with a diverse teaching faculty, skewed teacher-Student ratio and excessive syllabus in school, teachers might not get to know each Student individually, thereby making adolescents feel awkward to approach their teachers for seeking help in solving their problems in academics or in personal life. Another viable reason for difference in opinion, expectation and acceptable behaviour of adolescents with the adults in their life i.e parents and teachers is generation gap. Things which the adolescents feel and accept as normal behaviour may not be acceptable for their parents or teachers causing them to feel frustrated or misunderstood. This feeling of being unimportant or uncared, both by parents and teachers, can lead to adolescents feeling alienated from studies, school and peers and may lead them to depression. The state of poor mental wellbeing, inadequate Academic performance and resulting hopelessness for a reasonable future may lead them to seek solace in easier but high risk pitfalls like drugs, violence, sexual misconduct, etc. They could either become a recluse or a rebel; they might either start spending more time with peers or take respite in the virtual world of friends and games. Spending too much time with peers might alienate adolescents further from their parents deepening the gap while time on internet can cause them to fall prey to internet evils like pornography, frauds, addiction to games, etc. The 'Blue Whale Challenge' amongst others has been lately in news for targeting such susceptible adolescents and manipulating them to take their own lives. Events of such nature compel us to rethink the significance of parents and teacher's role in adolescents' life. There is a need to re-evaluate and revise the roles of parents and teachers according to changing times and requirement. Involvement of parents and teachers need a scrutiny and fresher perspective. Conscious efforts are required to understand the evolving needs of adolescents so as to facilitate parents and teachers to make necessary changes in their involvement for helping and guiding adolescents in a better way with the aim of achieving overall development.

All above aspects led the researcher to the need for finding the impact of parental and teacher involvement on behavioural adjustment and academic achievement of adolescent students.

1.4 Conceptual Framework

Adolescence is a noteworthy developmental period when foundation is laid for the transformation of a young child into an adult. It is a very vital and trying time for adolescents as they experience tremendous changes, both emotional and physical, that negatively or positively influence their life. The changes might develop a fresh dimension to adolescents' personality, which others, especially adults around them may fail to assess. The indifferent attitude of adults may lead to frustration in the adolescent and could affect his or her emotional wellbeing and / or concentration in Academic work. Therefore, it becomes essential to identify the constructs that influence development in adolescents.

The development stage is commonly the period from 10 to 19 years of age, between childhood and adulthood, when adolescents experience changes in biological, cognitive and socioeconomic domains. The period may cause radical changes in children's physical, mental and social aspects, adding new dimension to their personality.

The researcher studied plethora of models and theories by various eminent researchers and educators to form a framework of the current study. Few important studies that the researcher found indirectly or directly related to the current study are enumerated in the succeeding paragraphs.

1.5 Sinbadi's Development Indicators

Sinbadi A.M in Gicharu & Sinbadi (2013) classified development indicators of Adolescents into categories of Independent Variables, Dependent Variables and Intervening Variables.

Figure 1 illustrates development indicators by Sinbad A.M.

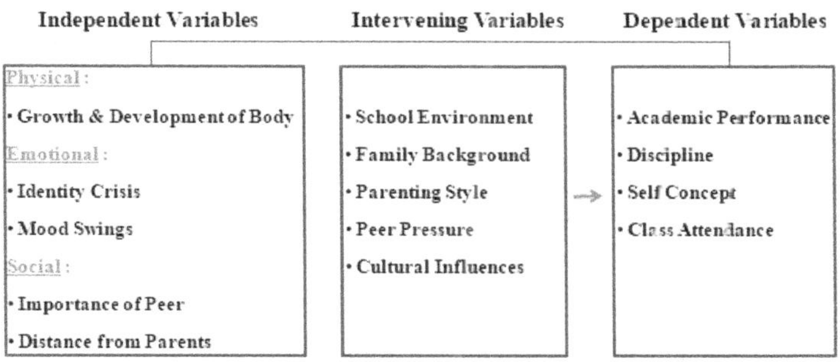

Figure 1. : Development Indicators of Adolescents as per Sinbad A.M.

https://www.ijsr.net/archive/v5i7/SUB158426.pdf

1.5.1 Independent Variables

The word 'adolescence' is derived from the Latin word 'adolescere' which means 'to grow'. So the essence of the word adolescence is growth, which represents a period of rigorous growth and changes in almost all aspects of an adolescents' physical, emotional, mental and social life. These variables do not get influenced by external factors and are intrinsic to adolescence in general and can therefore be termed as Independent Variables.

1. **Physical.** Adolescence is a phase with some remarkable visible physical changes like the deepening of voices and broadening of shoulders in boys while breast development and first menstrual periods for girls. It is noteworthy that physical appearance usually assumes overriding importance for both girls and boys although the timings for these physical changes might vary for different adolescents. They are observed to spend hours worrying about their appearance, predominantly in order to 'fit in' with the norms of the peer group they most identify with. At the same time, they yearn to have their own exclusive style, and may be found spending hours in the bathroom or in front of the mirror trying to achieve this desire These changes could lead to anxiety, low self esteem and low self consciousness in adolescents resulting in Behavioural and Academic problems in them.

2. **Emotional Behaviour.** Emotional development during adolescence involves establishing a realistic and logical sense while relating to others, discovering to handle stress and emotional management. Adolescents may also suffer from identity crisis; this takes into account how adolescents perceive themselves right now and also what they may and would like to become. Hormonal changes sometimes may lead them to consider themselves as a child on some occasion while at other times they could

consider themselves as adults, consequently resulting in mood swings, anger, outbursts, frustration, etc.

3. **Social Behaviour.** One of the most apparent changes in adolescence is that the centre of adolescents' world, around which their whole life revolves, shifts from their family to their friends or peer group. Acceptance by peers is the primary priority for adolescents and they would be willing to do anything to get socially accepted by them. This might cause stress and loss of focus whilst attraction towards opposite sex may add confusion in their life and mind. Facing self crisis as they transcend from a child into an adult may cause indecisiveness and irritation

1.5.2 Dependent Variables

The most noteworthy fact about adolescence is that it is a phase of transition from childhood to adulthood. It has been observed that transition from one stage to another is always associated with some problems and adolescence is not an exception. Adolescents have to face few problems due to various changes in physical, emotional as well as social domains, also known as Independent Variables. There are other aspects which depend on external factors and these aspects can be categorised as Dependent Variables. A range of studies indicate that in absence of proper guidance, adolescents could easily divert to wrong activities which might lead to problems like Behavioural issues or indifference for studies. Santrock (2010) reveals that "Adolescents who are unable to establish positive identity may perform poorly in schools since they lack successful adult with whom to identify and may develop negative identity". Following can be classified as Dependent Variables :-

1. **'Academic Achievement'.** Academic Achievement has always been acknowledged as one of the significant goals of education around the world. It could be defined as the measured performance of a present level of Student knowledge through a series of standardised educational tests held in school. More frequently the term is used to depict performance in the curriculum subjects. 'Academic Achievement' or performance can be described as the degree to which a Student, teacher or the institution has accomplished their short or long-term educational goals.

2. **'Discipline'.** Discipline is derived from Latin word 'disciplina' which means "teaching, learning". This includes how adolescents obey rules and follow code of behaviour.

3. **'Self Concept'.** Self Concept is self-evaluation or self perception, a representation of sum of the individual's beliefs about his or her own attributes. It reflects how an adolescent evaluates himself or herself in domains like confidence, knowledge, friendliness, etc.

4. **'Attendance'.** It refers to students attending or missing school and their inclination to do the same.

1.5.3 Intervening Variables

The above described Dependent Variables are directly or indirectly affected by external factors or Intervening Variables namely parents, teachers, friends, home and school environment, etc. These Intervening Variables have an immense role to play and their endeavour should be able to redirect adolescents in a proper manner, positively affect the Dependent Variables and also help adolescents to cope up with the problems associated with the age.

1. **'School Environment'.** Role of school and teachers in adolescents' life cannot be undermined, for they spend a lot of time with them too. Teacher's Involvement can be defined as the process where they influence students learning and promote life skills by utilising their professional proficiency, personal attitude, and social abilities. Moreover, teachers can also contribute through participation in education management, by fortifying a democratic school culture and by participating in the design, implementation and assessment of education policies. Teachers can develop relationships with adolescents through emotional support, as well as by their approachability, in terms to regularity and uniformity to children's needs. Teachers predominantly are essential for adolescents who are going through profound shifts in their personality and are at the same time struggling to comprehend the changing relationships with their parents and peers. Teachers being at an advantageous position, away from these struggles, can provide a safer perspective for support and guidance and at the same time can convey the correct advice, adult value and perspective. Teacher's indifference to adolescents' problems, bias attitude, lack of ability to help them in academics, etc. may lead to frustration in children and may lead to further problems in Behaviour, emotional or Academic aspects.

2. **'Family Background' and 'Parenting Style'.** This includes degree and manner in which the parents express their interest in the schooling of their child through motivational, cognitive and affective support. 'Parental Involvement' in their child's life

includes various forms like providing a secure and stable environment, good Parenting at home, Parent-Child discussion, imparting positive social and educational values, intellectual motivation, inspiring for personal accomplishment and good citizenship. School level involvement of parents may include their participation in various school events, regular contact with teachers and schools to share information and participation in school management, etc. parents have an essential role in a child's life. They are the first teacher to their child; they not just facilitate them to build good character but also prepare them for formal schooling. Educators worldwide agree that an adolescents' Behaviour is affected by their family life and Parental support is a positive factor to bring out better Achievement in teenagers. The 'Parental Involvement' can be measured though regular communication with school, involvement in Parent Teacher meetings, following their child's progress, supervision of their homework and guidance in academics. There are certain factors that are predictive of misbehaviour among adolescents, for instance conflicts at home, negligent or passive Parenting styles, inept problem solving, etc. Adolescence being a phase of transition can be quite overwhelming and baffling for both adolescents and parents. In absence of proper understanding, acceptance and guidance, the relationship may get strained sooner or later, leading to emotional, social, psychological, Behavioural and Academic problems.

3. **'Peer Pressure'.** Peer pressure is the direct influence by peers on adolescents, the effect of getting encouraged to follow peers through changing their behaviour, values or attitudes to match to those of the influencing group or individual. The results can either a positive or negative effect, or both.

4. **'Cultural Influences'.** Culture is the societal system, values and beliefs that adolescents follow. It has strong influence on their development and behaviour. Family rituals and good communication can have a positive effect on adolescents. Parents instilling positive cultural values and beliefs in their children could help improve their self-esteem and academic success.

1.6 Keith et al Model

Keith et al.(1993) in the very widely cited study collected data from about 22,000 8th grade students with the aim of establishing causal relationship between Parental support and 'Academic Achievement' of adolescents. The model hypothesises a well examined and pan-culture relationship of 'Parental Involvement' and 'Academic Achievement' using Structural Equation Modelling (SEM) technique. Four variables were observed to show best fit for the causal model relating to parental involvement and students' achievements. Figure 2 illustrates variables underlying 'PI Constructs' in Keith et al.

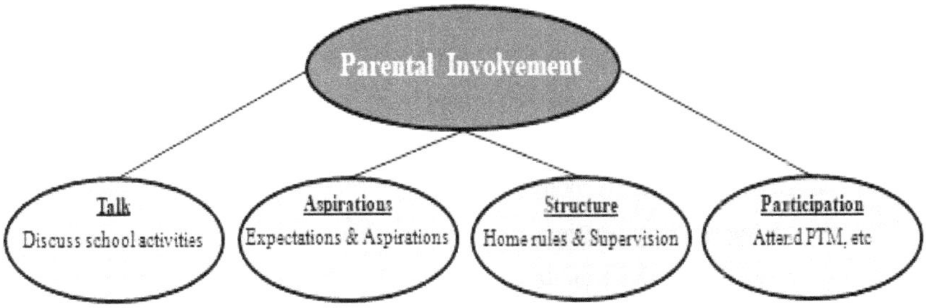

Figure 2. : Variables Underlying 'PI Construct'

1.6.1 Variables of the study

The variables underlying 'PI Constructs' in Keith et al shows different types of 'Parental Involvement' which are as follows :-

1. **Talking about school.** Parent-Child communication regarding school and related activities come under this variable. It was observed that such talking improved relationship between parents and children and also developed better understanding between them. Communication between parents and child was found to be associated positively with better 'Academic Achievement'.

2. **Aspirations / Expectations.** Aspiration and expectation of parents for their child's future was established as a variable to play a key role in their 'Academic Achievement'.

3. **Structure in the Home.** This variable reflected the extent to which the environment at home was structured in the form of rules. Positive home environment helped the students to concentrate better, which would in turn motivate them to improve their 'Academic Achievement'.

4. **Participation in school Activities.** Teacher Parent communication was also found to be a major variable for students' achievements. This includes parents' participation in school activities like Parent-Teacher meetings, Parent-Teacher activities, volunteer work, fund raising, attending school events, etc.

1.7 Epstein's Six Types of Involvement

Epstein et al. (2002) has developed a recognised framework in the world of education which is valuable for 'Parental Involvement'. She has identified as well as defined six types of 'Parental Involvement' across a spectrum which includes all levels of participation. In the framework, Epstein implied that guardians who were conversant and engaged in their children's trainings can bring positive impact in their child's attitude and performance. The six types of involvement interactions in the framework classify Behaviours, responsibilities and deeds performed by the parents with the aim of improving academic achievement of their children. As per Epstein, some parents engage in multiple activities from the defined types while some are able to focus on only one of the types. Figure 3 shows the types of parental involvement.

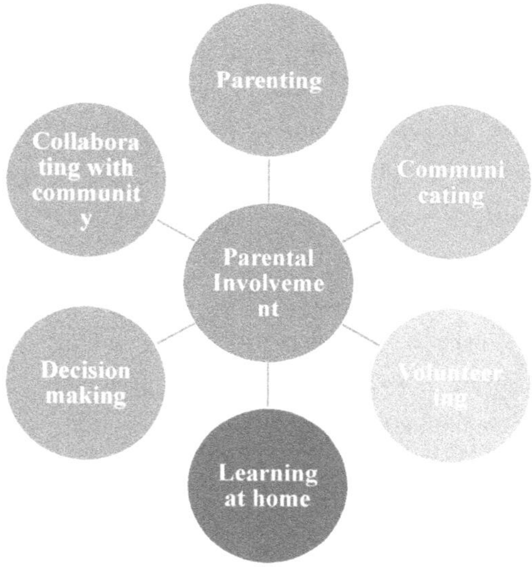

Figure3. : Types of Parental Involvement

17.1 Parenting.

Parenting is very vast term including parents' activities facilitating children from their birth till they attain adulthood and are mature enough to take their own decisions. Following are few examples covering parenting :-

(a) Child-rearing skills i.e. how parents adapt to the situations and aid their child to grow.

(b) Understanding the child and adolescent development and assist accordingly.

(c) Setting home conditions supporting children at each and every stage of their Academic life.

1.7.2 **Communicating.**

Communication is an integral part of 'Parental Involvement'. It includes parents' interaction with school and vice a versa about school programs and their child's progress. It is imperative to have meaningful interaction between parents and school.

1.7.3 **Volunteering.**

It includes parents volunteering in various activities at school or outside so as to support their child and school. The activities can range from accompanying to school trips, giving motivational lectures, etc.

1.7.4 **Learning at Home.**

'Parental Involvement' at home in their child's Academic work like helping in homework or project completion, curriculum related activities and facilitating in taking Academic related decisions are all part of supporting Student learning at home.

1.7.5 **Decision Making.**

This focuses 'Parental Involvement' in school decision making through PTA, school council, committees and other Parent organisations. Parents' initiative in giving advice for school governance, advocacy and policy making is included in decision making.

1.7.6 **Collaborating with Community.** This involves parents' willingness and efforts to coordinate with society to use their resources and services for betterment of students and to fulfil their requirements. The effective collaboration with community with the aim of helping the students is taken into account.

1.8 Hoover-Dempsey and Sandler Model

The model represents decades of research on family involvement by Hoover-Dempsey and Sandler through various models designed in the years 1995, 1997, 2005, and 2010.

Figure 4 illustrates Hoover-Dempsey and Sandler Model of the Parental Involvement Process. The model is structured in five levels and tries to answer three vital questions :-

1. Why do or don't families become involved in their children's life ?
2. What families do when they are involved ?
3. How family involvement makes a positive difference in student's outcome ?

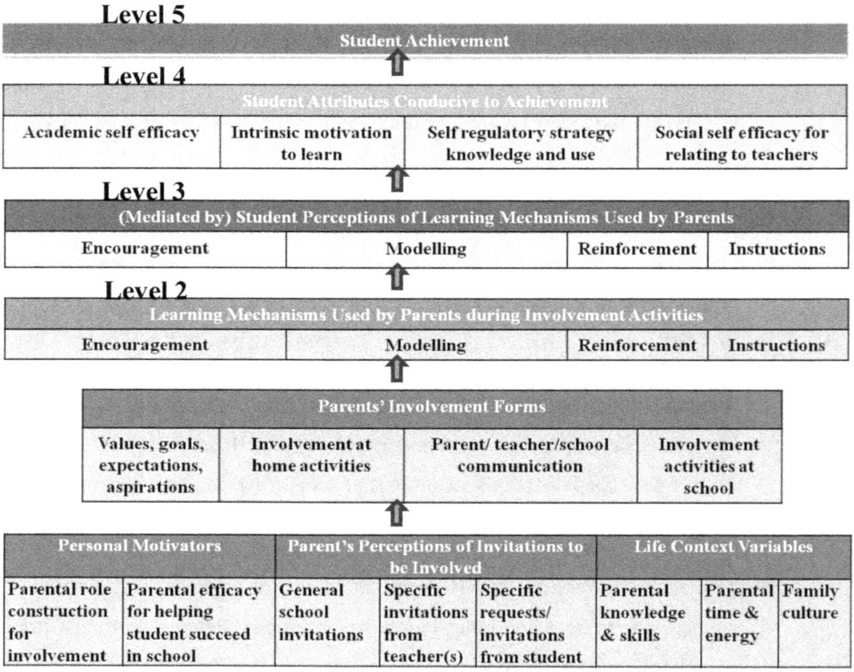

Figure 4. : Hoover-Dempsey and Sandler Model of 'Parental Involvement'

https://www.researchgate.net/publication/270509163_Model_of_Parent_Engagement_in_Academic_Support_Focus_on_students_with_Disabilities/figures?lo=1

1.8.1 Level 1.

The model begins with parents' motivation for involvement in their children's education (Level 1) with following parameters :-

(a) **Personal Motivators**. Parents' motivation for involvement, which is a key reason, is based on the social systems to which they belong. For instance, parents' role Structure and sense of usefulness are influenced by their own childhood experience of family and Academic experiences, their family systems or one of the experiences in the school systems that their children attend.

(b) **Parents' Perceptions of Invitations to be involved.** 'Parental Involvement' depends quite a much on their perception of invitation from school (school feels welcoming, staff members are cordial, etc.), Teachers (Teacher's invitation to attend Parent Teacher meeting, specific request for providing support at home for learning, etc.) and their own child (explicit invitation – showing disinterest in attending school, asking help specifically; implicit invitation – struggling to complete a project or procrastinating homework).

(c) **Life Context Variables.** An important variable influencing 'Parental Involvement' is their understanding of their own skills and knowledge. Parents may be reluctant to get involved if they believe their skills or knowledge are inadequate. Time and energy available with parents also play a role in their getting involved. Family culture may also play a significant role in how parents get involved in supporting their child's learning.

(d) **'Parental Involvement'.** The model further defines several forms of involvement :-

(i) **Values, Goals, Expectations and Aspirations.** This involves parents' communication about their values, expectations and aspirations from their children for Student learning. This communication of goals and expectations shapes the students' beliefs and Behaviour related to learning (as seen in Level 4).

(ii) **Involvement in Activities at Home.** The model also recognises the involvement of families at home in supporting the Student learning at home and also monitoring and reviewing home work.

(iii) **Family school Communication.** Students' academic progress is influenced by effective family school communication characterised by careful listening, mutual respect and school responsiveness to parents' questions, ideas and suggestions.

(iv) **Participation in school Based Activities.** Sometimes teachers assume that parents who are not at school are not involved but as we study the model further we get important cue that involvement at school is not necessarily a good indicator of parents' actual span and level of involvement.

1.8.2 **Level 2.**

The model argues that parents influence the Student aspects necessary for school success through four kinds of activities namely :-

(a) **Encouragement.** This involves parents' unequivocal support for students' active engagement in activities related to school projects and learning.

(b) **Modelling.** Parents, as role model for students, can influence through their interests, attitudes and Behaviours which can be linked to successful learning (e.g. motivation to learn, use of goal setting and strategy Adjustment).

(c) **Reinforcement.** This involves parents' use of positive and appropriate reward to children for their learning Behaviours and efforts.

(d) **Instruction.** These involve parents' actions with children in form of giving instructions either in indirect manner (e.g. home Structure) or direct (e.g. teaching).

1.8.3 Level 3.

In this level, the model states that the 'Parental Involvement' activities are of no use until and unless students perceive their parents' actions. Student perceptions of their parents' use of the four mechanisms is an essential measure of how parents' beliefs and Behaviours get translated into qualities that lead to Academic success.

(a) **Encouragement.** When children perceive the encouragement done by their parents, it will contribute to their success.

(b) **Modelling.** Parents attending meetings and events at school or asking their child about the school day are a way of modelling the importance of education to their child.

(c) **Reinforcement.** This involves children working hard or getting motivated due to promised rewards and positive reinforcement by parents.

(d) **Instruction.** When children take the instructions given by parents in a positive manner, it will aid in better leaning outcome.

1.8.4 Level 4.

The model describes the students as the creator of their Academic success. Following four beliefs and Behaviour of students are associated with their 'Academic Achievement' :-

(a) **Academic Self Efficacy.** This involves students' belief about their ability to complete school work successfully.

(b) **Intrinsic Motivation.** This involves students' interest in learning for their own sake rather than for external rewards.

(c) **Self Regulation.** This involves students' understanding and adopting Behaviour like self monitoring and goal setting which support successful learning.

(d) **Self Efficacy for Help Seeking.** This involves students' belief that asking for help along with interaction with teachers and knowledgeable elders will yield positive learning outcomes.

1.8.5 **Level 5.**

The ultimate goal of the Hoover-Dempsey and Sandler model is Student achievement. The model affirms that 'Parental Involvement', at different levels of the process, influences, and to some extent predicts, student outcomes.

1.9 PAR Theory

Parental Acceptance Rejection (PAR) theory by Rohner (2005) postulates that children respond mostly in the same way when they perceive themselves accepted or rejected by their parents or other important people irrespective of their socio-cultural or genders. Figure 5 represents Rohner's PAR theory.

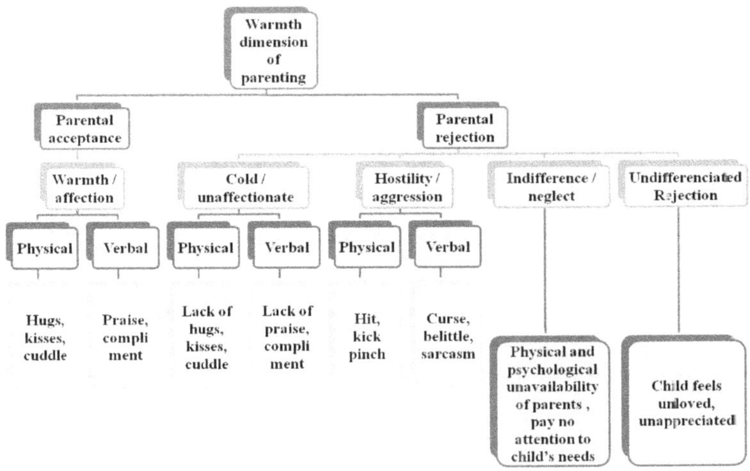

Figure 5. :Rohner's PAR Theory of Acceptance and Rejection
https://www.semanticscholar.org/paper/INTRODUCTION-TO-PARENTAL-ACCEPTANCE-REJECTION

1.9.1 Parental Acceptance.

Parental acceptance is parents' Behaviour expressing care, support and love for their children. It can be measured through the warmth quotient of parents as perceived by the children. PAR theory states that parents are affectionate when they act on their feelings of love. Affection or warmth can be shown either physically (e.g. hugging, kissing, etc.) or verbally (e.g. praising, complimenting, etc.).

1.9.2 Parental Rejection.

PAR theory asserts that Parental rejection can be experienced by any following four principle expressions :-

(a) **Cold and Unaffectionate.** The cold and unaffectionate Behaviour of parents is reflection of their internal or psychological state which can be classified into physical (lack of hugs, kisses, etc.) or verbal (lack of praise, compliments, etc.). Alternatively, children might perceive to feel unloved or uncared by their parents.

(b) **Hostile and Aggressive.** Parents acting on feelings of hostility, anger or resentment can be termed as aggression. Sometime parents can be physically aggressive (e.g., hitting, pushing, throwing things and pinching) while at other instances they may be verbally aggressive (e.g. sarcastic, cursing, mocking, etc.).

(c) **Indifferent and Neglecting.** Parents sometimes are unable to pay attention to children's need or they may be unavailable when required by them. Sometimes neglecting might be a way of parents trying to cope up with their anger towards their children.

(d) **Undifferentiated Rejection.** When children start believing that their parents do not love them or care about them, without giving any clear Behavioural indicators that the parents are neglecting, unaffectionate, or aggressive toward them.

1.10 Affective Teacher-Student Relationships (TSR) and students' school Outcomes - By Roorda D. L. et al.

Roorda D.L. et al. created theoretical model in 2012 to study Teacher-Student relationship and its effect on Student engagement and Achievement. The model is based on social-motivational and extended attachment perspectives observed through meta-analysis of various studies. The fundamental idea of Attachment Theory is that positive relationships between parents and children aids in promoting feelings of security in children. Emotional security has been considered as an indispensable prerequisite for exploration of environment. As per extended attachment perspective, sensitive teachers could serve as a secure foundation facilitating children in exploring school environment and help them to engage in learning activities. The theories stimulating social-motivation perspective are Self-System Theory and Self-Determination Theory. According to the theories, children need three basic psychological needs fulfilled to get motivated: the needs are relatedness, competence and autonomy. Teachers supporting these needs would facilitate children to increase their engagement activities of learning and in turn improving 'Academic Achievement'. The model includes variables from both perspectives. Figure 6 illustrates theoretical model of TSR and students' school Outcomes.

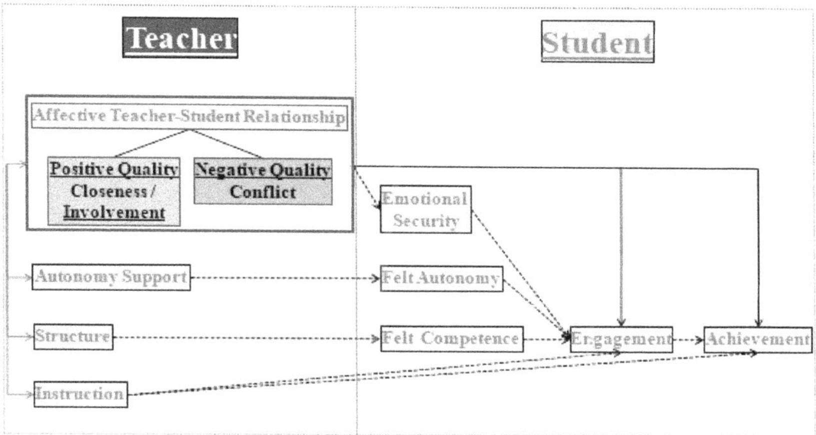

Figure 6. : Theoretical Model of TSR and students' school Outcomes

1.10.1 Teacher's Involvement

1. **Affective Teacher-Student Relationship**. Affective TSR includes positive and negative dimensions derived from Parent-Child Attachment Theory.

(a) **Positive Quality**.

(i) Includes Closeness, Empathy, and Encouragement for learning, etc.

(ii) Showing Involvement:- This parameter from socio-motivational perspective is included in positive quality of TSR and Includes caring, and expressing interest in the Student.

(b) **Negative Quality**. Includes Conflict, dependency, etc.

2. **Emotional Security**. It is a moderator between teacher's support and children's engagement in learning tasks. Hence, positive TSR could stimulate learning Behaviour in children and support them to deal with demands of the school environment. On the other hand, negative TSR reveals lack of security and could hamper or interfere with the child's efforts to cope up with school demands.

3. **Autonomy Support**. Giving students freedom to make their own choices and observing connections between schoolwork and students' interests.

4. **Structure.** Include setting clear rules and its consequences.

5. **Instruction.** Clear instructions by teachers about expectation, teaching, etc.

1.10.2 Outcome Variables for students

1. **Students' school Engagement.** Students' engagement in learning is often found to mediate between TSRs and 'Academic Achievement', as described in social-motivation perspective, while engagement concept included various aspects that are :-

(a) **Behavioural.** Include participation in academics, extracurricular activity.

(b) **Emotional.** Include feelings and reactions to school, academics, teachers and classmates.

(c) **Cognitive.** Include thoughtfulness and willingness to invest in mastering of difficult skills and comprehension of complex ideas.

However, due to heterogeneity within and overlap between the components, the model therefore uses engagement as one and multidimensional concept.

2. **'Academic Achievement'.** 'Academic Achievement' predicts additional school success in terms of grades, marks and future career opportunities.

1.11 Epstein's Overlapping Spheres of Influence Model

Epstein et al. (2002) states repeatedly in their work that "school, family, and community partnerships are better term than 'Parental Involvement' to understand that parents, educators and others in the community share responsibility for students' 1learning and development".

The theory of 'overlapping spheres of influence' asserts that students learn more when parents, educators and others in the community work together to guide and support students' learning and development. In this model, home, school and community are the three categories which overlap with unique and combined influences on children through multi-variant interactions of parents, educators and community. Figure 7 illustrates the theory of overlapping spheres.

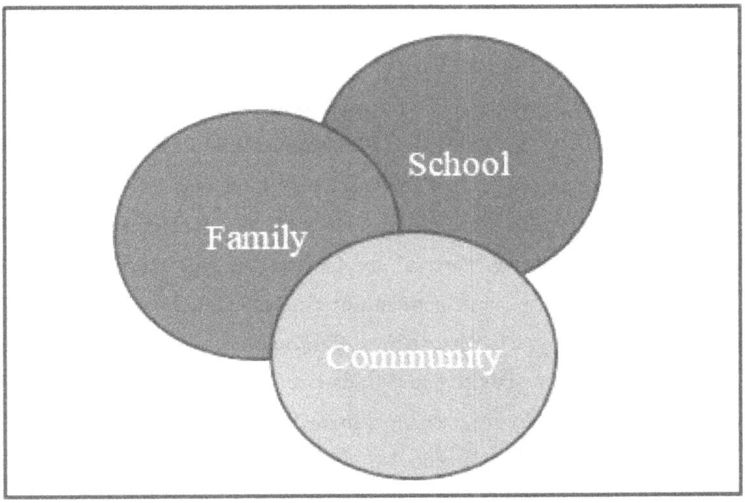

Figure 7. : Theory of Overlapping Spheres

https://theroadlesstravelledby.com/2017/09/28/schools-families-and-community-overlapping-spheres-of-influence/

Theory of overlapping spheres of influence shifts attention from the narrow focus of 'Parental involvement', from what an individual Parent does, to a broader, more realistic representation of how influential people in the three categories may work together to contribute to students' education and development. The model emphasises and recognises the importance of relationship between family, school and community in an adolescents' life for their development in a collaborative and complementary manner.

School and family's partnership including number of shared activities maximise interaction between the two spheres. The model highlights reciprocal relationship amongst teachers, families and students. It also recognises that students are the core agent in school family relations.

1.11.1 **Overlapping Spheres**

The spheres are influenced by three factors that may push them together or pull apart :-

1. **Force A – Time.** The spheres were found to overlap more during students' preschool and primary school years as parents were more eager to interact with teachers to know about their child's progress in school or any problem faced. The interaction decreased with the middle school. Parents generally have a tendency to give more attention to the child who is doing well or just started to have problems rather than one who has been experiencing difficulties for a long time.
2. **Force B – Characteristics, Philosophies and Practices of the Family.** The overlapping of spheres increases with increase in parents' participation in their child's education. For example if parents get involved in school activities overlapping increases. An important reason for 'Parental Involvement' in their children's education at home and at school is their perception of encouragement by the teachers and school.
3. **Force C – Characteristics, Philosophies and Practices of the school.** Similarly, teacher's activities also influence 'Parental Involvement' in school. For example, a teacher may seek 'Parental Involvement' by asking children to find out about the work their parents do. school family partnership programs implemented by the school have proved to be the greatest predictors of 'Parental Involvement'.

The model presumes that exchange of interest, skills and abilities between parents and Teachers is based upon mutual respect and sharing of common goals of benefitting children's learning and development.

1.12 Rationale of the Study

The Parent-Child -Teacher relationship has received considerable attention, with special emphasis on impact of Parental and Teacher support on the life of children. Over the years, researchers have examined the influence that children's experiences with these relationships may have on their functioning.

Findings indicated that Teacher and 'Parental Involvement' were primary predictors of 'Academic Achievement'. Parental support was apparent in a home environment where the child's self-determination or the experience is nurtured thereby improving their understanding, perceived competence and self-regulation. Ample researchers have found positive relationship between 'Parental Involvement' and 'Academic Achievement' of adolescents (Keith et al., 1993; Shute et al., 2009; Green et al., 2007).

Various studies have been done to find links between Parent-Child 'relationship quality' and 'relationship Adjustment' during the Student life of pre-elementary and middle school as well as in later adolescence (Fan , 1999; Gonzalez et al., 2005; Shute et al., June 2009; Badri et al., 2014; Smith , 2011).

Similarly, countless literature suggests that teachers play an imperative role in students' development, 'Academic Achievement' and psychological Adjustment (Pianta, 1999; Wentzel, 2002; Cattley, 2004; Fredriksen & Rhodes, 2004; Blazer, 2016). These research studies support the view that children having better teacher relationship perform better and achieve more than those who have disturbed or casual relationship. Children may look to their teachers for the same kind of security and emotional response as they do to their Parent. It was observed that changes in "perceptions of Teacher's support" predicted changes in both self-esteem and depression among middle school students, such that students who perceived increasing teacher support showed corresponding decrease in depressive symptoms and increase in self esteem and vice versa (Fredriksen & Rhodes, 2004). Therefore, the school and the family serve as the most sustaining and influential context that surrounds and shapes a child's development in today's world.

When parents, teachers, students and others view one another as partners in education, a caring community forms around students and begins its work (Epstein et al., 2002).students behaved better when they perceived responsiveness and care from teachers along with support and encouragement from parents to perform well in school (Sanders, 1998). Studies across the culture reiterate that simultaneous support from family and school positively affect child's attitude about self, academics and society as a whole.

In today's fast changing world, the dynamics of the relationship between adolescents with their parents as well as teachers has also changed. Busy lifestyle, working parents, peer pressure, digital distraction, nuclear family, changing concept of school, teacher's detachment, teaching styles, etc. are some of the aspects affecting these relationships.

The present study thus aims at learning about the relationships with the aim of finding best practices that positively affect the adolescents' 'Academic Achievement' and 'Behaviour Adjustment' to the best of their capability.

The present study aims at collecting data through specially designed questionnaires from adolescents, parents and teachers about their view on impact of both Parental as well as Teacher's Involvement on 'Academic Achievement' and 'Behaviour Adjustment', and then to find best practices and parameters through analysis of collected data.

Since most of the available research studies, while considering the impact of each of the variables in isolation, have only recommended but not adequately analysed the cumulative impact of all the variables, thus there exists a gap to study and analyse the combined impact of Teacher's support and 'Parental Involvement' on the 'Academic Achievement' and 'Behaviour Adjustment' of Adolescents.
The inter-related gaps which have been analysed in this research are as follows :-

1. Impact of Parental & Teacher's Involvement on Adolescents.
2. Impact on 'Academic Achievement' as well as 'Behaviour Adjustment'.
3. Comparative assessment of responses from :-
(a) Adolescents and Parents.
(b) Adolescents and Teachers.
(c) Parents and Teachers.
4. Gender difference in perception of Adolescents.
5. Explicit definition of Constructs of PI.
6. Explicit definition of Constructs of TI.

1.13 Aim of the Study

The aim of the current study is to analyse data from the viewpoint of adolescents, teachers and parents to find the impact of involvement by both parents and teachers on 'Behaviour Adjustment' and 'Academic Achievement' of adolescents so as to identify constructs that positively facilitate in improving both the aspects of adolescents. These constructs would not only act as a guide to parents and teachers in assisting the adolescents to improve their 'Behaviour Adjustment' as well as 'Academic Achievement' but also be a valuable addition to the body of knowledge for researchers worldwide.

"Impact of Parental & Teacher Involvement on Behaviour Adjustment and Academic Achievement in Adolescent students."

1.14 Statement of the Problem

To find the impact of Parental and Teacher Involvement on Behaviour Adjustment and Academic Achievement in Adolescent students.

1.15 Objectives of the Study

The objectives of the current study are :-

1. To study the impact of Parental Involvement on Academic Achievement of the students in their Adolescent years.
2. To study the impact of Parental Involvement on Behaviour Adjustment of the students in their Adolescent years.
3. To study the impact of Teacher's Involvement on Academic Achievement of the students in their Adolescent years.
4. To study the impact of Teacher's Involvement on Behaviour Adjustment of the students in their Adolescent years.
5. To compare responses from adolescents, parents and teachers.
6. To ascertain gender difference of adolescents in the following variables :-

(a) Parental Involvement.

(b) Impact of Parental Involvement on Academic Achievement.

(c) Impact of Parental Involvement on Behaviour Adjustment.

(d) Teachers Involvement.

(e) Impact of Teacher's Involvement on Academic Achievement.

(f) Impact of Teacher's Involvement on Behaviour Adjustment.

7. To ascertain which constructs of Parental Involvement impact Behaviour Adjustment of the students in their adolescent years.
8. To ascertain which constructs of Parental Involvement impact Academic Achievement of the students in their adolescent years.
9. To ascertain which constructs of Teacher's Involvement impact Behaviour Adjustment of the students in their adolescent years.
10. To ascertain which constructs of Teacher's Involvement impact Academic Achievement of the students in their adolescent years.

1.16 Research Questions

Following questions have been addressed with the help of this research :-

1. How do Adolescents rate Parental Involvement in their life, both at home and at school and its impact on their Academic Achievement and Behaviour Adjustment?
2. How do Adolescents rate Teacher's Involvement and its impact on their Academic Achievement and Behaviour Adjustment?
3. How do parents' rate their involvement in their child's life, both at home and at school and its impact on their Academic Achievement and Behaviour Adjustment?
4. How do Teacher's rate their involvement in their student's life, and its impact on their Academic Achievement and Behaviour Adjustment?
5. How do parents rate Teacher's Involvement and its impact on their Adolescent child's life?
6. How do Teachers rate Parental Involvement and its impact on their Adolescent child's life?
7. Which constructs of Parental Involvement do adolescents perceive to positively impact Academic Achievement of Adolescents?
8. Which constructs of Parental Involvement do adolescents perceive to positively impact Behaviour Adjustment of Adolescents?
9. Which constructs of Teacher's Involvement do adolescents perceive to positively impact Academic Achievement of Adolescents?
10. Which constructs of Teacher's Involvement do adolescents perceive to positively impact Behaviour Adjustment of Adolescents?
11. How can parents and teachers improve their involvement to achieve better Academic Achievement and Behaviour Adjustment of Adolescents?

1.17 Hypothesis Formulation

Following 'Null Hypotheses' have been considered for the research :-

1. There is no significant impact of Parental Involvement on Academic Achievement for total adolescent sample.
2. There is no significant impact of Parental Involvement on Behaviour Adjustment for total adolescent sample.
3. There is no significant impact of Teacher's Involvement on Academic Achievement' for total adolescent Sample.
4. There is no significant impact of Teacher's Involvement on Behaviour Adjustment' for total adolescent sample.
5. There is no significant relationship in the mean scores of adolescents' response and parents' response towards Parental Involvement.
6. There is no significant relationship in the mean scores of adolescents' and teachers' response towards Teacher's Involvement.
7. There is no significant relationship in the mean scores of parents' response and teachers' response towards Parental Involvement.
8. There is no significant relationship in the mean scores of parents' response and teachers' response towards Teacher's Involvement.
9. There is no significant relationship between the mean scores of adolescents' response and parents' response towards impact of Parental Involvement on Academic Achievement.
10. There is no significant relationship between the mean scores of adolescents' response and parents' response towards impact of Parental Involvement on Behaviour Adjustment.
11. There is no significant relationship between the mean scores of adolescents' response and teachers' response towards impact of Teacher's Involvement on Academic Achievement.
12. There is no significant relationship between the mean scores of adolescents' response and teacher's response towards impact of Teacher's Involvement on Behaviour Adjustment.
13. There is no significant gender difference of adolescents in the following variables :-

(a) Parental Involvement (PI).

(b) Impact of PI on Behaviour Adjustment (BA).

(c) Impact of PI on Academic Achievement (AA).

(d) Teacher's Involvement (TI).

(e) Impact of TI on Behaviour Adjustment (BA).

(f) Impact of TI on Academic Achievement (AA).

14. There is no significant impact of following constructs of PI on BA as perceived by adolescents :-

(a) Emotional.

(b) Aspiration.

(c) Structure.

(d) School & Studies.

(e) Friends.

15. There is no significant impact of following constructs of PI on AA as perceived by adolescents :-

(a) Emotional.

(b) Aspiration.

(c) Structure.

(d) School & Studies.

(e) Friends.

16. There is no significant impact of following constructs of TI on BA as perceived by adolescents :-

(a) Emotional.

(b) Interaction with parents.

(c) Instrumental.

(d) Structure.

17. There is no significant impact of following constructs of TI on AA as perceived by adolescents :-

(a) Emotional.

(b) Interaction with parents.

(c) Instrumental.

(d) Structure.

1.18 Variables the study

Following variables are included in the current study-

1.18.1 **Independent variables-**

1. Parental Involvement
2. Teacher Involvement

1.18.2 **Dependent variables-**

1. Behaviour Adjustment
2. Academic Achievement

1.19 Conceptual Definition of Key Terms

1.19.1 Parental Involvement.

According to Brito & Waller (1994) parent's involvement includes various activities ranging from an impersonal once a year visit to school to regular parent-teacher meetings and active participation in school governorship. Tomlinson (1991) upholds that parental involvement in schools might take one of four forms namely exchange of information; personal involvement in educational matters; formal involvement in school governing; and informal involvement in administrative matters through the parent association. Fullan (1982) on the other hand also identified four forms of parent involvement such as instruction at home, instruction at school, school governance, and community service.

1.19.2 Teacher Involvement.

According to Vieno et al. (2005) teacher support is a measurement of school connectedness and bonding. It is related to student's sense of belongingness, being accepted and receiving help when required within the school. Furman (1996) and Furman & Buhrmester (1985) identified elements of teacher support as bonding, social support, instrumental support and shared activities.

1.19.3 Behaviour Adjustment.

Behavioural performance or adjustment, as described by Carey (2009) deals with the following six BASICS elements namely Behavioural competence (Relation with others), Achievement (school work and play), Self- relation (Self assured or troubled), Internal status (thoughts and feelings), coping (adaptive or coping style or ability) and symptoms (any physiological functions or dysfunctions).

1.19.4 **Academic Achievement.**

According to APA Dictionary of psychology, Academic achievement in educational psychology is "A level of proficiency in scholastic work in general or in a specific skill, such as arithmetic or reading. Evidence of future academic achievement is usually based on the results of standardized ability tests and assessment of performance by a teacher or other supervisor".

1.20 Operational Definitions

1.20.1 **'Parental Involvement'.**

In the present research study 'Parental Involvement' includes looking after, or monitoring a child's activities at home and in school during Adolescent years. Following constructs of 'Parental Involvement' have been used in the present study :-

1. Emotional Involvement (helping in personal problems, counselling, etc.).
2. Aspiration (discussing future goals, motivation to achieve them, etc.).
3. Structure (keeping a tab on TV/internet usage, making timetable for studies, etc.).
4. School & Studies (helping in assignments, track progress in Academic).
5. Involvement with friends (inviting friends at home, getting to know friends, etc).

1.20.2 **'Teacher Involvement'.**

In the present research study 'Teacher Involvement' includes motivating, monitoring and influencing a child's activities in school during adolescent years. Following constructs of 'Teacher Involvement' have been used in the present study :-

1. Emotional (to know likes/dislikes of students, help in personal problems, etc.).
2. Interaction with parents (PTM, updating on important issues, etc.).
3. Instrumental (Innovative teaching, use of aids, etc.).
4. Structure (deciding rules of the class and explaining its importance, maintaining discipline, etc.).

1.20.3 **Impact on 'Academic Achievement'.**

In the present research study 'Impact on Academic Achievement' is the extent to which students achieve their short or long term educational goals. Grades of previous exam along with responses from questionnaire given to adolescents, parents and teachers were taken into consideration to measure impact on academic achievement.

1.20.4 **Impact on 'Behaviour Adjustment'.**

In the present research study 'Impact on Behaviour Adjustment' is the extent in which the adolescents are able to cope up to ever changing environment at home, outside and in school. Responses from questionnaire given to adolescents, parents and teachers were taken into consideration to measure impact on behaviour adjustment.

1.21 Procedure

For the present research study, theoretical models were developed by the researcher on the basis of extensive study conducted on the related existing body of knowledge. Further, a set of questionnaire was formulated by the researcher and vetted by seven renowned experts for adolescents, parents and teachers each. The data was then collected from adolescents, their parents and teachers of class 9th from CBSE schools of Mumbai city. Once the data was collected, it was analysed by the researcher using various descriptive and inferential analysis techniques and hypothesis was tested. The final stage involved documenting the results and inferences of the research. The models designed by the researcher which enabled her research are enumerated in the succeeding paragraphs.

1.22 Model 1

For Measuring Impact of Parental Involvement

A model is an abstract way of schematising a process, so that the strategy can be generalised to solve similar problems in other fields. This model is inspired by PI Constructs' in Keith et al. and is aimed at finding the relationship between 'Parental Involvement' and 'Behaviour Adjustment', 'Parental Involvement' and 'Academic Achievement'.'Parental Involvement' is further divided into five constructs namely 'Emotional Involvement', 'Aspiration of Parents', 'Structure by Parents', and 'school & Studies Involvement'.

'Emotional Involvement' is the support parents give to their child to help him / her emotionally during adolescent years, 'Aspiration of Parents' refers to how the parents convey their future aspirations for their child so as to inspire and motivate them. 'Structuring by parents' takes account of the daily routine and timetable parents make to organise their child's life. 'School & Studies Involvement' consists of the activities parents participate with respect to their child's school and studies. 'Involvement with

Friends' comprises the extent to which the parents involve themselves with their child's friends.

The model tries to establish impact of 'Parental Involvement' with the help of above constructs on 'Behaviour Adjustment' as well as 'Academic Achievement' in adolescent students. Figure 8 shows the proposed model for measuring impact of 'Parental Involvement' on 'Behaviour Adjustment' and 'Academic Achievement'.

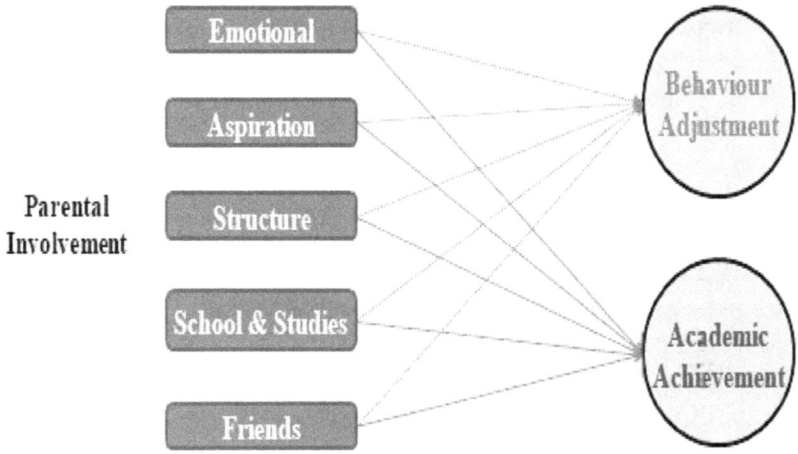

Figure 8 : Model Measuring impact of 'Parental Involvement' on 'Behaviour Adjustment' & 'Academic Achievement'

1.22.1 **Research Questions**

Following research questions will be answered through the above model :-

1. Whether Parental Involvement (PI) will impact 'Academic Achievement' (AA) ?
2. Whether Parental Involvement (PI) will impact 'Behaviour Adjustment' (BA) ?
3. Whether Emotional Involvement, Aspiration, Structure, school & Studies, and Friends will impact 'Academic Achievement' (AA) ?
4. Whether Emotional Involvement, Aspiration, Structure, school & Studies, and Friends will impact 'Behaviour Adjustment' (BA) ?

1.22.2 **Hypothesis**

1. PI will positively impact AA.
2. PI will positively impact BA.
3. Following constructs of PI will positively impact AA :-

(a) Emotional Involvement.

(b) Aspiration.

(c) Structure.

(d) School & Studies.

(e) Friends.

4. Following constructs of PI will positively impact BA :-

(a) Emotional Involvement.

(b) Aspiration.

(c) Structure.

(d) School & Studies.

(e) Friends.

1.22.3 **Model Fit**

Model Fit is comparing the theoretical model with sample data. Five Fit Indices have been used to assess the Model Fit. Fit Indices used to assess the Model Fit are CMIN / DF, CFI, GFI, PNFI and RMSEA.

1.22.3.1 **Definitions**

Definition of Fit Indices (Table 1) are as follows :-

1. **CMIN / DF (Minimum Discrepancy as Indexed Chi-square).** CMIN [chi-square statistics (χ 2)] is the minimum value of discrepancy. In case of maximum possibility estimation, CMIN contains the chi-square statistics. The overall measure of how many implied moments differ from sample moments is known as chi-square statistic.

2. **CFI (Comparative Fit Index).** The Comparative Fit Index (CFI) is the analysis of the Model Fit by examining the discrepancy between data and the hypothesised model and in the process adjusts the issues of sample size inherent in the chi-squared test of Model Fit and the scaled Fit Index.

3. **GFI (Goodness of Fit Index).** The Goodness of Fit Index (GFI) is a measurement of fit between observed covariance matrix and the hypothesised model. The GFI range between 0 and 1, with a value of over 0.9 is generally indicative of acceptable Model Fit.

4. **PNFI (Parsimonious Normal Fit Index).** Parsimonious Normal Fit Index (PNFI) adjusts degrees of freedom. It is considered lower in goodness as compared to other indices. Though there is no threshold level for PNFI but value greater than 0.5 is acceptable.

5. **RMSEA (Root Mean Square Error of Approximation).** The Root Mean Square Error of Approximation (RMSEA) is used to avoid issues of sample size by analysing the discrepancy between optimally chosen construct estimates and the population covariance matrix with the hypothesised model. The RMSEA ranges from 0 to 1, wherein smaller values indicate better Model Fit.

Table 1 shows the Fit Indices of the Model.

Table 1 : Fit Indices of the Model

Fit Indices	Observed	Criteria for Acceptable Fit	Result
CMIN/DF (Minimum Discrepancy as Indexed Chi-square)	1.701	Less than 5	Acceptable Fit
CFI (Comparative Fit Index)	0.957	More than 0.9 for Good Fit. Between 0.9 to 0.8 for Borderline Fit.	Acceptable Fit
GFI (Goodness of Fit Index)	0.953	More than 0.9	Acceptable Fit
PNFI (Parsimonious Normal Fit)	0.568	More than 0.5	Acceptable Fit
RMSEA (Root Mean Square Error of Approximation)	0.053	Less than 0.08 for Adequate Fit. Between 0.08 and less than 0.1 for Borderline Fit.	Acceptable Fit

1.22.3.2 **Result of Fit Indices**

As revealed in Table 1, all the five Fit Indices (CMIN/DF, CFI, GFI, PNFI and RMSEA) show a good fit between the hypothetical model and the sample data. Model Fit summary is attached in Appx D.

1.22.4 **Model Validation on Using Path Analysis**

Path analysis is a minor version of Structural Equation Model (SEM) developed by Sewall Wright, a geneticist in 1918. With time, it is now widely used in other areas in physical science, social science and sociology. Path analysis can be conducted using statistical programs including SPSS, STATA, etc. The method is also known as causal modelling, analysis of covariance structures, and latent variables models. It is an advanced statistical tool used to establish relationship between several variables simultaneously. It is a form of multiple regression analysis used to evaluate causal models which examines the relationship between dependent variable with two or more independent variables. This method can estimate both magnitude and significance of causal connections between the variables. Path analysis has following major benefits over other predictive models :-

1. It can fit theoretical model to sample data.
2. It can study direct, indirect and total impact.
3. Use of maximum probable techniques to compute path analysis.
4. Better understanding of causal relationship between independent variables with dependent variable.
5. Useful to evaluate causal hypothesis.
6. Clarifies correlation.
7. Indicates the strength of causal hypothesis.

1.22.4.1 **Assessing the Significance of Path**

In Path analysis, a path diagram is constructed where relationship between variables and causal direction between them are laid out. Before conducting a path analysis, an input path diagram is constructed which illustrates the hypothesised relationships where the researcher uses arrows to show relationships between variables. For instance if an arrow points from A variables to B, it implies that A variable is hypothesised to influence variable B. Data is then fed into the variables and hypothesis testing is done on it. The path coefficients, standard errors, and P values are calculated with statistical software (The researcher used SPSS Statistical Software) With P values, frequently the criterion $P < 0.05$ is used instead $P \leq 0.05$ for accepting a hypothesis.

The p-value for each term tests the null hypothesis. If the coefficient is equal to zero, it indicates no impact. A low p-value (< 0.05) indicates that the null hypothesis can be rejected while a higher p-value (> 0.05) indicates that the null hypothesis can be accepted.

Figure 9 illustrates the Path Coefficients for all the linkages of the Model.

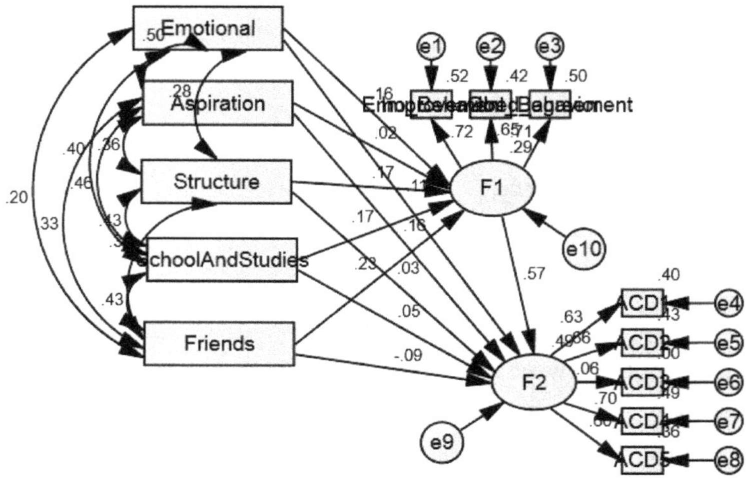

Figure 9 : Path Coefficients of the Model

1.23 Model 2

For Measuring Impact of Teacher's Involvement

Figure 10 illustrates 'Model for Measuring impact of 'Teacher's Involvement' on 'Behaviour Adjustment' and 'Academic Achievement' and is inspired by the theoretical model of Affective Teacher-Student Relationships (TSR) and students' school Outcomes by Roorda D. L et al.

1.23.1 Research Questions

Following research questions will be answered through the above model :-

1. Whether Teacher's Involvement (TI) will impact 'Academic Achievement' (AA) ?
2. Whether Teacher's Involvement (TI) will impact 'Behaviour Adjustment' (BA) ?
3. Whether Emotional Involvement, Interaction with Parents, Instrumental Support & Structure will impact 'Academic Achievement' (AA) ?
4. Whether Emotional Involvement, Interaction with Parents, Instrumental Support and Structure will impact 'Behaviour Adjustment' (BA) ?

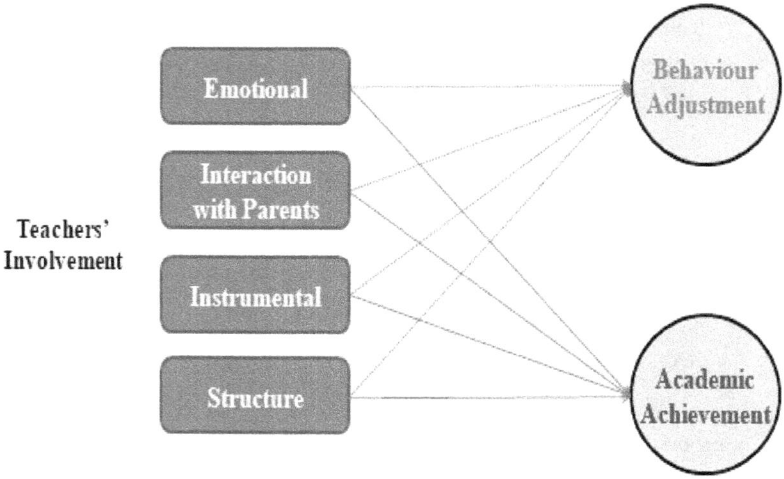

Figure 10 : Model Measuring impact of 'Teacher's Involvement' on 'Behaviour Adjustment' & 'Academic Achievement'

1.23.2 Hypothesis

1. TI will positively impact AA.
2. TI will positively impact BA.
3. Following constructs of TI will positively impact AA :-

(a) Emotional Involvement.

(b) Interaction with Parent.

(c) Instrumental Support.

(d) Structure.

4. Following constructs of TI will positively impact BA :-

(a) Emotional Involvement.

(b) Interaction with Parent.

(c) Instrumental Support.

(d) Structure.

1.23.3 Model Fit

Model Fit is comparing the theoretical model with sample data. Five Fit Indices have been used to assess t he Model Fit. Fit Indices used to assess the Model Fit are CMIN / DF, CFI, GFI, PNFI and RMSEA.

Table 2 shows the Fit Indices of the Model.

Table 2 : Fit Indices of the Model

Fit Indices	Observed	Criteria for Acceptable Fit	Result
CMIN / DF (Minimum Discrepancy as Indexed Chi-square)	2.32	Less than 5	Acceptable Fit
CFI (Comparative Fit Index)	0.86	More than 0.9 for Good Fit. Between 0.9 to 0.8 for Borderline Fit.	Borderline Fit
GFI (Goodness of Fit Index)	0.915	More than 0.9	Acceptable Fit
PNFI (Parsimonious Normal Fit)	0.59	More than 0.5	Acceptable Fit
RMSEA (Root Mean Square Error of Approximation)	0.073	Less than 0.08 for Adequate Fit.. Between 0.08 and less than 0.1 for Borderline Fit.	Acceptable Fit

1.23.3.1 **Result of Fit Indices**

As revealed in Table 2, all the five Fit Indices (CMIN / DF, CFI, GFI, PNFI and RMSEA) show a good fit between the hypothetical model and the sample data. Model Fit summary is attached in Appx E.

1.23.4 **Assessing the Significance of Path**

Figure 11 illustrates the Path Coefficients for all the linkages of the Model.

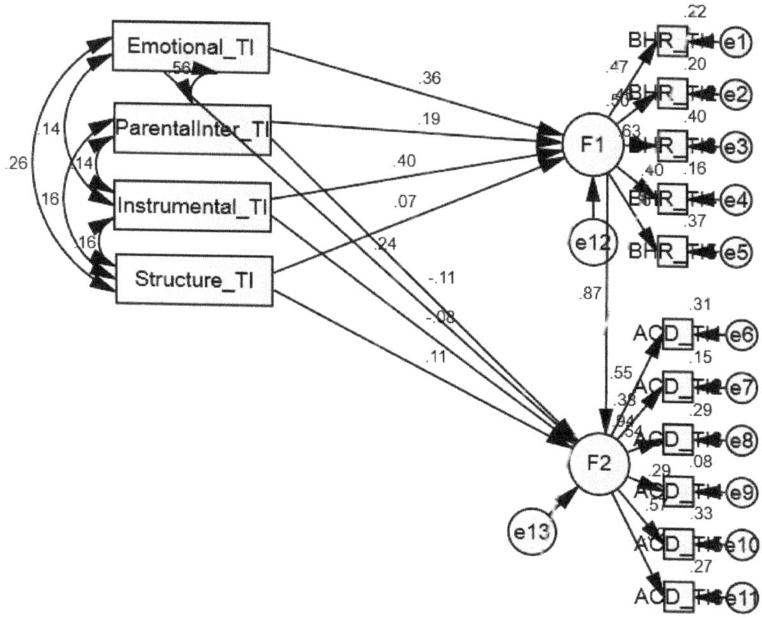

Figure 11 : Path Coefficients of the Model

1.24 Model 3

For Measuring Impact of Parental & Teacher Involvement

The model is inspired by Development Indicators of Adolescents from Sinbad A.M. PI Constructs' in Keith et al. and theoretical model of Affective Teacher-Student Relationships (TSR) and students' school Outcomes by Roorda D. L et al. The endeavour of the model is to find relationship between Parental and Teacher's Involvement with 'Academic Achievement' and 'Behaviour Adjustment'. Figure 12 illustrates 'Model for measuring impact of Parental and Teacher Involvement on 'Behaviour Adjustment' and 'Academic Achievement'.

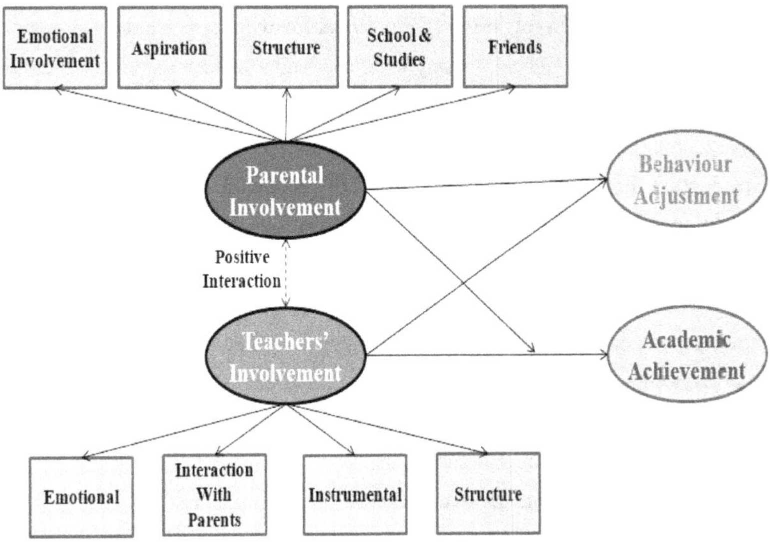

Figure 12 : Model Measuring impact of Parental & Teacher Involvement on 'Behaviour Adjustment' & 'Academic Achievement'

1.24.1 **'Parental Involvement'**

In the present research study, the researcher has considered 'Parental Involvement' as activities including looking after or monitoring a child's activities at home and in school during adolescent years. She further classified Parental Involvement into following constructs :-

1. **Emotional Involvement.** Emotional Involvement includes emotional wellbeing of adolescents through expressing love, care and understanding to their child so that he / she feel confident to share his / her problems and emotional needs with them. Their availability of time, interest and emotional support is reflected in adolescents' perception for their parents' emotional involvement which was measured through questions like "My parents take out time and sit with me whenever I have faltered", etc.
2. **Aspiration.** This involves parents' discussing about their as well as their child's ambitions and aims in life. Parents guiding and explaining different options that can be pursued by their child which will help him / her to choose a goal and decide his / her aspirations. Perception of adolescents with relation to Aspiration of Parents as an indicator of Parental Involvement was measured through questions such as "My parents discuss with me my career options", etc.
3. **Structure.** This involves parents' monitoring and Structuring their child's daily activity or routine for studies, sports, screen time, etc. Stating clear expectations and rules; maintaining discipline via mechanisms as taking out time and explaining the mistake and motivating him / her to correct and using punishment as a last resort can be termed as Structuring by Parents. Adolescents were asked to rate their parental involvement for Structuring at home through questions like "My parents keep a tab on my daily usage of TV / internet", etc.
4. **School & Studies.** It includes parental involvement in their child's studies and school activities, their organised and unorganised interaction with teachers and guidance at home for studies. Adolescents rated parents for their help and guidance to improve their grades and accomplishments in school activities through questions such as "My parents take out time to teach me and help me in my assignments", etc.
5. **Friends.** Friends being a very crucial element of being an adolescent can't be ignored. Adolescents tend to get affected by how their parents treat their friends. Involvement of Parents in The present research study includes parents' interaction with their child's friends, organising events and activities with them, knowing them personally or guiding their child about whom to be friends with. adolescents perceived

their parental involvement with their friends through questions like "My parents get involved in all the activities with my friends like movie, picnic, etc", etc.

1.24.2 **Impact of Parental Involvement on 'Behaviour Adjustment'**

Adjustment can be described as the process by which living organisms maintain a balance between the needs and the circumstances Shaffer L.F(1961). Kulshrestha S.P. (1979) explained that the Adjustment process is a way for individuals to deal with tensions, stress, conflicts, etc., that come along the way to meet his or her needs. In this process, the individual also attempts to maintain a harmonious relationship with the environment. UNICEF (2011) report estimated that around 20 percent of the world's adolescents have mental health or behaviour problems. To understand 'Behaviour adjustment' in adolescents, problem behaviour and social competence are important criteria. Social competence can be measured in school through participation in class discussions, cooperation with classmates, completion of work, etc. while at home the parameters could be spending time with family, discussing personal issues and following instructions, etc. Problem Behaviour in class can be assessed though analysing items such as anxiety, disruption in class and difficulty following directions. Similarly, at home, lack of socialising, tantrums and aloofness can be signs of problem Behaviour.

In the present research study, 'Behaviour Adjustment' has been considered as the extent to which the adolescents are able to cope up to ever changing environment at home, outside and school.

Adolescents' perception of Parental' Involvement and its impact on Behaviour was observed through constructs like supportive emotional environment at home that made adolescents comfortable to ask questions or share their personal problems, improvement in Behaviour due to parents' intervention, discipline and rules for life.

Perceived impact on 'Behaviour Adjustment' was measured through questions like "My problems get solved whenever I approach my parents", etc.

1.24.3 **Impact of Parental Involvement on 'Academic Achievement'**

'Academic Achievement' has been explained as measured performance of a present level of Student knowledge through a series of standardised educational tests held in school. More frequently the term is used to depict performance in the curriculum subjects. 'Academic Achievement' or performance can be described as the degree to which a Student, teacher or the institution has accomplished their short or long-term

educational goals. It is also an indicator of mental wellness of an adolescent and unexpected fall in the performance could be a precursor of mental stress owing to some external factors. Numerous methods are useful in measuring the Academic performance including standardised Achievement test scores, report cards, grades and teacher ratings. In the present research study, the researcher has considered 'Academic Achievement' as the extent to which students achieve their short or long term educational goals. Cumulative marks or grades are also representative of 'Academic Achievement'.
students' descriptions of Parental' involvement and maintaining a supportive environment, that help and guide them to perform better academically and / or help them achieve their short term and long term goals for 'Academic Achievement', were used to measure impact of Parental' involvement on 'Academic Achievement'. Perceived impact on 'Academic Achievement' was measured through grades in previous exams along with questions like "My parents monitoring of my grades motivates me to perform better academically", etc.

1.24.4 **Process of Analysis of Questionnaires**

1.24.4.1 **Adolescents' Questionnaire**

The response set for all the questions utilised a 5-Point Likert Type Scale in order to match the previous items and be easier for students to use with choices ranging from 'Never' to 'Very Often'. The negatively worded items were reverse coded for scoring purposes.

The items in the section of the adolescents' questionnaire asked adolescents to react to various statements regarding 'My parents' wherein they were instructed to consider about either of the Parent or both, as applicable, for individual questions before they started marking the answers.

1.24.4.2 **Parents' Questionnaire**

Parents' questionnaire carried same questions but worded from parents' point of view to compare the perception of parents and adolescents for 'Parental Involvement' in all sub groups namely emotional, aspiration, structure, school & studies and friends.

1.24.5 **'Teacher's Involvement'**

In the present research study, the researcher has considered 'Teacher's Involvement' as activities including motivating, monitoring and influencing a child's activities in school during adolescent years. She further classified Teacher's Involvement into following constructs :-

1. **Emotional Involvement.** 'Emotional Involvement' involves teacher's support and interest in students' wellbeing along with their Academic progress. Teachers spending time, showing interest in students' life, their sense of caring and emotional support are some parameters which exceeds the 'required' teaching Behaviours and is reflected in students' perception of teacher's attempts to connect on an emotional level. Students were requested to rate their teacher's care for their wellbeing via questions like "My class teacher gives personal attention to every Student in the class", etc.
2. **Interaction with Parents.** 'Interaction with Parents' includes communication of teachers with parents in the form of feedbacks, counselling session, PTMs, etc. It also includes whether the teacher is able to recognise students' Academic and / or emotional distress. Students' perception about the interaction was measured using questions like "My class teacher keeps my parents updated about my performance in school", etc.
3. **Instrumental Support.** 'Instrumental Support' involves teaching practices which teachers incorporate to impart Academic concepts to the entire class and individual students, using diverse strategies (e.g. smart boards, group discussions, etc.) to provide additional learning experience. Students rated teachers for their help and guidance to improve their classroom grades and accomplishments through questions like "My class teacher uses teaching aids and innovative techniques (e.g. smart board, quiz, crossword, etc.) while teaching in class", etc.
4. **Structure Support.** 'Structure by Teacher's involves stating clear expectations, providing rewards, fair treatment and consequences, feedback for mistakes and ways for improvement, maintain discipline via mechanisms as taking out time and explaining the wrongdoer his / her mistake and motivate him / her to correct it and using punishment only as a last resort. Questions were asked to measure the perceived Structure support by Teachers as "My class teacher separately counsels me when I make any mistake", etc.

1.24.6 Impact of Teacher's Involvement on 'Behaviour Adjustment'

In the present research study, the researcher has considered as 'Behaviour Adjustment' as the extent to which the adolescents are able to cope up to ever changing environment at home, outside and school.

students' descriptions of Teacher's Involvement and creation of supportive emotional environment that made them comfortable to share their personal problems, ask questions, adjust their Behaviour as per rules, lead disciplined life, etc. were used to measure the impact of Teacher's Involvement on Behavioural Adjustment as perceived by adolescents. Perceived impact on Behavioural Adjustment was measured through questions like "I find my Teacher's instructions about the rules and its importance helpful to mould my Behaviour positively", etc.

1.24.7 Impact of Teacher's Involvement on 'Academic Achievement'

In the present research study, the researcher has considered 'Academic Achievement' as the extent to which students achieve their short or long term educational goals. Cumulative marks or grades are also representative of 'Academic Achievement'.
students' descriptions of Teacher's Involvement and creation of supportive environment, that help and guide them to perform better academically and / or help them achieve their short term and long term goals for 'Academic Achievement', were used to measure impact of Teacher's Involvement on 'Academic Achievement'. Perceived impact on 'Academic Achievement' was measured through grades in previous exams along with questions like "With constant monitoring of homework and assignment by my class teacher, I complete my homework and improve my assignments on time", etc.

1.24.8 Process of Analysis of Questionnaires

1.24.8.1 Adolescents' Questionnaire

The response set for all of the items utilised a 5-Point Likert Type Scale in order to match the previous items and be easier for students to use with choices ranging from 'Never' to 'Very Often'. The negatively worded items were reverse coded for scoring purposes. The questions in the section of the adolescents' questionnaire asked adolescents to react to various statements regarding "My teacher". However, since multiple teachers through the day taught participants, students assumed 'Class Teacher' as that teacher for marking the answers to avoid any confusion.

1.24.8.2 Teacher's Questionnaire

Teacher's questionnaire had same questions but worded from teacher's point of view to compare the perception of teachers and adolescent for Teacher's Involvement in all sub groups namely emotional, Interaction with Parents, Instrumental and structural support.

1.25 Limitations and Scope of the Study

The impact of Parental and Teacher Involvement was limited to adolescents' 'Academic Achievement' and Behaviour Adjustment only. The other variables like self concept, self esteem, creativity, study habits, stress, family dynamics and school type, etc. were not included This research was restricted to the students of standard 9th and did not include those studying at any other level of education in school or college. The present research study involved only the students studying through the CBSE Board and not ICSE, SSC, IGCSE or IE.

The variable 'Academic Achievement' was studied with respect to adolescents' 'Academic Achievement' in their previous exam along with responses from participants (parents, teachers and adolescents) related to increased interest / keenness to work towards 'Academic Achievement'. The 'Academic Achievement' under other existing cognitive domains was not under the scope of this study.

The variable 'Behaviour Adjustment' was studied with respect to adolescents' ability to adjust to their environment at home and school only, which could be confirmed by them or their parents and teachers. The Behaviour Adjustment included constructs as listed in the research definitions only. The unobserved 'Behaviour Adjustment', as well those that happened at places other than home and school were not under the scope of the present research study.

The sample included students from public and private schools of the CBSE Board. Schools situated in Greater Mumbai were only included for the present research study. The schools coming under the jurisdiction of Navi Mumbai and Thane were not included. The present research study was conducted in English medium schools and it excluded schools with other mediums of instruction such as Marathi, Hindi.

The present research study includes gender difference of adolescents response with respect to parents' and teacher's involvement and its' impact. No other constrains like financial status, parents' education level, parental style, home environment, social stress of the students, gender difference of parents & teachers, etc. were considered for the present research study. The present research study focused only on impact of parental and teacher's involvement on 'Behaviour Adjustment' and 'Academic Achievement' of adolescents. It purposefully did not include involvement by others and their impact, nor did it include variables other than 'Academic Achievement' and 'Behaviour Adjustment' which may have also got affected by Parental and Teacher's Involvement.

1.26 Significance of the Study

Adolescents are the bearers of humanity for the future generations of the free world. With such onerous responsibility lined up for their delicate shoulders, it becomes vital that they are raised as healthy, happy individuals and to achieve this it is imperative they get appropriate support from parents and teachers.

Over time, parental involvement and teacher involvement have proved very pertinent, keeping both practitioners and theoreticians in the field of education busy. The researcher observed that many national and international literature claimed that everyone concerned – students, parents, teachers, schools, society as a whole – will benefit if parents and teachers are convinced to get involved in their children's education.

The present research study advocates that, in spite of the popularity of the concept, parental involvement and teacher involvement concepts are still vague, and their impact is rather unclear. This research study shall prove beneficial in understanding the scope of parental involvement and teacher involvement and also their impact on behaviour adjustment and academic achievement in adolescents. Parents are willing to give their support to their adolescent child at home and at school too but are often apprehensive or clueless as to how they could participate in their child's life. This research study helps them to not only understand their role but also how to guide their adolescent child to gain maximum benefit.

The research study also provides teachers with a framework to aid their students to improve their academic performance and interpersonal interactions. The significance of the present study is to facilitate all round development of adolescents with focus on 'Behaviour Adjustment' and 'Academic Achievement'. The researcher emphasises that parents and teachers should shoulder responsibility to show adolescents the right direction to improve themselves and this research helps in the same.

The present research study focuses on parental and teacher's involvement on adolescents studying in class 9th and its impact on adolescents' 'Behaviour Adjustment' as well as 'Academic Achievement'. Since scarcely any studies have been done in the past on this topic and it is the gap in the existing body of knowledge, the present research study is beneficial in filling these gaps.

The present research study is helpful to the schools, parents, teachers and students as it gives an understanding about how exactly the parental and teacher involvement in adolescent years can help in quantifiably improving the 'Academic Achievement' and 'Behaviour Adjustment'.

This research study throws light upon various constructs of parental and teacher involvement which facilitates in recommending parental and teachers involvement procedures beneficial for the 'Academic Performance' and 'Behaviour Adjustment' of adolescents, with collaboration of all stakeholders in the field of education like students, parents, teachers and school.

The present research study is especially significant in bringing to the fore the relatively lesser addressed inter-dependent variables, and in turn the multiple constructs, which cumulatively have a cascading effect in the shaping of adolescents as robust and capable citizens of the future world.

Chapter 2

LITERATURE REVIEW

2.1 Meaning of Literature Review

Literature review gives the current knowledge about a particular topic through substantive findings, as well as theoretical and methodological contributions. It involves locating, reading and evaluation of previous studies, observations and opinions related to the planned studies.

A literature review is an evaluation report of the studies found in writing, identifying with the chosen area. The review should describe, recapitulate, evaluate and elucidate the literature. It should offer a theoretical base for the survey to help determine the nature of the research. It is imperative to select a limited number of studies that are central to the subject rather than trying to collect a large number of studies which are not so closely related to the subject area.

Related literature refers to those studies which are directly associated to the problem or previous studies that investigated similar constructs, variables, research questions, theories or empirical testing of theories and practices. Comprehensively researched topics in education usually have adequate studies relevant to the research topic. Novel or rarely researched topics usually require reviews of literate, related in fundamental manner, to provide a rationale or conceptual framework for the present study. Literature review when conducted with care and presented well helps in understanding the chosen problem and in placing the results in historical perspective.

2.2 Purpose of Literature Review

A literature review is not limited to searching the information but also includes recognising and expressing the relationships between the literature and its research field. Even though there are various forms of literature review with different types of studies, the essential purposes remain same which are as follows :-

1. To provide research context.
2. Justification of investigation.
3. To ensure the research is not being replicated.
4. Helps in identifying gaps in the literature.

5. Helps in getting information already existing in same field of research.
6. Exemplifies the way subject has been previously studied.
7. Creates a picture of what is known and what is unknown in the research area.
8. Provides context or framework to the research.
9. Helps in refining, redirecting or even alter the subject.

Research utilises information gathered in the past by other researchers. Research cannot be done in isolation from other works which have already been done on the similar topics and issues, which makes survey of literatures an important procedure. "A survey of related literature is necessary for the proper planning, execution and right concept of the problems and solutions. It provides guiding hypothesis, suggestive methods of investigation and comparative data for interpretative purpose".

2.3 Characteristics of good Literature Review

A good literature review enables gaining insight into the study and has following characteristics :-

1. Relevant.
2. Clear and concise.
3. Synthesises available research.
4. Evaluates critically.
5. Referenced correctly.
6. Appropriate insightfulness.
7. Use of consistent and rigorous methods.

2.4 Steps Involved in Reviewing Literature

For research, review of literature by researcher involved the following steps :-

1. **Analysis of Problem Statement.** The first step was to make a detailed study of variables and concepts of the study.

2. **Transform the Problem Statement into Research Language.** The Problem Statement was reworded into a formal language in order to make it a dependable and reliable research. This would also allow others researchers to follow this study.

3. **Select Appropriate Index for Reference Services and Database.** To find most relevant and vital primary literature, all variables and concepts were cross

referenced with index to identify studies in database namely Research Gate, Academia.edu, Shodhganga, Eric, Google Scholar & Springer.

4. **Search and Read Relevant Literature.** Next was to read various literatures from primary sources like research papers, journals, dissertations, e-journals and surveys. The researcher searched many databases manually and through internet for the purpose. This helped in providing a brief review of the topic as well as facilitated in defining the research problem more precisely.

5. **Studying the Important Primary and Secondary Literature.** After reading and studying the primary and secondary literatures, the researcher made brief analysis relevant to the problem.

6. **Organised Notes.** Notes were further organised into two categories :-

(a) Variables.

(b) Studies carried out in India and abroad.

7. **Writing the Review.** Final stage was to write the literature review with researcher's investigation and analysis.

2.5 Sources of Literature Review

The intention of the review of literature from research work existing in the same area is to understand types of past studies which have been done and also scope for future studies. For the present study, the researcher used books, research study, journals, articles, handbooks; dissertations and website for reference and review. The researcher first and foremost is required to identify the gaps in existing body of knowledge, along with various means and ways to gather significant information keeping in mind the outcomes obtained in earlier studies on the current subject. This chapter covers various studies that drove the researcher's thoughts into this research field. The chapter highlights thoughts and influence of different scholars in the area of Adolescents' 'Academic Achievement' and 'Behaviour Adjustment' with relation to Parents and Teacher's support.

The researcher divided the reviews according to the following variables of the study :-

1. Research studies on impact of Parental Involvement on the following :-

(a) Academic Achievement.

(b) Behaviour Adjustment.

(c) Academic Achievement & Behaviour Adjustment.

(d) Other Variables.

2. Research studies on impact of Teacher's Involvement on the following :-

(a) Academic Achievement.

(b) Behaviour Adjustment.

(c) Academic Achievement & Behaviour Adjustment.

(d) Other Variables.

3. Research studies on impact of Parental and Teacher's Involvement on following :-

(a) Academic Achievement.

(b) Behaviour Adjustment.

As findings in social studies are generally found to have no universal validity and are socially relative in nature, the studies reviewed here are classified into two sections :-

(i) Research studies conducted in India.

(ii) Research studies conducted Abroad.

2.6 Research Studies on Impact of Parental Involvement Conducted in India

2.6.1 Impact on Academic Achievement

Bhavna & Kaur (2015) conducted a research on 200 students which highlighted that parents played a key role in shaping students' achievements and also concluded that motivation and support from parents helped adolescents to achieve better Academic results. Boys' perception of motivation from parents was more than that perceived by girls but still, girls were found to be better achievers in academics than boys. The study recommended further research with variables that are directly or indirectly related to the academic achievement of adolescents like school environment, home environment, parent education and parental encouragement, study habits, interest, attitude, intelligence, etc.

Bora & Ahmed (2008) conducted a study on class 9th students of Assam district to find the effect of parental involvement on 'Academic Achievement' focusing on their mathematics scores. Parental involvement was divided into five factors namely parents Communication with schools / teacher's, communication with teenager, personal development, helping with homework and attitude towards mathematics. Communication with teenager was observed as a significant factor for teenagers' mathematics Achievement. Personal development factor and attitude towards mathematics were found to be highly significant factors while helping with homework and communication with school / teacher were observed as non significant factors. Overall analysis suggested that parental involvement positively affected teenagers' academic achievement in mathematics.

Kumar & Lal (2014) examined 200 adolescents and the results indicated that children with healthy family environments were found to have higher academic achievement in comparison to children belonging to low family environment. The academic scores of girls were found to be better than boys while rating by boys for family environment was higher. Moos (1974) Family Environment Scale (FES) was used to find family environment, and aggregate scores of last two classes were used as parameter for academic achievement. The perceived parents' support was found to be better in boys as compared to girls while the academic scores of girls were better. Family values like building trust and confidence, parental approval, sharing of ideas, parental approval and making discussions were observed as positive activities which built strong bonding between adolescents and parents. A secure and emotionally stable atmosphere helped adolescents to build confidence and attain better academic achievement.

Singh & Gera (2016) in their research classified parental involvement as both home based and school based. Home based involvement included taking care of needs of children and listening to their problems while school based involvement comprised of attending Parent Teacher meets. The study from 400 students brought out that parental involvement positively affected academic achievement of adolescents. It was also observed that senior secondary school boys and girls did not differ in their parental involvement but boys were revealed to be emotionally more stable than girls. Parents were found to be equally devoted and involved in academics of their children without any gender discrimination. Furthermore, parental involvement was observed to positively affect academic performance of children.

Talluri & Esther (2017) undertook a study of 576 class 9th students from Andhra Pradesh to find the impact of parental involvement on academic achievement of secondary school students. The study revealed that positive correlation existed between parental involvement and 'Academic Achievements' of the secondary school students. It was observed that mean score of boys was higher than that of girls in both conditions i.e. when parental involvement was observed to be low and also when it was observed to be high. The literacy of parents affected the academic performance of students. Students with literate parents scored higher as compared to the students whose parents were less educated or illiterate.

Vijayalakshmi & Muniappan (2016) focused their study to find relationship between parental involvement and academic Achievement of 200 secondary school students taking into consideration their social studies scores. They observed that most of the parents were moderately involved in academic activities of their children while they also reaffirmed that parental involvement had positive direct impact on academic achievement of students. The researchers found parents' interaction may include helping in reading, motivating them to do homework independently, monitoring their activities inside as well as outside home and also providing coaching to improve various subjects. Parents sometimes are not aware of how to get involved in their child's activities so the researchers also recommended that psychologists, teachers and mental health experts should encourage and guide parents to get involved in various education related activities with their children so as to bring out the best results.

2.6.2 **Impact on Behaviour Adjustment / Mental Wellness**

Arulsubila & Subasree (2016) used personality index and parental bonding instrument as the tools for the study. Two dimensions namely care and overprotection or control was used to measure parenting style as perceived by children. Personality development was measure by variables like social concern, value & culture, assertiveness, communication, leadership, and self confidence. The questionnaire was obtained on a 5 point scale. The data was analyzed with Pearson's correlation and 't' test where the result indicated that there was no significant difference between mothers and fathers on care and overprotection dimensions of parenting style. Positive relation was found between care as a parenting style of both mother and father with personality of children while negative relation was observed between overprotection of both mother and father and personality of children parents could be trained on positive parenting, which will further help them to equip positive skills and implement them for wellbeing of their adolescent child.

Arulsubila. & Subasree (2017) observed 100 adolescents from Trichi to establish a relationship between parenting and psychological wellbeing of adolescents. The researchers measured psychological wellbeing through six parameters as defined by Carol Ryff (1988) namely autonomy, environmental mastery, personal growth, positive relations with others, purpose in life and self acceptance. A control group of 30 parents were given training by counsellors with life skills and 30 parents were observed without counselling. The results suggested that parents who were counselled were found to have improved their parenting style and thus enhanced the adolescents' life skills and psychological wellbeing while the other set did not find any improvement in the wellbeing of their children. Psychological well being and life skills were found to get promoted by positive parenting and reared happy and confident children.

Bhatia (2012) in her study tried to find relation between family relationships with emotional intelligence of 340 secondary school students in Haryana. Family relationship included parents relation with their child measured through parameters as acceptance, concentration and avoidance. Emotional intelligence was assessed on the basis of dimensions such as self awareness, self motivation, empathy, managing relations, emotional stability, self development, integrity, self development, value orientation, commitment and altruistic behaviour. It was found that significant relationship existed between emotional intelligence and Parental acceptance while it was seen that children's overall wellbeing was negatively affected with parental avoidance. The study recommended that parents should be made aware of their role in their child's emotional wellbeing at home and at school.

Sandhu & Kaur (2012) studied adolescents' problem behaviour classified into internalising and externalising problems in relation to emotional autonomy and parent-child relationship from 200 adolescent boys from Patiala. Emotional autonomy comprised of non dependency on parents, de-idealisation of parents, individuation, etc. while parent-child relationship encompassed care by parents and overprotection by parents. Analysis of data revealed that emotional autonomy and parent-child relationships affected adolescents' behaviour. Few parameters were found to have positive correlation with adolescents' problem behaviour namely individualisation, care by father, de-idealisation of parents, non-dependency on parents and mothers' overprotection, while mothers' care and fathers' overprotection was observed to be inversely correlated with adolescents' problem behaviour.

Sharma & Sandhu (2006) collected data of 240 students from Patiala with the aim of finding relation between parenting dimensions and externalising behaviour. The researcher classified parental dimensions into seven sub categories namely connection, autonomy, regulation, verbal hostility, physical coercion, non reasoning / punitive and indulgence. Externalising behaviour of children was classified into aggressive behaviour, oppositional defiant behaviour, ODD and other behavioural problems recommended by psychologists and psychiatrists. It was found that lower level of parental regulation predicted aggression where as lower levels of connection predicted conduct disorder in children. Parents' response and sensitivity to children's needs and their close monitoring, along with inductive reasoning, emphasising of expected behaviours was noted to be linked with low levels of behavioural problems, specially delinquency and externalising Behaviours and also to predict psychosocial adjustment in children. Boys were found to be more aggressive than girls and the difference can be owed to genetic, hormonal and psychobiological influences.

2.6.3 Impact on Academic Achievement and Behaviour Adjustment / Mental Wellness

Bala (2016) assessed relationship of social competence and 'Academic Achievement' of adolescents in relation with home environment. From the study of 600 adolescents, it was clearly brought out that 'Academic Achievement' and social competence i.e. the ability of students to combine thinking, feeling and Behaviour so as to achieve social tasks and bring out valued outcomes was positively associated with home environment. It also revealed that boys were more socially competent while girls were found to be better in academics. On one hand peer-pressure affected negatively to boys while girls were found to benefit from the pressure. The study emphasised on the need to enhance good family environment and decrease the peer pressure on students, so that social competence, study habits and academic achievement of the students may be improved.

Bandhana & Sharma (2012) investigated 300 12th grade higher secondary school students which revealed that girls were mentally healthier than boys while there was no significant relation found between home environment and mental wellbeing of children irrespective of the gender. Home environment had insignificant impact on achievement of students, with mental health as dependent variable. Home environment inventory designed by Dr Karuna Shankar Misra with 100 questions, consisting of 10 parameters namely control, protective, punishment, conformity, social Isolation, reward, deprivation of privileges, nurturance, rejection and permissiveness were used to measure parental involvement. Likewise, mental health Battery Test consisting of emotional stability, overall adjustment, autonomy, security insecurity, self concept and intelligence was used for assessing the mental health of the students. For academic achievement, aggregate marks in class 10th were used.

Dsa et al. (2018) conducted descriptive epidemiological study on 380 pre-university adolescents and they concluded that parental involvement positively affected academic achievement and mental wellbeing of the students. The important constructs considered by the reviewers were parental involvement in home activities, participation in school events, monitoring and communication with children, parenting style and educational expectations. The study brought out that with increased parental involvement, the academic performance and mental wellbeing of adolescents also increased. Positive correlation was also found between mental wellbeing and academic adjustment of adolescents.

Gopakumar et al. (2017) in their research studied 130 adolescent girls in India's Thiruvananthapuram city to find relation between parental care and mental health as well as academic performance. The mental health was measured through Kutcher's Adolescent Depression Scale (KADS) and scademic achievement' was measured through questionnaire. The study revealed that parental care has a direct association in academic performance and extracurricular activities of adolescent girls. Parental support was also linked to lower level of depression in girls irrespective of the socio-economic status.

Kannamma (2014) opined that behavioural management for middle aged children should reflect their need for independence while still offering plenty of guidance. Guidance and counselling as concluded by many studies, leaves a positive impact on the academic achievement of children. Structure at home, praise and attention, rewards and rules with clear consequences of breaking them were found to be most effective parameters for parents in guiding adolescents at home. Incidentally, it was also found that there was no significant difference in guidance needs of rural and urban adolescents. The researcher also recommended more systematic and comprehensive study of children's need, as the guidance at home was found to be on a generalised model.

2.6.4 Impact on Other Variables

Deb et al. (2015) analysed mental health of adolescents with respect to parental pressure and discovered that majority of the higher secondary students in Kolkata experience academic stress and for which Parental pressure for better academic performance was found to be the most common cause. Criticism by parents, comparison with others or high expectations and demands of parents were factors responsible for stress. Low or middle income group students and students with lesser educational qualification were found to face more pressure from parents as compared to their counterparts. The researchers advocated school level stress management programs to create awareness about Academic stress in parents along with strategies to avoid it and ways to help adolescents cope with it.

Haldar et al. (2011) conducted a study to find relationship between parental involvement and clinical anaemia of children. A group of f parents were selected for intervention program where parents, especially mothers, were provided guidance to plan menu, proper cooking practices, maintaining good hygiene, etc. They were also informed about importance of including local iron containing food in the diet. The analysis revealed significant improvement in anaemic status of children whose parents were in intervention group while the other group showed no improvement. At the same time the study observed that the group was not affected by gender of the participants, occupation of father and literacy of mother. It was recommended that parental involvement in nutrition process is imperative and should be encouraged for the improvement of the dietary habits of the children.

Moitra & Mukherjee (2012) tried to assess the impact of parent-adolescent communication on the development of delinquent behaviour. 200 adolescents, in which 100 delinquent and 100 non delinquent children were observed, linked to the development of delinquent behaviour. The study concluded that satisfactory parental communication was critical to provide a protective factor against delinquency. It was also noted that satisfactory communication of mothers was much more important compared to the communication with fathers. The study recommended that parents should be encouraged to improve their communication skill with their children with the aim of developing a positive interpersonal as well as social support system within the family so as to help the adolescent develop more mature and responsible attitude towards society.

Sharma et al. (2011) in the study examined the relationship between parental styles and depression among adolescents. 50 male and 50 female adolescents along with their parents were given questionnaire to find parenting style and level of depression in the children. The results revealed that authoritarian parenting style had significant positive correlation with depression while permissive parenting style had significant negative correlation with depression. Adolescent children whose parents followed authoritarian parenting (reasonable demand and high responsiveness) of parenting were found to be less depressed as compared to those children with parents following permissive parenting (low demand and high responsiveness). Males and females were found to have significant difference on measures of depression.

Tehlan & Zha (2018) studied the effect of parental involvement on the level of aspiration of 100 adolescents from Rohtak city. The study revealed that positive and significant relationship existed between the parental involvement and aspiration of adolescents. It was also noticed that male students perceived parental involvement more than that of females while there was no difference noted in the level of aspirations in both male and female adolescents. The findings recommended that parents, teachers and policymakers could work to help the children to improve the aspiration levels.

2.7 Research Studies on Impact of Parental Involvement Conducted Abroad

2.7.1 Impact on Academic Achievement

Chowa et al. (2013) in their research analysed samples of 6,252 youth and 3,083 parents randomly from 100 schools across 10 districts of Ghana. Four constructs each were taken for parental involvement at home and school, while continuous assessment score and examination scores of Maths and English were taken as parameters of academic Achievement. For Parental school involvement, attending PTA, speaking to teachers, attending school functions and volunteering in school activities were recorded while for parental involvement at home, checking children's homework, helping with children's homework, talking about expectations for school work and talking about what youth learned in school were the parameters taken into consideration. Results indicated that parental involvement activities at home and in school are statistically significant predictors of youth's academic performance. However, the direction of the relationships differed between the two factors. On one hand at-home involvement associated positively with academic performance, while on the other hand in-school involvement associated negatively with academic performance. An interesting fact that came out was parents whose children performed well academically appeared to be more involved at home with their children's school work as compared to the parents whose children did not perform well academically.

Fan et al. (1999) in the meta-analysis of research studies focused on finding relationship between parental involvement and academic achievement, clearly stated that there exists a positive relationship between the two. However, it also pointed out that the relationship was stronger when the academic achievement was represented by Global Achievement Indicator (e.g. GPA) as compared to subject wise achievement indicators. It also revealed that home supervision played lesser role in students' achievements while parents' Aspiration and their expectation for their child's future played a major role in their academic Achievement. The meta-analysis recommends further studies to operationally define parental involvement and document it for better analysis. Further, it also recommends studying different dimensions of parental involvement separately and their effect Academic on achievements as a whole and also subject specific.

Ghysens (2009) in the study found high perception of parental involvement by pupil, teachers and parents, especially home based involvement. It was found that since teachers have little or no knowledge of what happened at home, they included all dimensions of parental involvement as one while pupils and parents differentiated each aspect which can be further classified in six categories namely performance Orientation, parent-teacher communication, participation in school, cognitive stimulating home environment, parent-child communication and structuring home climate. The rating of parents and pupil converged for most of the aspects with one exception of parent-teacher communication while lot of variation was found in teacher's rating. However, it was also established that the congruency increased with regular communication between parents and teachers. Furthermore, it was also stated that teachers were biased on their rating based on the child's family background and characteristics of the child expressed in school. Performance orientation and parent-child communication were found to be positively correlated to academic achievement from parents' and pupils' point of view while Cognitive stimulating home environment was the key factor for pupils' achievements. It was also established that teachers viewed parental involvement and students' achievements as directly related while parents and pupil viewed it as indirectly related as motivating factor leading to academic Achievement. For future research, subject specific measures are advised, for parental involvement as well as learning Achievement.

Keith et al. (1993) in their longitudinal study of 21,814 students and their parents of 8th standard suggested positive relation between parental involvement and academic achievement of students. The parental involvement was measured through educational aspiration, parent-child communication, amount of home structuring and participation in school activities. The data suggested that parents instead of getting more involved when their child performed poorly get involved more when they perform well in school. Homework and TV time were found to be mediating variables affecting learning indirectly. The research concluded that parental involvement had a strong positive effect on 8th grade students' achievements, especially in Maths and Social Studies. It was interesting to see previous achievements affecting the parental involvement, which in turn affected the current performance of students. The study suggested that educators and policymakers should find ways to improve parental involvement which will indirectly lead to better performance in middle school. For future research, the study recommended to control previous achievement and student's ability to find effect of parental involvement. It also suggested finding effect thought overall grades rather than individual subjects.

Shute Valerie J. et al. (2009) reviewed the literature on the relationship between parental involvement and academic achievement, specifically focusing on the secondary school (middle and High school) level. The findings of the review clearly states positive relationship between parental involvement and academic achievement. Following areas were found to have strongest relationship: (a) discussions about school activities between parent and child (positive), (b) parents' aspirations/expectations for their children (positive), and (c) parental styles, particularly authoritative style (positive) and authoritarian and permissive styles (negative). It was noted that children's perception of parental involvement was better predictor of academic achievement as compared to parents' perception. Moreover, it was suggested that effect of parental involvement decreases as the student progresses through school. It also found that genetics as well as peer influence also affected the academic achievement' of students but direct parental involvement can leverage these factors for betterment of the child including academic achievement.

Smith (2011), in his research on 'The impact of parental involvement on students' Achievements' has clearly stated that parents have a significant role in student's academic achievement. He also insisted that through training, opportunity can be given to parents to understand the education system which will enable them to help their child for better performance. He also states that not only parents but teachers should also be trained through workshops for helping parents with tools to increase their capacity to help their children achieve academic success. He also addresses certain organisational barriers like language problem, lack of education in parents, etc. which hinder parental involvement. He recommends an effective collaboration between school and the parents, with an understanding that activities in school and home affect each other equally. Both parents and teachers should work together with a common goal of improving students' achievements.

2.7.2 Impact on Behaviour Adjustment / Mental Wellness

Abdirahman et al. (2012) tried to understand the relationship between parental involvement with adolescents' mental health and bullying through a study conducted in Caribbean on 6780 adolescents. The study revealed that students who perceived their parents to be more understanding and were found to monitor their free time activities reported fewer mental health issues and were rather less prone to report being a victim of a bully. It was also noticed that students reported moderate levels of parental involvement in their life where nearly half of them reported that their parents knew how they spent their free time, while about one in three reported that their parents usually checked their homework and understood their problems. Parental understanding and Parental monitoring of free time were found to be associated with lower probability of mental health problems.

Badri et al. (2014) in their research studied 'The Causal Relationship between parental involvement and Children's Behaviour Adjustment to schooling'. The study affirms the relationship between positive parental involvement and significant decrease in their child's unwanted behaviour with respect to internalising, externalising and hyperactivity behaviour. The maximum influence was observed for reducing arguments by the child, easy distraction and also being depressed and lonely. The most effective ways of parental involvement which came out as positive reinforcement was parents' interaction with teachers on a regular basis.

Dmitrieva J et al. (2004) evaluated the effect of family relations with psychological outcomes of 1,696 adolescents studying in class 11th in four countries. Family relationship was categorised into perceived parental involvement, parent-adolescent conflict and perceived parental sanctions [Disapproval] of adolescent misconduct, while psychological outcome was divided into depression mood and problem behaviour. Results indicated that perceived parental involvement and parent-adolescent conflict intervened in adolescent problem behaviours. The study also revealed that parental involvement helped in controlling adolescents' internalising and externalising behaviour. There were few exceptions found due to minor cross cultural differences in the scale of associations among variables.

Pengpid & Peltzer (2016) assessed relationship between parental involvement and mental health from 44,231 adolescents of six countries. Violent or aggressive behaviour was found to decrease in all six countries with increased parental involvement. Higher levels of parental involvement was negatively associated with suicidal ideation in all six countries, loneliness in five countries and anxiety in four countries while preventing internalising problems like loneliness, anxiety and suicidal ideation. The effect on mental wellbeing seems to get stronger with increasing levels of parental involvement and thus was recommended by the researcher to be used by parents or guardians to improve various health behaviours of their adolescent children.

Pengpid & Peltzer (2018) assessed the association between parental involvement and mental health among adolescents in five Caribbean countries through 10,063 adolescents. It was observed that higher levels of parental involvement could help adolescents in learning how to cope with stress and increased perceived personal mastery and control, thereby improving their mental health while it was also found that parental involvement negatively associated with internalising problems like anxiety, loneliness and suicidal ideation among adolescents in all five countries. Parental involvement with adolescent population was identified to be effective in reducing poor mental health, especially risk for suicidal Behaviour in all five countries.

2.7.3 Impact on Academic Achievement and Behaviour Adjustment / Mental Wellness

Bean et al. (2006) studied the effect of three dimensions of parenting namely support, behavioural control and psychological control on adolescents' behaviour (depression, anti-social) and academic achievement, through sample of 202 African American adolescents. Paternal support was significantly (negatively) associated with depression and delinquency (antisocial Behaviour) while psychological control by both mothers and fathers was not found to be associated with delinquency, depression or GPA. It was observed that when adolescents experience their parents as accepting and supportive, they are less prone to depression despite their ethnicity, nationality or other socio demographic differences. It was further noted that close relationship with fathers as compared to mothers played a crucial protective factor against externalising Behaviour for both boys and girls. The findings of the study indicated that none of the three dimensions of parenting domains was found to be significantly related to academic achievement.

El Nokali et al. (2010) in their research collected data of 1,364 students from the 'NICHD Study of Early Childcare and Youth Development' to investigate children's trajectories of Academic and social development across 1st, 3rd and 5th grades. The main findings implied that parental involvement predicted improved social skills and decline in problem behaviour but did not predict changes in academic achievement. High involvement of parents was positively related to boost social functioning and lessen behaviour problems. Teacher's report of parental involvement strengthened this view. Parental involvement was measured through a questionnaire comprising of 10-12 questions from teachers and parents reflecting parental encouragement, parental investment and parental attitude. Academic performance outcomes were recorded from grades 1st, 3rd and 5th while Child Behaviour Check List (CBCL, Achenbach, 1991a)' for parents and Teacher's Report Form (TRF) from teachers were used to measure socio emotional development. Furthermore, socio emotional development was divided into two subscale scores of externalising and internalising problems where externalising problems included aggressive or delinquent behaviour, and internalising problems comprised of withdrawn, anxious or depressed behaviour. The analysis result showed that there were very few significant relations between parental involvement and academic achievement, with a special mention to children who had better maternal cognitive competence, were found to have higher average levels in academics. Male children scored lesser as compared to female counterpart in Maths and vocabulary. Teachers rated social skills to have improved and problem Behaviour to be marginally reduced with increased parental involvement. Classroom quality was found to affect the social skills positively. An important finding was that parents rated themselves more involved than teachers. It also reiterated the view of many other research studies that role of parents in later years of education receives lesser attention.

Mante et al. (2014) carried out their study at Adukrom Methodist Primary school for all six primary classes where a total population of 50 students and parents were used. It concluded that involvement of parents in academic activities of the children positively affect their academic performance. Four main instruments used to collect required data were Interview, Questionnaire, Survey and Classroom Report. From students' perception of parental involvement, it was concluded that majority of the students were in agreement that they worked harder for better grades when their parents interacted with teachers about their performance in school. Similarly, they also agreed upon making an effort to act and behave appropriately in class when there was communication between parents and teachers regarding the same. Parents also accepted that their children not only behaved better but also achieved better results when they were more involved with them. However, parents confided that lack of time; tiredness and resistance from children were foremost reasons for lack of their involvement. The teachers asserted that parental involvement was quite influential in leading to better pupil's performance in the classroom and completed more of their homework assignment while behaviour problems declined when the parents were kept informed about how their child was performing in class. The results of this study echo the findings of the multitude of researchers that previously examined the impact of parental involvement on improved student academic achievement and classroom behaviour.

Wang & Sheikh (2014) studied the relationship between parental involvement and student achievement and mental health in 1,056 adolescents from grade 10th and 11th. The study perceived parental involvement as a multidimensional construct which included school based involvement, home-based involvement and academic socialisation while the effect was measured through adolescents' achievements and depression. The study also tested whether parental involvement could influence adolescent outcomes by increasing their Academic engagement in school. It was found that parental involvement improved academic and emotional functioning in adolescents. It was observed that academic socialisation and school based involvement influenced depression directly and also indirectly through emotional engagement in school while home based involvement was observed to influence academic achievement directly and indirectly through behavioural engagement. Also, parental involvement predicted adolescent academic success and mental health both directly and indirectly through behavioural and emotional engagement.

2.7.4 Impact on Other Variables

Dietricha & Salmela (2013) investigated parental involvement in career goals' pursuit of adolescents by studying 807 students twice, once at high school and second at their graduation. It was observed that support from parents positively affected both goal motivation and goal attainability while goal stress was found to be positively linked to parents' lack of career related engagement with adolescents. Warmth of parents was observed to have positive effect on career motivation while it negatively affected career related stress. It was concluded that at both stages adolescent perceived warmth and career specific parental involvement were associated with goal related stress, though weakly.

Flouri (2000) tried to understand role of parents on money management of adolescents by observing 2,722 adolescents in Britain. It was observed that lower parental involvement significantly and independently contributed to poor money management. The relationship between parental involvement and money management was found to be same for both boys and girls. Boys were observed to have better money management as compared to girls while adolescents from lower socio economic backgrounds were likely to report better money management. The association between parental involvement and money management was weaker when children experienced family disturbance than when they were in a stable home environment.

Gonzalez et al. (2005) in the study examined the relationship between parental involvement and Student motivation to achieve better results. After reviewing many related literature, the researchers came to the conclusion that parental involvement both at home and in school has positive relation with motivation of the students. It recommends that having meaningful and qualitative parent-teacher interaction is important rather than increasing the number of times they interact. The strongest relationship between competence and motivation was found to be their perception about their parents' view about learning and achievement. Moreover, it was also found that parents who communicated achievement as worthwhile enterprise motivated the students more. It recommends further studies to be conducted on different forms of parental involvement and its effect on students' achievements with respect to diverse population. It also encourages further research to be done on various parenting styles and their effect on students' motivation.

Ruholt et al. (2015) examined parental support and parental involvement's effect on both self esteem and academic self efficacy. 250 adolescents from Kentucky were analysed and the results revealed that academic self efficacy and self esteem were both positively correlated with parental support and also with parental involvement. It was also established that the effect did not differ for boys and girls. Furthermore, it could be said that active involvement from parents and receiving emotional support were equally important for a child's perceived worth, confidence and self-sufficiency in school.

Worthington (2014) assessed impact of parenting on school violence in 948 middle school adolescents. The parental involvement was categorised into parenting, communicating, volunteering and decision making while the dependent variable was the Student aggression. The researcher studied 948 middle school students and found that communicating significantly impacted on the decrease of school violence at the middle school level. Middle schools which offered regular scheduled parent-teacher meets and where parents were observed to participate in parenting program were observed to have fewer incidents of Student aggression.

2.8 Overview of Studies on Parental Involvement & Its impact

Reviewing research on parental involvement showed its relation with academic achievement, behavioural aspects and many more areas. Many longitudinal as well as cross cultural studies had been done to find effectiveness of the different types of involvement such as home involvement, school, friends, structural, emotional involvement, etc. for parents while emotional, instrumental, appraisal and involvement with parents, etc. were taken into consideration for teachers. While the reviews of research studies revealed effect of parental involvement in relation to academic achievement, behavioural aspects and numerous more areas, but rarely any study was found to have measured the effect on both Academic achievement and behaviour adjustment of adolescents. It was also discovered that rarely any research studies the effect of parental involvement from point of view of all three stakeholders namely adolescents, parents and teachers which can be considered as a major gap in the literature.

Most of the findings support the pre existing belief that parental support is significant as it offers a sense of security and comfort to adolescents striving for their development and find a sense of individuality in an unfamiliar world of adults. Parents support involves setting limits, encouraging and also acting as resource for children when they encounter various challenges every day in personal, social and academic domains. Parental involvement is a way to communicate to their children how important they are to them. Attending parent-teacher meets, open houses and other school activities is also representative of their concern and importance. The support from parents is especially imperative to adolescents who might be at risk of alienating themselves from school and society. In the perspective where parental involvement is lacking and with permissive Parenting style, at-risk adolescents might most likely turn to peers in excess, likely leading to negative outcomes in behaviours (such as improper social attitudes, depression, tantrums, mood swings, etc.) and / or academics (truancy, poor grades, disciplinary problems in school, dropouts, etc.).

Parental Involvement was measured through various parameters in different studies such as participating in parent-teacher meets, interaction with teachers, participation in school activities and functions, facilitating in academics and extracurricular activities at home, engaging in students' extracurricular activities, assisting in the selection of student's courses, track of children's academic grades, imparting moral values and attitudes about importance of hard work and academic success. Autonomy support at home and level of parental control in home environment also counts for parental involvement affecting adolescents. Most of the studies were observed to use survey method using questionnaire while few used interview for data collection. There were few studies which used experiment control groups for finding the impact of parental involvement comparing with non-control groups. The sample size ranges from 100-500 for most of the research studies while few longitudinal and multi-state or country had higher sample sizes. Data analysis was done using various statistical techniques ranging from mean, median and mode to T-test, ANNOVA , Pearson's Correlation, etc to establish relationship between variables.

2.9 Research on Impact of Teacher's Involvement Conducted in India

2.9.1 Impact on Academic Achievement

Chetri (2014) opined that motivation for Achievement has a perfect positive relationship with academic achievement. Level of intelligence was found to have risen when teachers encouraged the students to develop the problem solving ability, thinking, reasoning by participation in different activities and studying the creative work. The researcher recommended for organising different workshop training, refresher courses, in-service training courses, etc. for the teachers to help them to equip with necessary skills and competencies to enhance student's achievement motivation.

Kumar (2019) tried to understand the effect of traditional and non traditional teacher's quality variables on students' Maths performance. Traditional variables included teacher's qualification, teacher's certification and professional development while non-traditional qualities included positive attitude of teachers, accountability, strictness, etc. The traditional teacher's quality variables namely full time, fully qualified teachers and professional development showed significant relationship with students' performance in Maths and on the other hand non traditional teacher's quality variables, namely influence of poor teacher-student relationship and teachers being too strict with students, were observed to have a significant influence on student performance in Maths.

Shah (2009) observed 375 teachers and 1,500 students and assessed them through two questionnaires developed for collection of data. The study concluded that when the teachers adjusted themselves with the current situation and used different motivational techniques for teaching, students were observed to be satisfied and connected better with their teachers. The teacher's behaviour was found to be highly and positively significant to the academic achievement of students. Parameters of teacher's involvement that were found as positive contributors to academic achievement were adjustment with situations, striving for continuous improvement in their knowledge and skill, using different evaluation techniques while teaching, fair marking, equal participation of students in co-curricular activities' and appreciation when they performed well.

Sharma (2016) investigated 646 adolescents studying in class 10th in Chhattisgarh state of India to understand the effect of teacher's support on academic achievement.

Academic achievement was recorded from their overall marks in all subjects of class 10th exam while teacher's support was measured through a classroom environment scale consisting of nine dimensions. Teacher support is one dimension of classroom environment scale with 12 items. The study showed that teacher's support was significantly and positively associated to academic achievement of students. When teachers create an environment in class that not only supports effective teaching but also facilitates learning, it is bound to positively affect the academic performance. There was no significant difference noticed in academic performance with respect to gender.

Shashidhar et al. (2009) observed in the study of 1,230 adolescent students across classes 8th, 9th and 10th that it was feasible and valuable to identify the determinants of scholastic performance and plan intervention strategies at each school for improving academic achievement of students. The teachers were found to help students with their positive intervention. The study highlighted the importance of implementing newer strategies, focusing on strict study patterns and creating conducive school and home environment for study, so as to achieve better scholastic performances.

2.9.2 **Impact on Behaviour Adjustment / Mental Wellness**

Bharath & Kumar (2010) in their longitudinal study compared 600 students who were under a supervised program where their teachers taught them life skills vis-à-vis 423 students who were not involved in the program. Life skills included participatory learning methods of games, debates, role plays and group discussion by teachers. The adolescents in the program were found to be better adjusted in classroom as well as displayed positive behaviour and interaction as per their teachers as compared to their counterparts who were not imparted life skills. The available resources of schools and teachers were seen as an effective way of empowering adolescents. As teachers are the personnel who interact with the adolescents closely, so it was recommended to give adequate training to teachers, so that they could facilitate adolescents in coping up with stress and solve their problems.

Jayalekshmi et al. (2011) used Achenbach's classification of behavioural problems as externalising (aggression, bullying and fighting) and internalising (anxiety, withdrawal and loneliness). It suggested that teachers who listen to and assist early adolescents in learning can provide adolescents with critical skills that will prevent and reduce violence along with other behaviour issues. Teaching subjects by more interesting methods and participatory activities, emphasising self discipline, were found to be effective in improving academic and behavioural performance of adolescents. It recommended parents and educators support to make a positive learning environment for betterment of the students.

Khanna & Singh (2015) aimed to understand the teacher's and adolescents' perception of issues relevant to adolescent well-being.900 students and 17 teachers were interviewed about adolescents' problems and interventions. Adolescents response were categorized into three sub-groups pertaining to life at school, factors affecting well-being and changes that adolescents suggest to improve their well-being while teacher's responses were categorised into main factors that disturb well-being of adolescents', target areas for classroom based positive psychology interventions for adolescents' and best approach to deliver interventions in the classroom. Most of the adolescents placed enjoyment and friends as the best aspect of school life while academic stress, overly materialistic, lacking parental guidance, peer pressure, phase of transition and influence of media and technology were revealed to be the key points affecting well-being of adolescents. Building confidence, importance of education, real world exposure and value education were observed as parameters of intervention programme of teachers that helped in improving well-being of students. Best approaches as recommended by teachers were collaborative (building rapport with students), Interactive (interesting innovative teaching techniques), need for regular repetition (Reinforcing positive messages through repetition), need for separate time (structured special time for well-being orientation initiatives). Another prominent factor enhancing as well as disturbing participants' well-being was influence of peer.

Rajeswari & Eljo (2013) in their research reiterated that adolescence is a difficult phase filled with stress and turbulence, thus making adolescents easy prey for emotional disturbances. From the study of 200 adolescents it was found that 70% of the population shared cordial relationship with their teachers but only 15% confided their problems with their teachers, while 77% of the population confided their problems with their friends. More so, 70% got educational guidance from their teachers and 20 % from their friends, from which 91% were satisfied from the guidance they got. The study revealed no significant difference in gender with relation to school adjustment. The researcher further discovered that life skill abilities developed through various innovative teaching methods by teachers would enable them to cope with their emotional challenges and also enhance their adjustability, which would further lead to positive development and mental health.

Vranda (2015) in her study discussed methodology adopted in developing and standardising school mental health model with teachers as facilitators, as existing resources. It has been found that school based interventions program are more effective means of promoting mental health of students and prevent the development of unhealthy behaviour. The program focused on increasing the psychological competence and resilience of children to minimise risk through experimental learning. The study found that teachers as existing resource are found to have capabilities to effectively deliver mental health promotion intervention in schools. It also recommends for further evaluations of program to determine the long term impact on various multi component aspects of mental health and psychological wellbeing.

2.9.3 Impact on Academic Achievement and Behaviour Adjustment / Mental Wellness

Elumalai & Nagaraja (2013) revealed in their research that teachers have two faceted responsibilities towards students, one being educational and the other being extensional which includes involvement of teachers in day-to-day life of students. The modern teachers are also required to organise different co-curricular activities like sports and games, debates and discussions, publications and literary activities, cultural and recreational activities, aesthetic and social activities, which were identified as modes to improve personality of students. Innovative teaching methods were found to be more effective for understanding. Personal counselling was identified as a major role player in helping students adjust to the environment or for solving their problems.

Mercinah & Nirmala (2016) brought out that adolescents' mental health is imperative and can be achieved by teacher's support. Motivation by teachers, clear communication, cordial relationship, clear and consistent discipline model, innovative and interesting teaching techniques, interesting class activities and mutual respect were some important factors which the study highlighted for improved Teacher-Student relationship which in turn will enhance the mental health of adolescents and also Academic results. With improved teacher-student relationship, adolescents imbibe important social values such as building friendship, gaining respect for peers and adults and learning social skills. These side by side help the Student get good academic records and performance.

Monique, Jethwani & Keyser (2008) examined 125 secondary and higher secondary teachers for their perception of their involvement on student' academic stress and welfare. The study revealed that students get motivated through innovative teaching methods like field visit, project work and usage of audio visual aids in the schools which was confirmed by more than 95% of the sample teachers. Teachers also suggested that reward system in the schools along with punctuality and taking classes seriously helped students to feel less anxious and improved their wellbeing. Reduction of load of home work was also found to reduce academic stress.

Shewkani (2016) revealed that students' cordial relationships with teachers not just improved the children socially but also improved their academic performance. Positive better relationship with teachers was found to serve as a secure base for young children as they are better able to work and play with the confidence that if they are upset, they can count on their teachers to recognise and respond to their problems. In schools where teachers were given allotted time to discuss with children their problems, they reported 40-50% decline in school dropout, maintenance of achievement levels and fewer student and teacher reported behavioural or emotional problems. It was recommended to study about teacher-student relationships for low income students to decrease high school dropout, and improve students' social emotional development.

Yadav & Iqbal (2009) concluded in their study of 60 students that life skill training showed positive results in bringing change in adolescents' attitude, thought and Behaviour by providing supportive environment to them by their teachers. It was found that children not only adjusted better but also improved in academics after three months program where teachers held group discussions, role plays and case studies. Children developed a clearer perspective which helped them in better understanding, to sympathise with others leading to lesser stress. It was recommended to further experiment involving parents along with teachers to help children cope social pressures outside school.

2.9.4 Impact on Other Variables

Bajaj (2011) explored the role of teachers in Human Rights Education (HRE) where 118 HRE teachers and 625 students were observed. The study revealed that as several semi literate communities hold teachers and textbooks in high regard, their advocacy of human rights would prove Instrumental for HRE to go beyond the school walls.

Teacher training which is appropriate, contextualised and engaging, promotes participation of both, the teachers and their students. Teachers and textbooks can provide legitimacy for human rights and can be vital community resources for intervening in abuses.

Dahiya (2015) studied 260 secondary school students to measure teacher-student interaction and its effect on emotional security of the students. The researcher noted that secondary school students being all adolescents are in the phase of emotionally intense and stressful period and thus require caring and friendly relationship at home and school. Teacher-student interaction as described in the study is the communication between teacher and a student, a way to deal and share information with each other in the classroom or outside. The study concluded that students who had positive and high teacher-student interaction were observed to be more emotionally secure than the students who have low and negative interaction with their teachers. It was found that positive interaction provided students with a sense of belongingness, improved motivation to learn, decreased misbehaviour and also improved the school environment.

Idhaufi & Ashari (2017) analysed relationship between students' motivation and teacher's teaching style at secondary schools in Kulai. The data was collected through questionnaires from 160 students from two different schools. The findings of the study showed that students' preferential style of teaching was personal model which affected students' motivation the most. Female students seemed to be more motivated to engage in learning as compared to boys. Result revealed that there was a moderate relationship between students' motivation and teacher's teaching style.

Singh & Punia (2018) tried to assess effect of implementing value base d education by teachers on delinquency at school. The study revealed that effective implementation of value based education was found to be necessary for juveniles at school level in India where juveniles' crimes have been increasing. Value based education provided a positive focus for redirecting juveniles' inappropriate behaviour and helped to create a collaborative and cohesive school community which helped in identifying and solving juveniles' problems effectively. It was further found to enhance quality teaching, give sense of care to students and at the same time making students more cooperative, tolerant and responsible towards their goal making student-teacher relationship trustworthy.

Tanveer et al. (2012) studied influence of teachers on students' learning motivation. The findings of the study revealed that there were numerous aspects of teacher's behaviour and teaching styles which were found to influence learning motivation of students. The study showed that teachers of management sciences could successfully motivate their students by keeping in view techniques as formal lesson planning, promoting active participation, lesson elaboration, de-emphasising grades, students' counselling, and emotional support. Positive behaviour and appropriate teaching techniques could increase students' learning motivation level.

2.10 Research on impact of Teacher's Involvement Conducted Abroad

2.10.1 **Impact on Academic Achievement**

Archambault et al. (2012) explored the effect of teacher's expectations and sense of efficacy on the relationship between students' cognitive engagement and achievements. They conducted a longitudinal study with sample of 79 Maths teachers and 1,364 secondary school students from 33 schools in Canada. The results indicated that students' academic experience was directly influenced by teacher's self reported beliefs. However, there was no significant difference in the influence on low achieving students and high achieving students. The findings suggested that in schools having students from low socioeconomic status, the teachers should be made conscious of the role their attitudes can play on students' achievements and cognitive engagement. School authorities should make efforts to help teachers develop positive attitude towards all students.

Fredriksen & Rhodes (2004) aimed at finding the role of teacher relationship in lives of students. It highlighted that relationship with teachers can affect students' learning and academic achievement. Supportive relationship from teachers can motivate students to learn and perform well even in those subjects which interested them the least. With increased participation, change in attitude for the subject is likely through increased efficacy, interest and perceived utility. Perceived support from teachers also help students in psychological adjustment and emotional wellbeing. It was observed that changes in perceptions of teacher support predicted changes in both self esteem and depression among middle school students, such that students who perceived increasing teacher support showed corresponding decreases in depressive symptoms and increases in self esteem and vice-a-versa. Students exhibiting problem behaviours including inattention, internalising, disruptive and aggressive behaviour, are likely to have negative relationships with their teachers. Further, it can be said that good teacher-student relationships are characterised by low levels of conflict and high levels of closeness, supporting children's motivation to explore, as well as their growing ability to regulate social, emotional and cognitive skills. It was reiterated in the study that teacher-student relationship deteriorates as the students reach middle school, so efforts are needed at the school level to make policies and change the system so as to improve teacher-student relationship.

Gurganious (2017) evaluated the relationship between teacher's autonomy to make decisions about classroom teaching practices and specific science curriculum, with school based students' achievements in science and students' Social Economic Status (SES). Data was collected from 108 students of 16 different schools studying in class 8th. The study revealed scores of science were found to increase with teacher's better perceptions of their ability to make decisions about the science curriculum they teach in their classroom and their autonomy. Teacher's perception about their autonomy to decide teaching practices also helped in better achievement by students while SES was not found to have any effect on science achievement of students. The key finding of the study showed that when teachers are allowed autonomy and to make decisions about their teaching practices and curriculum in the classroom, Student achievement scores tend to increase.

Konishi et al. (2010) studied 27,217 students aged 15 years and 1,087 school principals to understand the relationship between teacher-student connectedness and academic performance. Results of the analysis revealed that Maths achievement was positively related to teacher-student connectedness. Boys were observed to have better effect of teacher-student relationship on academic performance as compared to girls. The study also recommended that if teachers tried to improve their relationship with students, it would aid in improving their academic performance.

Kosir & Tement (2014) studied teacher-student relationship with academic achievement of adolescents through 816 students. The result indicated positive relationship between teacher's personal support and academic achievement though to low or medium level, while teacher's acceptance was found to positively affect significantly to academic achievement of children. Furthermore, it was noticed that teacher's acceptance had positive relation with teacher's support too. The study also brought out that the students who had higher academic achievement at the start of the school year reported better teacher personal support at the end of the school year and when students perceived higher levels of teacher personal support at the start of the year were found to be more accepted by their teachers at the end of the session. Similarly, students when perceived higher teacher acceptance and support at the beginning of the year had higher achievements at the end of session and students with higher achievements at the beginning of the school year were more accepted by their class teacher at the end of the school year.

2.10.2 **Impact on Behaviour Adjustment / Mental Wellness**

Blazar & Kraft (2017) assessed teacher's effect on Behaviour and attitude of students. Teacher's parameters were classified into emotional support and classroom organisation while students' attitude was measured through Behaviour in class and happiness in class. Emotional support that included sensitivity, regard to students' perspective and a positive climate in class was observed to influence happiness in class. Classroom Organisation which captured teacher's behaviour management skills and productivity in delivering content was positively related to self reported students' behaviour in class while it was negatively associated with happiness in class. Overall it was observed that teachers had a positive relationship in behaviour as well as attitude of students.

Cattley (2004) in her study in Australia and Japan focused on the role of teacher support in teacher-student relationship and its impact on students' wellbeing during their adjustment to the middle years of schooling. It concluded that students perceived steady amount of high support throughout their middle schooling years. While the amount of perceived support from parents vary at different levels but remains higher than perceived teacher's support with respect to students wellbeing. It was also found that as students' progress in class to middle school, the perceived support from teachers gets lower as compared to perceived parents support. This decline was observed to be cross cultural and in both the nations. Reasons for this decrease might be nature of teacher's role in middle school, curriculum demand, low teacher efficacy or lack of teacher attention to students' emotional wellbeing, possibly due to environmental and structures within the middle school setting. This can also be due to emotional changes in adolescents which cause increased desire for autonomy and dislike for too much restrictions. As it was established that teachers have a multidimensional role in an adolescents' life and have higher potential in influencing emotional wellbeing and mental health of adolescents, ways and means should be found to improve teacher-Student relationship in middle school. To do the same, in South Australia, a trend was found to be emerging to organise the time table in the middle years of schooling so that the students are with the same teacher for much of the day. The researcher recommends further studies focusing on questions like 'What would contribute to teachers being more relevant in their students' lives ?' and "How can teachers best be supported in increasing students' sense of well-being ?'.

Gregory & Ripski (2008) examined high school students' behaviour with respect to their trust on teacher's authority. Data was collected through interviews and surveys from 32 teachers and 32 students. The study revealed that association between adolescents' perceptions of their teachers as trustworthy authority figures positively affected their behaviour. It was also observed that students saw themselves as cooperative and also indulged in activities and course material in class when teachers built relationship with students. Furthermore, it was recommended that teachers could earn the trust and cooperation of students through relationship building, with the aim of preventing discipline problems.

Suldo et al. (2009) conducted a research where 401 students participated in self report to measure Subjective Well Being (SWB) and social support by teachers. Furthermore, 50 students also participated in focus groups to unearth students' perceptions of teacher's behaviour that offers support. Findings of the study indicated that perceived emotional and instrumental support distinctively predicted SWB for both boys and girls. Students perceived teachers to be supportive largely when they attempted to connect with students on an emotional level through usage of innovative teaching strategies, by acknowledging and boosting students' academic success, demonstrating fair behaviour during interactions with students and also encouraging a classroom environment where questions are encouraged. Gender differences emerged during the qualitative stage where girls were observed to perceive emotional support as indicator to teacher's support predicting SWB while boys were observed to find fair behaviour, creation of environment to encourage questions and giving manageable academics workload as strategies communicating social support. On the other hand, lot of academic workload, presence of too many rules and regulations were indicative of low social support from teachers.

Wang, Brinkworth & Eccles (2013) examined teacher-Student relationships and the concurrent and longitudinal impact on emotional and behaviour adjustment of adolescents. Data was collected from 1,400 urban youths about their depressive symptoms and misconduct while teacher-student relationship data was collected from teacher report. Positive teacher-student relationship was found to protect adolescents against depression and misconduct throughout their adolescence. Furthermore, positive teacher-student relationship acted as a buffer for parent adolescent conflicts .Warmth and trust of teachers moderated the negative influences of adolescents' misconduct and helped at-risk adolescents in emotional and behaviour adjustment.

2.10.3 Impact on Academic Achievement and Behaviour Adjustment / Mental Wellness

Berman-Young & Sarah (2014) in the study took a survey through self reporting instrument from 102 middle school students and 15 teachers of an urban school, which included students' perception of teacher's support and their self reported engagement. Teacher's caring and support was further classified into two sub categories i.e. teacher's support for the needs of competence, autonomy, and relatedness and teacher's support for academic press and mastery goal orientation. Students' engagement, behaviour outcome as well as academic achievement were measured too from both students' and teacher's point of view. For behavioural outcome as well as academic scores, teacher's caring and support and teacher's press for academic thought were both found to be significant predictors, where girls were found to display more positive behaviour as well as score better GPAs than boys. Though teacher's caring and Support and teacher's press for academic thought were both found to be positively and strongly correlated to students' academic and behavioural success at school, but teacher's press for academic thought was observed to be more predictive of academic and behavioural outcomes than teacher's caring and support.

Blazar (2016) studied relationship between individual teachers and students' Maths performance along with their self reported, self efficacy in happiness and behaviour in class and also in Maths. The researcher found that concept and inquiry based teaching style positively adopted by teachers, affected academic performance of students while classroom environment or management had no effect on academic achievement. Teachers were observed to affect the happiness in class as reported by students. Furthermore, teacher's emotional support had positively associated constructs, namely self efficacy in Maths and happiness in class, where emotional support by teacher included sensitivity to students, consideration for students' viewpoint and the degree to which they create a positive climate in the classroom. It was interesting to note that while high quality instruction as a sub construct of classroom organisation positively affected students' self reported behaviour in class, it negatively affected their happiness in class.

Crosnoe, Johnson and Elder (2004) in their study found that integration bonding between teachers and adolescents in secondary school has a strong relationship with Behaviour outcomes in relation to the academic achievement and disciplinary issues. It states that students across the board showed better results and fewer problems in school when they had positive views about their teachers and vice-a-versa. The study shows that when school has safer environment, it affects the bonding of teachers and students positively. When children are around same ethnic crowd then they tend to have better relation with teachers and in turn better performance. It also brings out that parents' education also somewhat affects the bond between teachers and students. The study recommends that with stronger integration bonding in schools, problems of students becoming alienated or disengaged in secondary schools can be dealt.

Hamre & Pianta (2006) in their book discussed that students' relationships with teachers are fundamental to their success in school and these relationships should be explicitly utilised in school based prevention and intervention efforts. Teacher-student relationship develops over the course of the school year and once a strong and supportive relationship is formed, students feel safer and more secure in the school setting. It facilitates the students to have positive connections with peers and achieve greater academic progress. In contrast, conflict with teachers may lead students on a trajectory of school failure wherein they are unable to cope up academically and socially within classrooms and school. Relationship of adolescents' with teachers and other adults may facilitate their transition to adulthood. A conceptual model of teacher-student relationships presented by Pianta (1999) was discussed wherein the three primary components of relationships between teachers and students were found as features of the individuals and their representation of the relationship, processes by which information is exchanged between the relational partners' and external influences of the systems in which the relationship is embedded.

Roorda (2011) found that positive teacher-student relationship affected school engagement and academic achievement, while negative relationship adversely affected students' engagement and academic performance. School engagement, that is the social behaviour of students, was found to have more impact of teacher's relationship than academics. It was also revealed that older children felt the teacher-student relationship to be more important for academic achievement. Boys were found to have stronger effects for both positive and negative relationships and engagement. In contrast, for positive relationship and achievement, associations were stronger in studies with more girls. The study recommended adding parameters as emotional security, autonomy, structure, etc. along with cross sectional studies and multiple informants and methods for data collection for future research.

Wentzel (2002) in her research study assessed the teacher's role with respect to their modelling of motivation and to Baumrind's parenting dimensions of control, maturity demands, democratic communication and nurturance. The effect was measured in terms of students' academic performance and social adjustment. It brings out clearly the positive effect of teacher's motivation with students performance and behaviour. It also states that negative feedback given by teachers to the children affects them negatively. It emphasises that teacher's role in influencing students' behaviour in a classroom is far more as compared to parents. The effect of social motivation by teachers was rated higher than academic motivation for better performance in middle school. The study recommends that collaboration with parents through parent intervention programs can ensure social competence and academic excellence in early adolescents.

2.10.4 **Impact on Other Variables**

Breuer (2016) studied impact of perceptions of teachers on mental health and adolescents' depression. The researcher analysed 92 high school teachers to find about their views about adolescents' mental health and depression and their ways to deal with it. It was found that by increasing teacher's awareness related to the issue, helped adolescents' access to mental health services to reduce depressive symptoms. Female teachers were observed to be more mindful of their students' mental health than male teachers. Teachers with more awareness about mental health were found to be more willing to refer student for mental health counselling services as compared to teachers who regarded mental health as stigma or were unaware of its importance. Thus, the study recommended that teachers should be educated about the importance of mental health of adolescents to take notice of it in class and then put effort to help them.

Ibrahim & Zaatari (2020) in their study explored teacher-student relationships in one UAE school district from perspective of 650 students and 65 teachers and its influence on adolescents' sense of school belonging. The perspective was classified into rigid classrooms, interpersonal communication, lack of effective support, punishment and relationships with friends or peers. Positive teacher-student relationship was observed to enhance students' development and supported their sense of belonging to the school. However, in the present study, cooperation or reciprocity was not happening; respect, care, and love were not present and power balance was challenging which made students find school frustrating and had low sense of belonging. Teachers were not able to provide psychological and academic support as expected by students while students had problem behaviours which made teachers weary. The study recommended educating teachers and students both about their role in education system.

Nugent (2009) analysed student and teacher interaction as well whether or not these interactions significantly impacted motivation and achievement. The results of the study indicated that teacher-student interaction was significantly related to student motivation. Interaction between teachers and students was also found to positively affect academic achievement while motivation was found to be negatively associated, though slightly, with academic achievement. It was observed that teacher's rated themselves higher than students, especially for being less strict and friendlier. The study recommended that teachers should be provided with the appropriate assistance and resources to appropriately meet the needs of their students outside academics

Patricia & Sullivan (2009) assessed teacher's perceptions and classroom practices in motivating adolescents in high school. Data was collected from 96 participant teachers in 15 high schools in USA where teacher's perceptions were measured through supportive classroom environment, students' general motivation, causes for students' lack of motivation, teacher's self efficacy for motivating students, interpersonal style and motivating strategies. Teacher's efficacy for diagnosing and intervening for students' motivation and their interpersonal motivating styles were observed to predict their strategy for motivation. Both internal and external underlying perceptions explained important parts of variance in teacher's perceptions of students' overall motivation. Strategies that teachers use, in turn, predicted the supportiveness of their classroom environments. Surprisingly, teacher's perceptions of causes of motivation did not predict either environment or strategy selection.

Reddy, Rhodes & Mulhall (2003) in their longitudinal study brought out positive relationship between perceived teacher's support by adolescents and their adjustment in middle school with relation to depression and self esteem. It observed that girls had lower self esteem as compared to boys when starting middle school however both boys and girls were equally affected by teacher's support in later years. The study mirrored result of various studies that said adolescents tend to experience loss of teacher's support over time during middle school. The reasons may be due to psychological changes in adolescents, multiple teachers teaching various subjects rather than single teacher, larger class size, standardised testing, dense curriculum, etc. It recommended schools to give opportunities for increasing supportive relationship between teachers and children through practices like home assignments, advising, multiyear teacher placements and smaller class size. The study also emphasised on future studies to be conducted on teacher's role in academic efficacy of students, effect of relational process in school with adolescents' adjustment in school.

2.11 Overview of Research Studies on Teacher's Involvement and its Impact

The transition phase of adolescence is believed to be a particularly difficult time for children and teachers could play a pivotal role in helping them navigate this transition successfully. Numerous studies claimed and observed that teacher's Involvement had a positive impact on children. With teachers forming positive bond with students, it was found that classroom gets converted into a supportive space facilitating students academically as well as socially (Hamre & Pianta,2006). The integration bonding between teachers and adolescents was found to have a strong relationship with behaviour outcomes, academic achievement and disciplinary issues (Wentzel; Crosnoe, Johnson, and Elder). Studies brought out positive relationship between the perceived teacher's support by adolescents and their adjustment, with relation to depression and self esteem (Reddy, Rhodes and Mulhall, 2003). Through secure relationship, students were observed to become confident, have improved self esteem, better relationship with peers and became better equipped to take academic challenges and improve on emotional and social development. Students learnt about socially appropriate behaviour as well as about academic expectations and ways to achieve them. Lack of teacher's support was linked to disciplinary problems, under confidence, insecurity, academic difficulties, etc. in some adolescents.

Most of the studies focused on academic achievement or behaviour adjustment while there were few which studied impact of teacher's Involvement on both behaviour adjustment and academic achievement. The researcher could find only a handful of studies that examined the teacher and student relationship from the perspective of both adolescents and teachers, and they mostly included some limitations, while could find none comparing the data obtained from parents, teachers and adolescents. The gap in the literature motivated the researcher to study the perception of teachers, adolescents along with parents.

Teacher's Involvement can be measured through parameters as motivation, warmth, positivity, friendliness, security, academic prowess, teaching methodology, communication with parents, emotional and Academic guidance, etc. Most of the studies used survey method using questionnaire and few also used interview for data collection. In some studies experiment control groups were formed to find the impact of teacher's involvement by comparing with non-control groups. The sample size ranges from 60-500 for students while teacher's sample size was usually 15-50. Few of the research studies which were longitudinal in nature or spanned in multi-state or country had higher sample sizes. Data analysis was done using various statistical techniques ranging from mean, median and mode to T-test, ANNOVA, Pearson's Correlation, etc to establish relationship between variables.

2.12 Research studies on Impact of Parental and Teacher's Involvement on Academic Achievement and Behaviour Adjustment / Mental Wellness

2.12.1 **Conducted in India**

Parmar et al. (2010) studied a sample of 217 high school students in India to find the relationship between Indian adolescents' perceptions of their teacher's and parents' acceptance and behavioural control, students' conduct in school and students' psychological adjustment. It was noticed that the more care the children perceived from parents and teachers, the better was their psychological adjustment. In school conduct, boys and girls were found to have positive effect from parents' support while teacher's support was found to be nonexistent in boys as compared to girls. Both boys and girls found parents and teachers to be firm in behaviour control. 4-point Likert type scale was used to find Parental support for parameters namely paternal warmth / affection, hostility / aggression, indifference / neglect, undifferentiated rejection and Behavioural control (permissiveness strictness). To assess the children's personality, PAR theory's personality sub theory (Rohner 2004) was used for evaluating parameters like hostility / aggression, emotional responsiveness, dependence or defensive independence, self esteem, self adequacy, emotional stability and worldview while their school conduct problems were evaluated by teachers through questions regarding disruptive Behaviours such as defying teacher's authority, cheating, lying, stealing and disobedience. On the other hand, parameters used to understand teacher's Behaviour were warmth / affection, hostility / aggression, indifference / neglect, undifferentiated rejection and overall acceptance rejection and level of under-control / over-control.

Barmola (2013) for the research on 300 adolescents measured mental health through different parameters namely resilience, flexibility, balance and self actualisation while grades of formative assessment was taken into consideration for academic achievement. The study showed significant effect of guidance from parents and teachers on academic performance while no significant effect was found on mental health of students. Recommendation for developing techniques with help of present and related findings in academic setting to properly manage the student life with reference to academic performance, mental health was done.

Thirukkovela & Dhanalakota (2015) found it important to provide suitable emotional, physical and intellectual environments in which a child will have the sense of acceptance, equality and security. The study brought out that adolescents studying in the schools face stress from severe competition at academics and constant comparison at home and school. Lack of recreational activities, vast curriculum, home work and defective examination system were found to emanate stress in adolescents at school, while poor conditions of the family, health problems, problems in understanding the subjects, lack of support from the siblings and parents were noted to cause disturbance in the mental health of the students. The researchers revealed that school teacher and parents played major role in preserving and promoting positive health of students through proper counselling and guidance. Innovating teaching methods by teachers and open communication at home were found to have positive effect on adolescents while effective physical exercises, recreational activities, value education, meditation and yoga were recommended for adolescents to maintain their mental health and adjust to the environment better.

Srinivas & Venkatkrishnan (2016) considered scholastic achievement as an index of child's future in this highly competitive world and tried to find relationship between academic performance, with home environment and teacher's influence. Well educated parents showed positive influence on academic achievement of children, while the home environment with facilitating factors like separate study room, table, etc. also affected the Academic performance of adolescents positively. 60% of adolescents who had help from parents for their studies were reported to have better marks than those children who did not get any help from home .Furthermore, family disharmony showed negative influence on scholastic performance. Teachers also were found to play a vital role in the academic performance of children as 52.7% of adolescents with good academic grades accepted that their teachers were encouraging. Girls were found to be better performer than boys. The study recommended forming an association among parents, teachers, school management and educational authorities to help students in academics as well as emotionally by creating supportive environment and providing personal counselling and behaviour therapy, as and when required.

Madhavan (2016) stated that adolescent period is usually accompanied with new stress, behavioural change and lack of relationship between the family members, which affect their psychosocial development and can cause adjustment issues. Degree of adjustment to the environment was linked to the level of mental health of students. Data analysis of 50 adolescents brought out that mothers' education had significant positive effect on the adolescents' mental health whereas the institutions like family and school were observed to play a vital role to mould the adolescents. The study also discovered that parental support was essential for students' motivation to have a high desire to achieve, while academic institution was also found to play imperative role in personality development and opportunities to improve students' self concept and vision.

Sarkar et al. (2017) in their study at Tripura highlighted that support from parents and teachers aided in academic as well as behavioural excellence of adolescents. It also brought out that girls were better emotionally adjusted than boys while boys were found to be comparatively better than girls in academic adjustment. It recommended that parents and teachers should provide intellectual, social and emotional support to children at the time of stress and also that every secondary and senior school should have a comprehensive programme of guidance, especially educational and vocational.

2.12.2 **Conducted Abroad**

Eccless, Jacquelynne & Harold (1993) in their study on parent school involvement during Early adolescent Years' confirmed the positive impact of parents' role during adolescent years. Furthermore, she added that parents and teachers play a vital role in positive development of adolescents if they work together. She noted that there is a trend of decrease in the collaboration of parents and teachers as children move into adolescent age, which is alarming and needs to be addressed through adopting effective ways to involve parents to work with teachers as a team. She emphasised the importance of parental involvement during adolescent years to avoid youngsters choosing a wrong path or having behavioural problems.

Sanders (1998) in their research on 867 8th grade African American adolescents found that students behaved better when they perceived responsiveness and care from teachers along with support and encouragement from parents to perform well in school. The study also brought out that involvement of church, parents and school has a positive effect on students' behaviour and attitude, more so on school conduct and academic perception. The study thus recommended that guidance and encouragement from adults in the family, school and church can facilitate in developing right attitude and behaviour required for school success in adolescents. The teacher's support was a positive motivator for classroom behaviour. However, the effect of combined support from church, parents and school was found to be profound on academic achievement and attitudinal variables as compared to any of the institution alone i.e. school, church or family. With the above findings, it was concluded that with simultaneous support from all three sources i.e. family, school and church, the effect on their attitude about self, academics and importance of school increases manifolds. Moreover, it was worth noting that the students realised the importance of family-school-community for their academic success and overall wellbeing. The study highlights that family, school and community positively affect Behaviour and academic achievement in adolescents even after considering factors like age, sex, poverty level and family structure. With proper collaboration of all three working towards a common goal of helping students succeed in school, students will be triply benefited.

Chirkov & Ryan (2001) studied effect of perceived parental and teacher autonomy support on academic motivation and wellbeing on 264 high school students from Russia and United States. It was observed that Russian adolescents perceived parents and teachers to be more controlling than their counterpart students in U.S. while in both samples, adolescents perceived autonomy support as a precursor for better academic self motivation and wellbeing. Parental autonomy support was found to be a positive predictor of wellbeing in both the countries as compared to teacher's autonomy support, which was found to be significantly low. For academic motivation, both parental and teacher's autonomy support was positively linked to internal motivation (based on fun or enjoyment for school work) and identified regulation (based on perceived worth of school and studies) of adolescents, wherein teacher's support was rated to affect the internal motivation along with academic regulation in general for students higher than that of parents. The main difference that was observed in the adolescents with regards to country was that Russian adolescents reported higher intrinsic motivation for school than their U.S. counterparts. On the other hand, U.S. students were reported to have higher scale in both forms of internalised motivation, than the Russian students.

Hill and Craft (2003) observed in their study that parental involvement in education related activities both at home and at school, along with the teacher's perceptions about parents' dedication to education, appeared to improve children's school performance. Teachers support to parents and children predicted improved academic skills and competence in social interactions. It was found in the study of 103 KG students that academic behaviour skills of parents mediated the relation between parent school involvement and school achievement. Specifically, parental involvement at school, including volunteering in the classroom and sending materials to school, improved children's academic skills, which in turn improved Maths performance for African American children. For Maths achievement, school involvement, home involvement and valuing education were significant predictors while only perceived value for education was significantly related to reading score.

Soenens & Vansteenkiste (2005) in their study examined 285 adolescents for parents' and teacher's autonomy support from Belgium with relation to their adjustment and levels of self determination in various life domains. Autonomy support parenting was observed to be positively related to GPA in adolescents and also scholastic competence. Teacher's autonomy support was also significantly associated with GPA as well as their exploration and commitment. Along with that, teacher's support was also positively associated with self determination for vocational or job competency. Girls were found to report higher autonomy support from their mothers, higher self determination for school and friendship and also achieved greater GPA, while they displayed lower level of social competence as compared to boys.

Sumbleen (2011) clearly brought out the importance of parents and teachers in a child's life irrespective of their gender. The study indicated that perceived negative parents' support or rejection seriously affects the psychological development and personality of adults (Khaleque and Rohner, 2002) which can further have consequences like depression, aggression, low self esteem, delinquency, emotional instability, etc. in adolescents. On the other hand, perceived positive parental support aids in development of pro-social behaviour, general happiness quotient and low psychological stress in children and also improves peer relation in adolescents. Perceived teacher support was found to be affecting the motivational beliefs and achievements of students thereby improving their psychological adjustment. The researcher further recommended that teacher Parent interaction should be improved for betterment of children. This interaction will not only help teachers in improving their teaching method and better understanding of students but also help parents in realising the importance of their role in children's life. Similarly, policies should also be made to improve school home relationship.

2.13 Overall Conclusion from the Reviews

The review revealed that focusing on Parent teacher partnership might be able to help improve adolescents' academic achievement and also to understand their problems better so as to guide them adjust their behaviour. When students perceived their family support for academic achievement, it also positively influenced their behaviour (Sanders G. Mavis, 1998) while Teacher-Student relationship provided the framework which positively impacted them academically, behaviourally, socially and emotionally. Therefore, many schools aim at improving students' behaviour and academic performance through focusing on a program partnered with parents (Sanders and Sheldon, 2009). Few studies also found that with view on improving students' behaviour and performance, more than often schools only focused on teacher's work at school, ignoring partnership with parents and the community.

Previous studies suggested that cooperation of everyone is required to lessen problematic behaviour and improve learning in school. Sheldon and Epstein claimed that in schools where partnership programs were improved with parents and the community, had reported fewer students being sent to the principal and also got less detentions or suspensions (Sanders and Sheldon, 2009).

Researchers around the globe agreed that adolescents required both parental and teacher's support and involvement to achieve best results. It was suggested that the parents and teachers partnership activities should be deliberated to motivate, connect, uplift and guide students to accomplish success, not just academically but also behaviourally (Epstein et al., 2002). It was also recommended and suggested that schools should ensure to make teachers aware of importance of parental support and guide them through in-service Teacher training to motivate parents for involvement (Green et al., 2007).

Taking into account above parameters, the researcher tried to include all of them by classifying them into emotional involvement; involvement through aspiration, involvement through structure, involvement with friends and school involvement for this study. Questions related to involvement at home included "My parents take out time to listen to my problems", "My parents discuss with me my job aspirations", "My parents keep a tab on T.V. / Internet viewing", "My parents invite my friends at home", "My parents help me in my assignments and projects", etc. The same sets of statements were given to parents to find a comparative assessment of parental involvement for the defined parameters. Teachers were also asked to rate parental involvement in school and studies for robust analysis of data.

Keeping in mind the above parameters, the researcher classified teacher's Involvement into emotional involvement, involvement with parents, instrumental support and structural support. To measure teacher's involvement, researcher asked questions from adolescents such as "My teacher gives personal attention to me", "My teacher updates my parents about my progress", "My teacher uses innovative teaching techniques", "My teacher councils me when I make a mistake", etc. Teacher's perception was taken into account through same set of questions worded differently for comparative analysis. Parents' views were also taken for teacher's involvement for analysis of data.

Taking cue from the review, the researcher tried to incorporate questions firstly to assess the impact of parental and teacher Involvement from the viewpoint of adolescents, parents and teachers through questionnaire (Appx A, B and C). Adolescents were asked to rate impact of parents and teacher's involvement on the basis of statements like "My problems get solved whenever I approach my parents", "The regular interaction of my parents and teachers guides me to improve myself academically", "My class teacher arranges for remedial classes for the subjects I am weak in which helps me in coping up".

Parents' view were taken on impact of their own involvement as well as teacher's involvement through statements like "My child is attentive whenever I try to give our perspective towards life", "I have seen changes in my child's Behaviour with teacher's support". Similarly teachers were asked to rate statements like "parents of my class attend all scheduled events and are always ready for interaction", "My students enjoy and appreciate my class when I use teaching aids and innovative techniques", "I find positive improvement in my student's Behaviour after my counselling". After analysing the collected data, researcher tried to propose best techniques and parameters of parental and teacher's involvement to facilitate adolescents' academic Achievement and behaviour adjustment.

Review of related literature indicated that there is research gap in studies done in India and abroad, as only handful of studies have been conducted on impact of both parental and teacher involvement, but they also had limitation with regard to dependent as well as intervening variables. The researcher was unable to find any relevant study which considered point of view of parents, teachers and adolescents to find parameters positively affecting adolescents' academic achievement as well as behaviour adjustment. This gave an impetus to the researcher for taking this subject as the final research topic which would not only add to the already existing body of knowledge but also enable all the stakeholders in the education system to create a partnership program facilitating adolescents in both academic achievement and behaviour adjustment.

CHAPTER 3

DESIGN OF THE STUDY

3.1 Meaning of Research

The meaning of word 'Research' is to search again and again. Hence research can be defined as an organised process or investigation with the aim of gaining new knowledge of the already existing information. It is the search for knowledge, or a systematic investigation, aiming to establish new facts or solve new or already existing problems, or to prove new ideas, or for developing new theories with an open mind.

According to Best (2006) "The secret of our cultural development has been research, pushing back the areas of ignorance by discovering new truths, which in turn lead to better ways of doing things and better products".

It is a systematic and organised way to find answers to questions. It is systematic as definite set of steps and procedures need to be followed. To get the most accurate outcome, many things are to be followed in the research process. It is not a spontaneous process but a planned procedure with a focus and limited to a specific scope. Overall aim of the research is to find answer. Research is called as a successful one when it is able to finds solutions to problems and also validates the applicability of theories.

Educational research refers to an array of methods by which individuals can evaluate different aspects of education including but not limited to "learning of students, methods of teaching, training of teacher, and classroom dynamics".

3.2 Research Design

Webster's Dictionary describes 'design' as a 'blueprint'. It further defines a 'design' to be a 'creation and nature of the forms, parts, or details of something according to a plan'. A blueprint or design is a concrete form of an abstract idea to make it feasible, cost efficient and mainly executable. Once identification of the problem is done along with formulation of hypotheses, the next vital phase is to decide on the strategies, methods and steps that the researcher would be using to study the problem objectively.

These strategies, methods and steps comprise the blueprint or plan prepared for carrying out the study by the researcher. These plans or blueprints are known as the research design.

According to Selltiz "A research design is the arrangement of conditions for collecting and analysing data in a way that aims to unite relevance to the research purpose with economy in procedure".

According to Kothari (2004) "Research design" can be defined as "the conceptual Structure within which research is constituted. It includes the blueprint, the measurement and also the analysis of data". Research design is required to facilitate smooth functioning of various research operations thus, making research as proficient as possible, producing maximum information with least time, money and effort.

The design allows the researcher to arrange his thoughts in a form where he is able to search for any insufficiencies and imperfections. Furthermore, great care should be taken for preparation of the research design as any error in the design might disturb the entire project.

3.3 Purpose of a Research Design

Following are the purpose of research design :-

1. **Minimise Expenses.** The design of the research significantly influences the reliability of the results attained and provides a solid foundation for all investigations. Preparing the plan before conducting any research helps in minimising the effort, money and time for providing maximum information.
2. **Facilitate the Expansion.** The research design facilitates the expansion of different research operations making the research as efficient as possible.
3. **Collect Relevant Data.** The research design involves prior planning of methods and techniques of data collection relevant to its use in the analysis, also keeping in mind the purpose of the research and availability of resources like personnel and money.
4. **Provide Strategy for the Plans.** The design of the research aids many research operations for working well. It provides in advance the techniques and plans to collect relevant data and analyse it for preparation of the research project.
5. **Provide Information to Other Experts.** A research design offers an overview of complete research process. It can help in taking opinions of experts in

this field as he can understand the research better. The design helps the researcher to organise their ideas, which helps to recognise and repair their mistakes.

6. **Provide Guidance.** A research design provides guidance to other researchers and experts who help in the process.

3.4 Methods of Research

The problem statement and goal of research decides the research method which a researcher follows. With the change in research goal and problem, diverse methods of research can be utilised. The methodologies for research in behavioural and social sciences mostly rely on sociology, psychology and anthropology. As research in these fields emphasise on logical positivism using experimental and quantitative research methods, most of the educational research utilises these methodologies.

Methods of research according to Good, Barr and Scats (1941) may be classified from numerous points of view namely the field to which applied (Education, Psychology, Philosophy, History, Biology etc.), type of research (subjective, quantitative, qualitative etc.), data collection methods, nature and type of test rating scales and questionnaires etc, mathematical symbols or language symbols deployed in recording describing or treating results, forms of thinking (deductive, inductive etc.), control of factors, control and uncontrolled experimentation methods used to establish causal relationship for agreement / difference, etc.

3.5 Research Approaches

In social science, research attempts at understanding social phenomena consisting of complex network of factors connected with each other. The interaction of these interlinked variables can be studied using two approaches :-

1. **Quantitative Approach.** The approach that focuses to study relation between two or more concepts in an accurate manner through use of quantification and statistical techniques is known as quantitative approach.
2. **Qualitative Approach.** The approach that focuses on studying the phenomenon in its totality with the use of verbal discussion and not using any sensible technique is known as qualitative approach.

The present study has used the quantitative approach of research.

3.5.1 Categories of Quantitative Approach

Quantitative approach can be classified into following three main categories :-

1. Descriptive Research.
2. Experimental Research.
3. Correlational Research.
4. Causal-Comparative Research.

1. **Descriptive Research.** Descriptive Research offers a method of investigation, discovery, description and interpretation of what exists in present by understanding the existing conditions' nature and degree. It has undeniably been the most accepted and widely used research method for research studies in education as its studies are designed to gain specific information relating to the current status of phenomenon and draw valid general conclusions from discovered facts whenever possible. Descriptive studies endeavour to find information useful to answer local problems and at the same provide data to form the basis for research which is more fundamental in nature.

It explains data and characteristics of the phenomenon or population being studied. Descriptive research tries to answer the questions of who, where, why and how. It focuses on formulation of hypothesis, testing and the analysing the relationship between non manipulated variables to uncover answers to numerous questions and its goal. It aims at developing generalisations, theories and principles having universal validity. It also concerns with functional relationship. Descriptive studies select and observe the variables already existing or have occurred. The procedures and variables are explained as completely and accurately as is possible to enable the replication of study by other researchers. Data relevant for the purpose of study and capable of finding significant similarities, differences or relationships are measured, classified, analysed, compared and interpreted.

2. **Experimental Research.** Experimental Research offers research methods which enable to understand the basic relationship of phenomenon under controlled conditions. In other words, it aids in identifying the conditions causing the occurrence of a given phenomenon. Experimental research studies involve manipulation of an independent variable .The impact of the manipulation of the independent variable on the dependent variable is studied by attempting to hold all other variables constant except the dependent variable. Experimental method is most useful to identify cause and affect relationships.

3. **Correlational Research.** Correational Research attempts to establish the extent of a relationship between two or more variables using statistical data. It will recognize trends and patterns in data, but would not analysis to prove causes for these observed patterns. The data, relationships, and distributions of variables are only studied only. It does not manipulate the variables but only go far in identifying and are studying them as they occur in a natural setting.

4. **Causal Comparative Method.** Causal Comparative Research endeavours to identify a cause-impact relationship between two or more groups. It aims at discovering possible causes and impact of a characteristics or Behaviour pattern by comparing subjects having the patterns with subjects without the pattern. It is sometimes also known as ex-post-facto research, because it studies the causes or the consequences of difference pre-existing in groups of individuals. Its effort is to attribute the change in the affected variable when manipulation of cause variable cannot be done. The most vital practical consideration in performing causal-comparative research is identification of two or more groups apparently different with each other in an educationally significant way.

3.6 Methodology of the Present Study

The selection of methodology of the study is based upon the aims of the study. The present study aims to study factors influencing students' 'Academic Achievement' and 'Behaviour Adjustment'. The present study applies quantitative and descriptive research. Quantitative paradigm is being used with quantitative methods to describe, analyse and interpret data and conditions that exist. It involves collecting data through self reporting tools for testing the hypotheses to find the relationship of 'Parental Involvement' and 'Teacher's Involvement' with 'Academic Achievement' and 'Behaviour Adjustment' of adolescents.

The present research study is also causal comparative as it studies difference in adolescents' scores of 'Academic Achievement' and 'Behaviour Adjustment' by the levels of scores in 'Parental Involvement' and 'Teacher's Involvement'. The researcher also studied the gender difference of adolescents in the scores of 'Academic Achievement' and 'Behaviour Adjustment' with respect to 'Parental Involvement' and 'Teacher's Involvement'.

3.7 Variables of the Study

According to Best and Kahn (1998, 2006), 'Variables' are the characteristics or conditions that the experimenter observes, controls or manipulates. "The independent variables can be described as those characteristics or conditions that the experimenter controls or manipulates in the attempt to ascertain their relationship with observed phenomena". The characteristics or conditions that change, appear or disappear in the phenomena as the experimenter changes, introduces or removes independent variables helps the experimenter to understand and deduce the result.

3.7.1 Variables of the Present Study

The present investigation includes the following variables :-

1. **Dependent / Outcome Variable.**

(a) Academic Achievement.

(b) Behaviour Adjustment.

2. **Independent / Predictor Variable.**

(a) Parental Involvement.

(b) Teacher's Involvement.

3. **Control Variable.** Variable held constant to assess or clarify the relationship between other variables :-

(a) IQ.

(b) Socio Economic Status.

(c) Gender and Educational Qualification of parents & teachers.

3.8 Sample

3.8.1 Population

Educational phenomena mostly consist of a large number of units. It would be quite impracticable, if not impossible, to observe, interview or test each unit of the population with controlled conditions, with the aim of arriving at generalisation which have universal validity. In some cases, population is so huge that the study would become expensive in terms of time, effort, money and manpower. Therefore, researcher chooses any group of individuals having one or more characteristics in common which interests the researcher and will be termed as population.

A population may also refer to any collection of particular group of human beings or of non human entities such as salaries, prices of commodities, objects, time units, geographical areas and educational institutions.

In the present study, the population comprises of students of standard IX from schools affiliated to the CBSE Board from Greater Mumbai, with medium of instruction as English.

3.8.2 **Sample**

As per Creswell (2002), a sample can be defined as a subgroup of the target population that the researcher is planning to study for the purpose. In the present study, the sample comprises of 250 adolescents, 40 teachers and 40 Parents from different schools of Greater Mumbai.

3.8.2.1 **Determining the Sample Size**

Sample size was determined using sample size determination by 'Mean Method'. Variables in study were measured using a 5-point measurement scale; hence the mean method was adopted.

3.8.2.2 **Formula**

Sample Size 'n' = $\frac{Z^2 S^2}{e^2}$

Where :-

'Z' is 'Standard Score' associated with Confidence Level (95% in current case).

Hence, Standard Score Z = 1.96 (borrowed from Normal Table).

'S' is the 'Variability' in the data set.

S = Range ÷ 6.

'Range' = 5 - 1 = 4 ('Maximum' minus 'Minimum' values in 5-point scale).

6 refers to ±3 'Standard Deviation' values on X axis of standard normal curve.

Hence, 'Variability' S = 4/6 = 0.66

'e' is the 'Tolerable Error'.

e = 8% (in the current study).

Sample size n1 = 324 for adolescents.

Sample size n2= 63 for parents.

Sample size n3= 56 for teachers.

Questionnaires were distributed to 324 respondent adolescents. However 74 questionnaires were discarded for incompleteness or redundant/multiple responses. Hence the final sample size was fixed at 250.

Questionnaires were distributed to 63 respondent parents. However 23 questionnaires were discarded for incompleteness or redundant/multiple responses. Hence the final sample size was fixed at 40.

Questionnaires were distributed to 48 respondent teachers. However, 8 questionnaires were discarded for incompleteness or redundant /multiple responses. Hence the final sample size was fixed at 40.

3.9 Sampling Techniques

Sampling is the process through which a relatively small measure of individual event, object or number of individuals are selected and evaluated in order to discover something about the entire population from which it was chosen. The proportion of the population representative of the entire population is called sample. The strategies applied by researchers during the statistical sampling process are called as statistical sampling techniques. Sampling may be defined as selecting a little part of an aggregate or totality on whose basis a judgment or inference about the aggregate or totality is made. It is the process by which selection of a sample from the population is done. To achieve this, the population is separated into different parts called as sampling unit.

3.9.1 Types of Sampling

There are two main types of sampling techniques :-

1. **Probability Sampling.** The sampling in which the sample is selected in a way that each unit within the population or universe has known chance of being selected is called as 'Probability Sampling'. Types of 'Probability Sampling' are :-

(a) Simple random sampling.

(b) Systematic sampling.

(c) Stratified sampling.

(d) Cluster sampling.

(e) Incidental sampling.

(f) Purposive sampling.

2. **Non Probability Sampling.** Non probability samples are the ones which use whatever subjects are available, instead of following an explicit subject selection process. Various types of non probability sampling are :-

(a) Convenience sampling.

(b) Quota sampling.

(c) Dimensional sampling.

(d) Snowball sampling.

3.10 Sampling Technique Adopted in the Present Research

In the present study, the researcher has uses a two stage sampling technique. At the first stage, schools selection was based on their geographical location using 'Stratified Random Sampling'. The selected strata were North Mumbai, South Mumbai and Western Mumbai. At the second stage, adolescents from these schools were selected using 'Cluster Sampling Technique' where the entire class of class IX was selected. The sample included 324 adolescents, 63 parents and 48 teachers; however 74 adolescents, 23 parents and 8 teachers had to be excluded from the present research study due to incomplete or redundant data. Thus the final sample size was 250 adolescents of 9th standard from schools affiliated to the CBSE Board including 160 boys and 90 girls, 40 parents and 40 teachers from English medium schools located in Greater Mumbai in Maharashtra.

Table 3 shows the number of adolescents, parents and teachers included in the present research study, the number of discarded forms and the accepted sample i e the final sample size.

Table 3 Sample Distribution

Categories	Included Sample	Discarded Sample	% of Discarded Sample	Accepted Sample	% of Accepted Sample
Adolescents	324	74	22.84%	250	77.16%
Parents	63	23	36.51%	40	63.49%
Teachers	48	8	16.67%	40	83.33%

Table 3 shows that the response rate of Adolescents was 77.16% which is fairly acceptable. The wastage rate of forms with respect to incomplete information or multiple responses was 22.84%.The researcher personally conducted the data collection giving all instructions that needed to be followed for the filling up of questionnaires clearly to the adolescents. In addition, students were also encouraged to get their doubts clarified while filling the questionnaires. The rush in filling or uncertainty for responses may be the cause of incompleteness or multiple responses in few questions leading to their dismissal.

Response rate of questionnaire for parents was 63.49% which is nearly average but acceptable. The wastage rate of forms with respect to incomplete information or multiple response was 36.51%.Whie the researcher had clearly mentioned all the instructions in simple and understandable manner in each individual questionnaire along with email and phone number to enable them to clarify their doubts, but probably due to rush in filling or uncertainty for responses may be causes of incompleteness or multiple responses in few questions leading to their dismissal.

Teacher's response rate was found to be 83.33% which is high, while the wastage rate of forms with respect to incomplete information or multiple response was 16.67%.Though researcher had clearly mentioned all the instructions in simple and understandable manner in each individual questionnaire along with email and phone number to enable them to clarify their doubts, but rush in filling or uncertainty for responses may be the cause of incompleteness or multiple responses in few questions leading to their dismissal.

Figure 13 shows sample distribution of adolescents, parents and teachers.

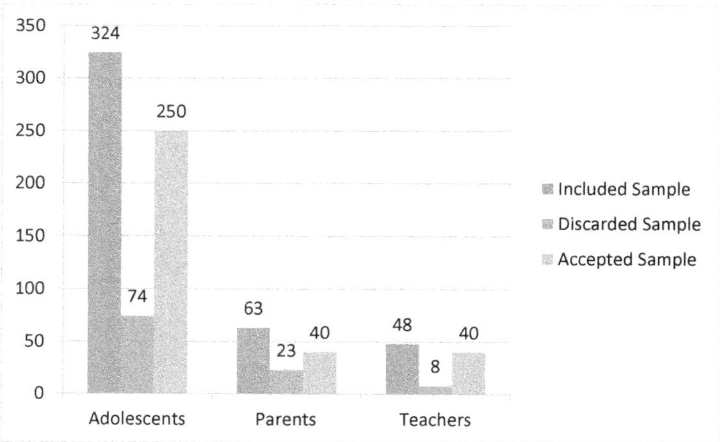

Figure 13 : Sample Distribution of Adolescents, Parent & Teachers

Table 4 shows the schools selected on the basis of geographical location from various strata identified.

Table 4 : Sample Size of schools by Geographical Location

Stratum	Sub Stratum	Number of school	%
Geographical Location	South Mumbai	4	40%
	Western Mumbai	3	30%
	North Mumbai	3	30%

Figure 14 shows the schools selected on the basis of geographical location from various strata identified.

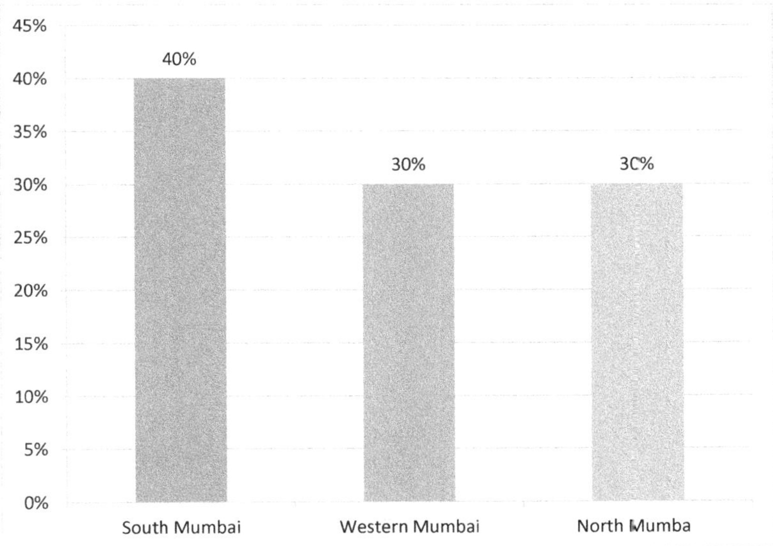

Figure 14 : Sample Size of schools by Geographical Location

Table 5 shows the number of Adolescents, Parents and Teachers selected from various strata identified on the basis of type of geographical location.

Table 5 : Sample Size of Adolescents, Parents & Teachers By Location

Stratum	Sub Stratum	No of Adolescents	%	No of Parents	%	No of Teachers	%
Geographical Location	South Mumbai	89	35.6%	15	37.5%	16	40%
	Western Mumbai	82	32.8%	13	32.5%	13	32.5%
	North Mumbai	79	32%	12	30%	11	27.5%
	Total	250	100%	40	100%	40	100%

Figure 15 shows the number of adolescents, parents and teachers selected from various strata identified on the basis of type of geographical location.

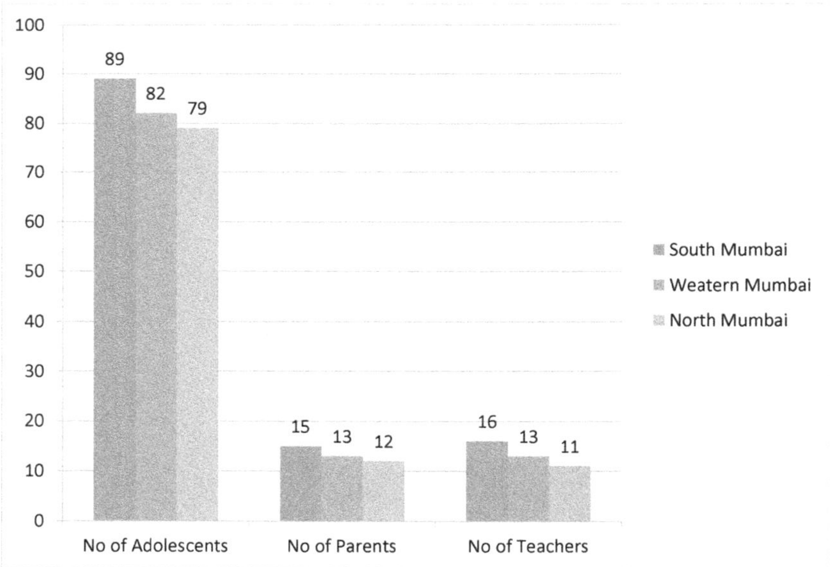

Figure 15 : Sample Size of Adolescents, Parents and Teachers By Location

Table 6 shows the sample size of Adolescents by gender.

Table 6 : Sample Size of Adolescents by Gender

Gender	Frequency	%
Girls	90	36%
Boys	160	64%
Total	250	100

Figure 16 shows the number of Adolescents selected from the various strata identified on the basis of gender.

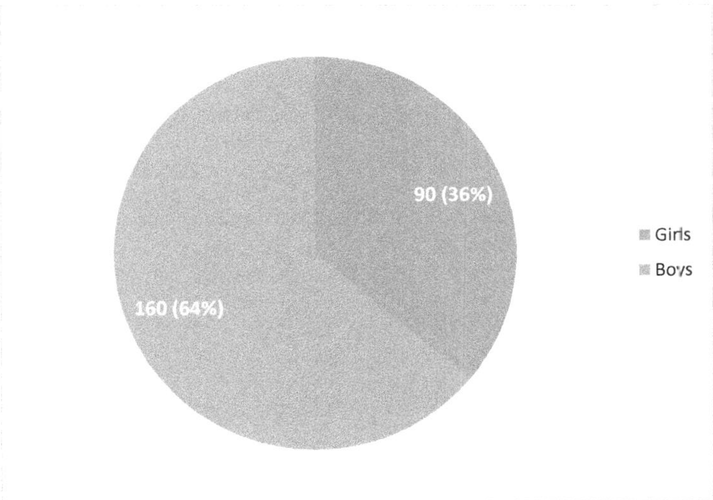

Figure 16 : Sample Size of Adolescents by Gender

3.11 Tools of the Study

According to Koul (1988), a researcher needs various tools for data collection which may vary in "design, complexity, interpretation and administration.".

A variety of tools are used for collecting data in a research. Some commonly used tools in educational research are as follows :-

1. Observation schedule.
2. Questionnaire.
3. Interview schedule.
4. Rating scale.
5. Score card.
6. Attitude scale.
7. Check list.
8. Psychological tests.

The present research study used self assessing questionnaires for data collection from adolescents, parents and teachers by the researcher which were vetted by seven different experts and also tested for reliability and validity before administering to respondents.

3.12 Reliability and Validity of the Questionnaire

3.12.1 Reliability

Reliability is the ability of the scale to produce consistent results. It is the extent to which the research instrument is trustworthy. For the current study, Cronbach's Alpha is used to examine reliability. Cronbach's Alpha is the most popular method of assessing reliability. It's a measure of internal consistency. It is the extent to which items of a construct correlate with each other while aligning the underlying construct. In the current study following thirteen constructs have been used to answer the research questions :-

1. Emotional Involvement of Parents.
2. Aspiration of Parents.
3. Structure by Parents.
4. School & Studies Involvement.
5. Involvement with Friends.

6. Impact of Parental Involvement on Behaviour Adjustment.
7. Impact of Parental Involvement on Academic Achievement.
8. Emotional Involvement of Teachers.
9. Interaction with Parents by Teachers.
10. Instrumental Support by Teachers.
11. Structure by Teachers.
12. Impact of Teacher's Involvement on Behaviour Adjustment.
13. Impact of Teacher's Involvement on Academic Achievement.

Cronbach's Alpha will range between 0 and 1. Values from 0.7 and above indicates 'Reliability', values between 0.6 and 0.7 are 'Borderline Acceptable'.

Table 7 shows 'Reliability Table' for various constructs of the questionnaire.

Table 7 : Reliability Table for Constructs

Construct	No of Items	Alpha	Result
Emotional Involvement t of Parents	4	0.627	Borderline Acceptable
Aspiration of Parents	3	0.718	Reliability Supported
Structure by Parents	3	0.646	Borderline Acceptable
school & Studies Involvement	4	0.626	Borderline Acceptable
Involvement with Friends	4	0.611	Borderline Acceptable
Impact of Parental Involvement on Behaviour Adjustment	12	0.703	Reliability Supported
Impact of Parental Involvement on Academic Achievement	5	0.656	Borderline Acceptable
Emotional Involvement of Teachers	5	0.657	Borderline Acceptable
Interaction with Parents	4	0.644	Borderline Acceptable
Instrumental Support by Teachers	5	0.654	Borderline Acceptable
Structure by Teachers	5	0.635	Borderline Acceptable
Impact of Teacher's Involvement on Behaviour Adjustment	5	0.651	Borderline Acceptable
Impact of Teacher's Involvement on Academic Achievement	6	0.641	Borderline Acceptable

3.12.2 **Validity Test**

Validity is the ability of the instrument to produce precise results. It is the extent to which the scale measures what it is invented to measure. Validity is quality assessment of a measurement instrument. If a scale is not valid or validated, the results are distrustful and incorrect. In the current study, 'Content Validity Index' and 'Content Validity Ratio' as recommended by Lawshe (1975) are used to compute and confirm the validity index. It is an crucial method for gauging concurrence among experts regarding how essential a particular item is. Lawshe suggested that each expert will respond to each item using a 3-point scale i.e. 'Essential,' Useful, but not Essential' or 'Not Necessary'. According to Wilson et al. (2012), who recalculated the critical values of Lawshe's Content Validity Ratio, a CVR value of 0.741 and above (for α = 0.05 and a two-tailed test and 7 experts) will indicate validity of an instrument. Below table shows responses from seven experts to thirteen constructs which are as follows :-

1. Emotional Involvement of Parents.
2. Aspiration of Parents.
3. Structure by Parents.
4. School & Studies Involvement.
5. Involvement with Friends.
6. Impact of Parental Involvement on Behaviour Adjustment.
7. Impact of Parental Involvement on Academic Achievement.
8. Emotional Involvement of Teachers.
9. Interaction with Parents by Teachers.
10. Instrumental Support by Teachers.
11. Structure by Teachers.
12. Impact of Teacher's Involvement on Behaviour Adjustment.
13. Impact of Teacher's Involvement on Academic Achievement.

All experts perceived the content of the question and response options to each question of the variable as 'Essential' (therefore CVR is 1) except for one construct, wherein one expert found contents to be 'Not Necessary', hence the CVR was 0.71.
However, the overall 'Content Validity Index' is 0.97, which is above the requisite threshold and validity of the instrument /questionnaire.

Table 8 shows Content Validity Ratio & Content Validity Index of constructs.

Table 8 : Content Validity Ratio (CVR) and Content Validity Index (CVI)

Variable Code	Expert 1	Expert 2	Expert 3	Expert 4	Expert 5	Expert 6	Expert 7	CVR
V1	X	X	X	X	X	X	X	1
V2	X	X	X	X	X	X	X	1
V3	X	X	X	X	X	X	X	1
V4	X	X	X	X	X	X	X	1
V5	X	NN	X	X	X	X	X	0.71
V6	X	X	X	X	X	X	X	1
V7	X	X	X	X	X	X	X	1
V8	X	X	X	X	X	X	X	1
V9	X	X	X	X	X	X	X	1
V10	X	X	X	X	X	X	X	1
V11	X	X	X	X	X	X	X	1
V12	X	X	X	X	X	X	X	1
V13	X	X	X	X	X	X	X	1
							CVI	0.98

X = Essential

NN = Not Necessary

3.13 Scoring of the Tool

Each item of the questionnaire was rated on a 5-point scale rating from 'Never' (1) to 'Very Often' (5). Table 9 shows scoring of the questionnaire. Table 9 shows the scoring for questionnaires.

Table 9 : Scoring Of Questionnaire

Response Category	**Score Value**
Never	1
Rarely	2
Sometimes	3
Often	4
Very Often	5

3.13.1 Adolescents Questionnaire

The adolescents' questionnaire had 65 questions, with 35 questions related to Parental Involvement and its impact and 30 related to Teacher's Involvement and its impact respectively.

Table 10 shows maximum and minimum score of each variable along with sub groups for Adolescents' questionnaire.

Table 10 : Maximum and Minimum Score for Adolescents' Questionnaire

Variable	Sub Groups	Min Score	Max Score
Parental Involvement	1. Emotional Support of Parents	4	20
	2 Aspiration of Parents	3	15
	3. Structure by Parents	3	15
	4. school & Studies Involvement	4	20
	5. Involvement with Friends	4	20
	Total	**18**	**90**
Impact of Parental Involvement on Academic Achievement		5	20
Impact of Parental Involvement on Behaviour Adjustment		12	60
Teacher's Involvement	1. Emotional Involvement of Teachers	5	25
	2. Interaction with Parents by Teachers	4	20
	3. Instrumental Support by Teachers	5	25
	4. Structure by Teachers	5	25
	Total	**19**	**95**
Impact of Teacher's Involvement on Academic Achievement		6	30
Impact of Teacher's Involvement on Behaviour Adjustment		5	25

Following are some examples of items included in adolescents' questionnaire :-

1. My problems get solved whenever I approach my parents.
2. I take parents counselling positively and change my behaviour accordingly.
3. With my parents help I am able to perform better in my academics.
4. My class teacher regularly checks assignment and homework given.
5. My class teacher arranges for remedial classes for the subjects I am weak in.

A copy of the questionnaire for Adolescents is given in Appendix A.

3.13.2 **Parents' Questionnaire**

Parents' questionnaire had 42 questions, with 38 questions related to Parental Involvement and its impact and 4 related to Teacher's Involvement respectively.

Table 11 shows maximum and minimum score of each variable along with sub groups for parents' questionnaire.

Table 11 : Maximum and Minimum Score for Parents' Questionnaire

Variable	Sub Groups	Min Score	Max Score
Involvement with Adolescents	1. Emotional Involvement	6	30
	2. Aspiration	5	25
	3. Structure	4	20
	4. school & Studies Involvement	6	30
	5. Involvement with Friends	4	20
	Total	**25**	**125**
Impact on Academics		2	10
Impact on Behaviour Adjustment		11	55
Teacher's Involvement		4	20

Following are some examples of items included in parents' questionnaire :-

1. I can make out if my child is upset or disturbed.
2. I keep a tab on my child's daily usage of TV / internet.
3. I invite my child's friends at home.
4. I find my child to be attentive while we discuss about his / her future.
5. I have seen changes in my child's Behaviour with teacher's support.

A copy of the questionnaire for parents is given in Appendix B.

3.13.3 **Teachers' Questionnaire**

Teacher's questionnaire had 24 questions, with 20 questions related to Teacher's Involvement and its impact and 4 related to Parental Involvement respectively.

Table 12 shows maximum and minimum score of each variable along with sub groups for Teacher's questionnaire.

Table 12 : Maximum and Minimum Score for Teacher's Questionnaire

Variable	Sub Groups	Min Score	Max Score
Involvement with Adolescents	1. Emotional Involvement	5	25
	2. Interaction with Parents	5	25
	3. Instrumental Support	7	35
	4. Structure	5	25
	Total	**22**	**110**
Impact on Academics		4	20
Impact on Behaviour Adjustment		4	20
Parental Involvement		4	20

Following are some examples of items included in Teachers' questionnaire :-

1. I try to give personal attention to every Student in the class.
2. I keep my students' parents updated about their performance.
3. I find my students to complete homework on time.
4. I find positive improvement in student's Behaviour after counselling.
5. Parents of my class attend all scheduled events.

A copy of the questionnaire for Teachers is given in Appendix C.

3.14 Data Collection

Data collection is a systematic way of assembling information from various sources to get a perfect and entire picture of the area of interest. It is an important activity which is required in concluding the research. It is an imperative and essential part of a research process for validating and verifying the hypothesis, inferences and generalisation as correct or untenable, thereby accepting or rejecting it respectively. This stage requires involving process of collecting and analysing information on variables of interest, in a recognised methodical fashion that enables the researcher to test the hypothesis and also evaluate the outcomes.

3.14.1 **Procedure Employed for Data Collection**

The researcher made a proper plan for administering the tools to the respondents. Once, all the tools were ready, the researcher first obtained a letter from Head of the Department requesting the school principals to grant permission to the researcher for administering and collecting data using the tools.

For collecting the data for present study the researcher approached principals of various CBSE schools requesting them the permission to administer the tool to class 9th students, teachers and parents. After lot of discussions and persuasion only few principals granted permission to the researcher. Most principals refused to give permission citing various reasons.

As per the discussed and decided schedule with the principals, the researcher then went to the respective schools. In each school, researcher first introduced herself and explained about the requirement and need of the study. The respondents were then explained about the process of choosing their response to the items on the tools. They were also assured that the collected data would be strictly kept confidential and would be put to use for research purpose only. The tools for adolescents and teachers were administered and collected on the same day while for parents it was given to children who volunteered. The teachers were found to be very cordial and cooperative and they helped the researcher in data collection process from students. The researcher noted the students to be highly enthusiastic and co-operational. After collection of data was done, the researcher expressed her gratitude to the respondent teachers and students for their whole hearted cooperation. The whole procedure of collecting the data took around 90 days for the researcher.

3.14.2 **Quantification of the Data**

After collecting the data, the responses of all three questionnaires were quantified by assigning fixed scale value to the items and organising the scores systematically so as to facilitate the ease of tabulation.

3.14.3 **Tabulation**

Tabulation is the process of putting ordered information into formatted frame. Tabulation is a tedious way of inserting classified data into tabular form. The whole raw data needs to be tested on the basis of the intention for which they are collected and tabulating only the usable as well as useful data. According to Garg (2002) the first step for the statistical treatment of data is tabulation. It presents the data in an organised form in orderly columnar display through charts or tables for allowing the measurement of one or more characteristics of the population. As per the application requirement, the tabulation will differ. There is no particular and fixed way to present data, depending on the nature of research and methodology applied multiple paths to understand the data can be employed.

The present study required the data to be tabulated on the basis of various variables (as defined in tables 10, 11 and 12) namely 'Parental Involvement', 'Teacher's Involvement', impact of 'Parental Involvement' on 'Academic Achievement', impact of 'Parental Involvement' on 'Behaviour Adjustment', impact of 'Teacher's Involvement' on 'Academic Achievement' and impact of 'Teacher's Involvement' on 'Behaviour Adjustment'. In addition, above tabulation was also done on the basis of gender wise composition of adolescents in 9th standard.

Some variables had sub dimensions, so data was tabulated as per requirement. The data was tabulated using the Microsoft Excel program.

3.15 Analysis of Data

Analysis is another imperative process of research. Analysis means studying the data tabulated with the aim of determining inherent facts or meanings. It is the process in which valid and statistical techniques are applied to express, evaluate, describe and summarise the data.

It is the process of breaking down the existing complex data into simpler parts and synthesising this data in new arrangements for the purpose of proper interpretation. The collected data is organised and then examined using tables, charts, narratives and graphs.

Good, Barr & Scates (1941) suggested following four useful modes to start with the analysis of data :-

1. To imagine in terms of noteworthy tables that the data permit.
2. To scrutinise the statements of the problem and the previous analysis carefully and to study the original records of the data.

3. To not just think about the data but understand the problem in a layman's perspective and also discussing the problem with others.

4. To evaluate the data by performing various simple statistical calculations.

3.15.1 **Statistical Techniques of Data Analysis**

Statistics can be called a mathematical science related to the collection, interpretation, analysis, explanation and presentation of the data. It helps the human mind to understand the scattered data in a structured format. Statistical analysis is the process of analysing the collected data with the aim of summarising it in a more usable and understandable manner. It also tries to make generalisation about the population on the basis of samples drawn from that population.

Statistics allows the researcher to view the data in two ways :-

1. Descriptive Analysis.
2. Inferential Analysis.

1. **Descriptive Analysis.** 'Descriptive Analysis' is the statistical method used to organise, describe and summarise a collection of quantitative data. It describes the shape of the data and explains the relationship within the data. The purpose of descriptive analysis in the study is to describe basic features of the data and also establish the normality of the data. They are employed for presentation of complex quantitative data in a convenient visual form. Some examples of basic numerical description include 'Mean' and 'Standard Deviation', while charts and graphs are examples of graphical summarisation. In the present investigation, the following measures of central tendency and variability were used for descriptive data analysis :-

(a) Measures of central tendency : Mean, Median and Mode.

(b) Measures of variability : SD, skew and kurtosis.

(c) Estimation of population parameters of 'Mean' and 'SD' of dependent variables.

2. **Inferential Analysis.** Inferential analysis is applied for testing the hypotheses for finding any relationship that exit between two or more variables and also to find difference among the two sample groups. It is very useful to draw conclusions. The tenability of the hypothesis formulated can be tested by using techniques like t-test, ANOVA, ANCOVA, etc. In the present study, statistical techniques that were employed to test the 'Null Hypothesis' are as follows :-

(a) Independent Sample t-Test.

(b) Pearson Correlation.

(c) Path Analysis.

(a) **The Independent Samples t-Test.** The Independent Samples t-Test is a parametric test which compares the means of two independent groups so as to determine whether there is statistical evidence that the means of two unrelated groups are significantly different. In the present study, t-Test was used in comparing following means :-

(i) Parental Involvement (PI) as perceived by Adolescents and Parents.

(ii) Teacher's Involvement (TI) as perceived by Adolescents and Teachers.

(iii) Parental Involvement (PI) as perceived by Parents and Teachers.

(iv) Teacher's Involvement (TI) as perceived by Parents and Teachers.

(v) Impact of PI on AA as perceived by Adolescents and Parents.

(vi) Impact of PI on BA as perceived by Adolescents and Parents.

(vii) Impact of TI on AA as perceived by Adolescents and Teachers.

(viii) Impact of TI on BA as perceived by Adolescents and Teachers.

(ix) Gender wise comparison of PI, TI, impact of PI on AA, impact of PI on BA, impact of TI on AA and impact of TI on BA.

Interpretation of t

The calculated t value is compared to the critical t value from the t distribution table with degrees of freedom $df = n_1 + n_2 - 2$ and chosen significance level. If the calculated t value is greater than the critical t value, then the null hypothesis is rejected. Here for N-2 degree of freedom, the critical ratio of t is read at significance level 0.05 i.e. α=0.05. P value is the sig. (2-tailed) value corresponding to the test statistic. When obtained P value is greater than the significance level (α) the null hypothesis is rejected, while null hypothesis is accepted when obtained value is lesser than the significance level. The obtained value of P is tested for N-2 degrees of freedom at 0.05 level of significance.

(b) **Pearson Correlation.** Pearson Correlation is the test statistics that measures the statistical relationship or association between two continuous variables through the method of co-variance thus making it the best method of measuring the association between variables. It measures the linear correlation between two variables X and Y and is also referred to as Pearson's r, or the bi-variate correlation. In the present study, Pearson Correlation is used to find relation between following variables as perceived by Adolescents, Parents and Teachers :-

(i) Parental Involvement (PI) and Academic Achievement (AA).

(ii) Parental Involvement (PI) and Behaviour Adjustment (BA).

(iii) Teacher's Involvement (TI) and Academic Achievement (AA).

(iv) Teacher's Involvement (TI) and Behaviour Adjustment (BA).

Interpretation of *r*

A Pearson Correlation is a number between -1 and +1 that indicates the extent to which two variables are linearly related. Value of +1 means that a linear equation describes the relationship between X and Y perfectly, where all data points lie on a line in which Y increases as X increases. A value of −1 indicates all data points lying on a line where Y decreases as X increases. Whereas a 0 value implies that there is no linear correlation between the variables.

(c) **Path Analysis of the Model.** Path analysis is a minor version of Structural Equation Model (SEM) developed by Sewall Wright, a geneticist in 1918. With time, it is now widely used in other areas in physical science, social science and sociology. Path analysis can be conducted using statistical programs including SPSS, STATA, etc. The method is also known as Causal Modelling, Analysis of Co-variance Structures and Latent Variables Model. It is an advanced statistical tool used to establish relationship between several variables simultaneously. It is a form of multiple regression analysis used to evaluate causal models which examine the relationship between dependent variable and two or more independent variables. This method can estimate both magnitude and significance of causal connections between variables. Path analysis has following benefits over other predictive models :-

(a) It can fit theoretical model to sample data.

(b) It can study direct, indirect and total impact.

(c) Use of maximum probable techniques to compute path analysis.

(d) Better understanding of causal relationship between independent variables with dependent variable.

(e) Useful to evaluate causal hypothesis.

(f) Clarifies correlation.

(g) Indicates the strength of causal hypothesis.

Usage of Path Analysis.

In the present study, path analysis was used to find relationship between following variables :-

(a) Impact of various constructs of Parental Involvement (PI) namely emotional, Aspiration, Structure, school & Studies and friends on Academic Achievement of Adolescents (AA).

(b) Impact of various constructs of Parental Involvement (PI) namely Emotional, Aspiration, Structure, School & Studies and Friends on Behaviour Adjustment of Adolescents (BA).

(c) Impact of various constructs of Teacher's Involvement (TI) namely Emotional, Interaction with Parents, Instrumental and Structure on Academic Achievement of Adolescents (AA).

(d) Impact of various constructs of Teacher's Involvement (TI) namely Emotional, Interaction with Parents, Instrumental and Structure on Behaviour Adjustment of Adolescents (BA).

Interpretation of Path Analysis. In Path Analysis, a path diagram is constructed where relationship between variables and causal direction between them are laid out. Before conducting a Path Analysis, an input path diagram is constructed which illustrates the hypothesised relationships where the researcher uses arrows to show relationships between variables. For instance, if an arrow points from variable A to variable B, it implies that A variable is hypothesised to influence variable B. Data is then fed into the variables and hypothesis testing is done on it. The path coefficients, standard errors and P values are calculated with statistical software (the researcher used SPSS Statistical Software). With P values, frequently the criterion $P < 0.05$ is used instead $P \leq 0.05$ for accepting a hypothesis. The P value for each term tests the null hypothesis. If the coefficient is equal to zero, it indicates no impact. A low P value (< 0.05) indicates that the null hypothesis can be rejected while a higher P value (> 0.05) indicates that the null hypothesis can be accepted.

3.16 Model 1

For Measuring Impact of Parental Involvement

A model is an abstract way of schematising a process, so that the strategy can be generalised to solve similar problems in other fields. This model is inspired by PI Constructs' in Keith et al. and is aimed at finding the relationship between 'Parental Involvement' and 'Behaviour Adjustment', 'Parental Involvement' and 'Academic Achievement'.'Parental Involvement' is further divided into five constructs namely 'Emotional Involvement', 'Aspiration of Parents', 'Structure by Parents', and 'school & Studies Involvement'.

'Emotional Involvement' is the support parents give to their child to help him / her emotionally during adolescent years, 'Aspiration of Parents' refers to how the parents convey their future aspirations for their child so as to inspire and motivate them. 'Structuring by parents' takes account of the daily routine and timetable parents make to organise their child's life. 'School & Studies Involvement' consists of the activities parents participate with respect to their child's school and studies. 'Involvement with Friends' comprises the extent to which the parents involve themselves with their child's friends.

The model tries to establish impact of 'Parental Involvement' with the help of above constructs on 'Behaviour Adjustment' as well as 'Academic Achievement' in adolescent students. Figure 17 shows the proposed model for measuring impact of 'Parental Involvement' on 'Behaviour Adjustment' and 'Academic Achievement'.

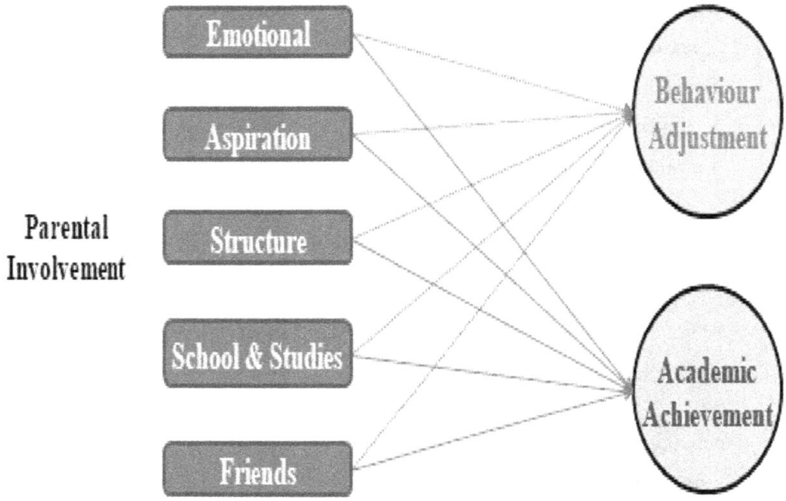

Figure 17 : Model Measuring impact of 'Parental Involvement' on 'Behaviour Adjustment' & 'Academic Achievement'

3.16.1 Research Questions

Following research questions will be answered through the above model :-

1. Whether Parental Involvement (PI) will impact 'Academic Achievement' (AA) ?
2. Whether Parental Involvement (PI) will impact 'Behaviour Adjustment' (BA) ?
3. Whether Emotional Involvement, Aspiration, Structure, school & Studies, and Friends will impact 'Academic Achievement' (AA) ?
4. Whether Emotional Involvement, Aspiration, Structure, school & Studies, and Friends will impact 'Behaviour Adjustment' (BA) ?

3.16.2 Hypothesis

1. PI will positively impact AA.
2. PI will positively impact BA.
3. Following constructs of PI will positively impact AA :-

(a) Emotional Involvement.

(b) Aspiration.

(c) Structure.

(d) School & Studies.

(e) Friends.

4. Following constructs of PI will positively impact BA :-

(a) Emotional Involvement.

(b) Aspiration.

(c) Structure.

(d) School & Studies.

(e) Friends.

3.16.3 Model Fit

Model Fit is comparing the theoretical model with sample data. Five Fit Indices have been used to assess the Model Fit. Fit Indices used to assess the Model Fit are CMIN / DF, CFI, GFI, PNFI and RMSEA.

3.16.3.1 **Definitions**

Definition of Fit Indices (Table 13) are as follows :-

1. **CMIN / DF (Minimum Discrepancy as Indexed Chi-square).** CMIN [chi-square statistics (χ 2)] is the minimum value of discrepancy. In case of maximum possibility estimation, CMIN contains the chi-square statistics. The overall measure of how many implied moments differ from sample moments is known as chi-square statistic.

2. **CFI (Comparative Fit Index).** The Comparative Fit Index (CFI) is the analysis of the Model Fit by examining the discrepancy between data and the hypothesised model and in the process adjusts the issues of sample size inherent in the chi-squared test of Model Fit and the scaled Fit Index.

3. **GFI (Goodness of Fit Index).** The Goodness of Fit Index (GFI) is a measurement of fit between observed covariance matrix and the hypothesised model. The GFI range between 0 and 1, with a value of over 0.9 is generally indicative of acceptable Model Fit.

4. **PNFI (Parsimonious Normal Fit Index).** Parsimonious Normal Fit Index (PNFI) adjusts degrees of freedom. It is considered lower in goodness as compared to other indices. Though there is no threshold level for PNFI but value greater than 0.5 is acceptable.

5. **RMSEA (Root Mean Square Error of Approximation).** The Root Mean Square Error of Approximation (RMSEA) is used to avoid issues of sample size by analysing the discrepancy between optimally chosen construct estimates and the population covariance matrix with the hypothesised model. The RMSEA ranges from 0 to 1, wherein smaller values indicate better Model Fit.

Table 13 shows the Fit Indices of the Model.

Table 13 : Fit Indices of the Model

Fit Indices	Observed	Criteria for Acceptable Fit	Result
CMIN/DF (Minimum Discrepancy as Indexed Chi-square)	1.701	Less than 5	Acceptable Fit
CFI (Comparative Fit Index)	0.957	More than 0.9 for Good Fit. Between 0.9 to 0.8for Borderline Fit.	Acceptable Fit
GFI (Goodness of Fit Index)	0.953	More than 0.9	Acceptable Fit
PNFI (Parsimonious Normal Fit)	0.568	More than 0.5	Acceptable Fit
RMSEA (Root Mean Square Error of Approximation)	0.053	Less than 0.08 for Adequate Fit. Between 0.08 and less than 0.1 for Borderline Fit.	Acceptable Fit

3.16.3.2 **Result of Fit Indices**

As revealed in Table 13, all the five Fit Indices (CMIN/DF, CFI, GFI, PNFI and RMSEA) show a good fit between the hypothetical model and the sample data. Model Fit summary is attached in Appx D.

3.16.4 **Model Validation on Using Path Analysis**

Path analysis is a minor version of Structural Equation Model (SEM) developed by Sewall Wright, a geneticist in 1918. With time, it is now widely used in other areas in physical science, social science and sociology. Path analysis can be conducted using statistical programs including SPSS, STATA, etc. The method is also known as causal modelling, analysis of covariance structures, and latent variables models. It is an advanced statistical tool used to establish relationship between several variables simultaneously. It is a form of multiple regression analysis used to evaluate causal models which examines the relationship between dependent variable with two or more independent variables. This method can estimate both magnitude and significance of causal connections between the variables. Path analysis has following major benefits over other predictive models :-

1. It can fit theoretical model to sample data.

2. It can study direct, indirect and total impact.
3. Use of maximum probable techniques to compute path analysis.
4. Better understanding of causal relationship between independent variables with dependent variable.
5. Useful to evaluate causal hypothesis.
6. Clarifies correlation.
7. Indicates the strength of causal hypothesis.

3.16.4.1 **Assessing the Significance of Path**

In Path analysis, a path diagram is constructed where relationship between variables and causal direction between them are laid out. Before conducting a path analysis, an input path diagram is constructed which illustrates the hypothesised relationships where the researcher uses arrows to show relationships between variables. For instance if an arrow points from A variables to B, it implies that A variable is hypothesised to influence variable B. Data is then fed into the variables and hypothesis testing is done on it. The path coefficients, standard errors, and P values are calculated with statistical software (The researcher used SPSS Statistical Software) With P values, frequently the criterion P < 0.05 is used instead P ≤ 0.05 for accepting a hypothesis.

The p-value for each term tests the null hypothesis. If the coefficient is equal to zero, it indicates no impact. A low p-value (< 0.05) indicates that the null hypothesis can be rejected while a higher p-value (> 0.05) indicates that the null hypothesis can be accepted. Figure 18 illustrates the Path Coefficients for all the linkages of the Model.

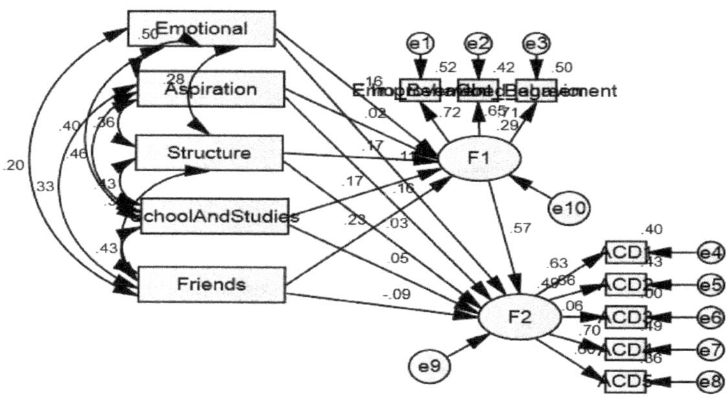

Figure 18 : Path Coefficients of the Model

3.17 Model 2

For Measuring Impact of Teacher's Involvement

Figure 19 illustrates Model for measuring impact of 'Teacher's Involvement' on 'Behaviour Adjustment' and 'Academic Achievement' and is inspired by the theoretical model of Affective Teacher-Student Relationships (TSR) and students' school Outcomes by Roorda D. L et al.

3.17.1 **Research Questions**

Following research questions will be answered through the above model :-

1. Whether 'Teacher's Involvement' (TI) will impact 'Academic Achievement' (AA) ?
2. Whether 'Teacher's Involvement' (TI) will impact 'Behaviour Adjustment' (BA) ?
3. Whether Emotional Involvement, Interaction with Parents, Instrumental Support & Structure will impact 'Academic Achievement' (AA) ?
4. Whether Emotional Involvement, Interaction with Parents, Instrumental Support and Structure will impact 'Behaviour Adjustment' (BA) ?

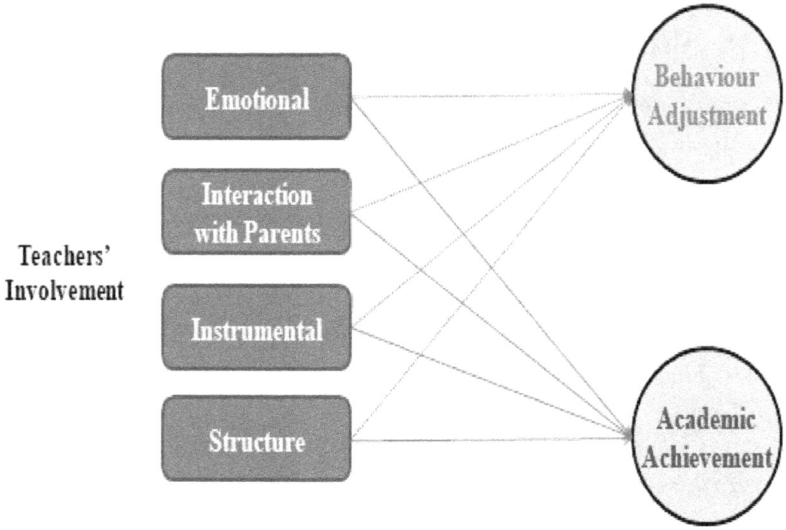

Figure 19 : Model Measuring impact of 'Teacher's Involvement' on 'Behaviour Adjustment' & 'Academic Achievement'

3.17.2 **Hypothesis**

1. TI will positively impact AA.
2. TI will positively impact BA.
3. Following constructs of TI will positively impact AA :-

(a) Emotional Involvement.

(b) Interaction with Parent.

(c) Instrumental Support.

(d) Structure.

4. Following constructs of TI will positively impact BA :-

(a) Emotional Involvement.

(b) Interaction with Parent.

(c) Instrumental Support.

(d) Structure.

3.17.3 **Model Fit**

Model Fit is comparing the theoretical model with sample data. Five Fit Indices have been used to assess t he Model Fit. Fit Indices used to assess the Model Fit are CMIN / DF, CFI, GFI, PNFI and RMSEA.

Table 14 shows the Fit Indices of the Model.

Table 14 : Fit Indices of the Model

Fit Indices	Observed	Criteria for Acceptable Fit	Result
CMIN / DF (Minimum Discrepancy as Indexed Chi-square)	2.32	Less than 5	Acceptable Fit
CFI (Comparative Fit Index)	0.86	More than 0.9 for Good Fit. Between 0.9 to 0.8 for Borderline Fit.	Borderline Fit
GFI (Goodness of Fit Index)	0.915	More than 0.9	Acceptable Fit
PNFI (Parsimonious Normal Fit)	0.59	More than 0.5	Acceptable Fit
RMSEA (Root Mean Square Error of Approximation)	0.073	Less than 0.08 for Adequate Fit.. Between 0.08 and less than 0.1 for Borderline Fit.	Acceptable Fit

3.17.3.1 **Result of Fit Indices**

As revealed in Table 14, all the five Fit Indices (CMIN / DF, CFI, GFI, PNFI and RMSEA) show a good fit between the hypothetical model and the sample data. Model Fit summary is attached in Appx E.

3.17.4 **Assessing the Significance of Path**

Figure 20 illustrates the Path Coefficients for all the linkages of the Model.

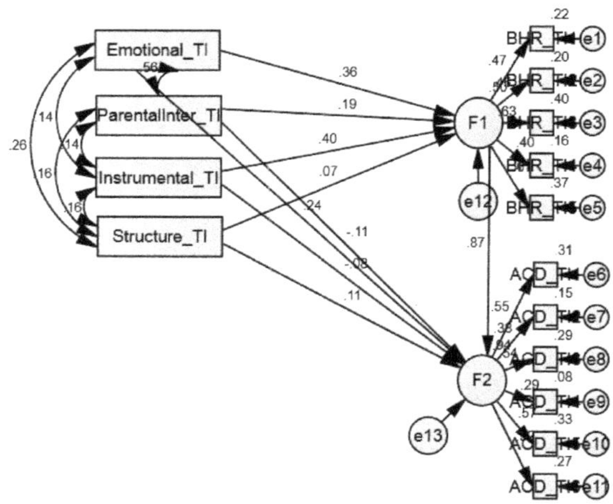

Figure 20 : Path Coefficients of the Model

3.18 Model 3

For Measuring Impact of Parental & Teacher Involvement

The model is inspired by Development Indicators of Adolescents from Sinbad A.M. PI Constructs' in Keith et al. and theoretical model of Affective Teacher-Student Relationships (TSR) and students' school Outcomes by Roorda D. L et al. The endeavour of the model is to find relationship between Parental and Teacher's Involvement with 'Academic Achievement' and 'Behaviour Adjustment'. Figure 21 illustrates 'Model for measuring impact of Parental and Teacher Involvement on 'Behaviour Adjustment' and 'Academic Achievement'.

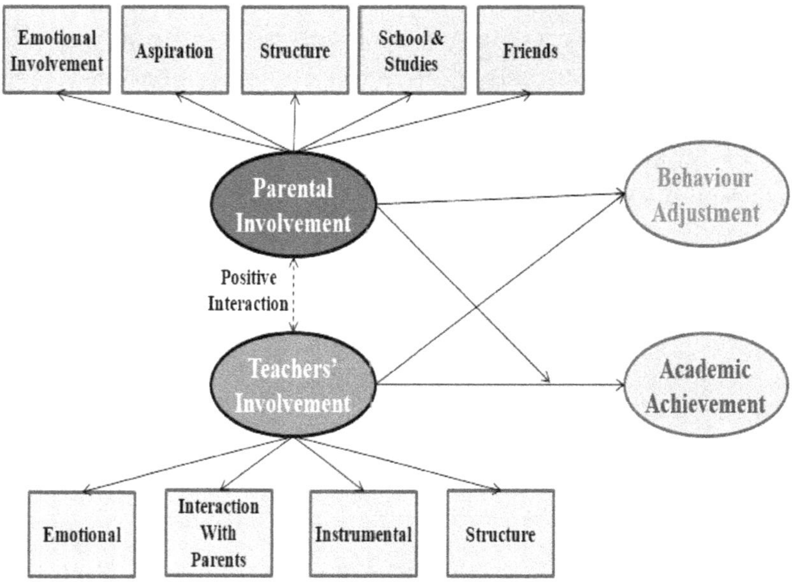

Figure 21 : Model Measuring impact of Parental & Teacher Involvement on 'Behaviour Adjustment' & 'Academic Achievement'

3.18.1 'Parental Involvement'

In the present research study, the researcher has considered Parental Involvement as activities including looking after or monitoring a child's activities at home and in school during adolescent years. She further classified Parental Involvement into following constructs :-

1. **Emotional Involvement.** Emotional Involvement includes emotional wellbeing of adolescents through expressing love, care and understanding to their child so that he / she feel confident to share his / her problems and emotional needs with them. Their availability of time, interest and emotional support is reflected in adolescents' perception for their Parents' emotional involvement which was measured through questions like "My parents take out time and sit with me whenever I have faltered", etc.
2. **Aspiration.** This involves parents' discussing about their as well as their child's ambitions and aims in life. Parents guiding and explaining different options that can be pursued by their child which will help him / her to choose a goal and decide his / her aspirations. Perception of adolescents with relation to Aspiration of Parents as an indicator of Parental Involvement was measured through questions such as "My parents discuss with me my career options", etc.
3. **Structure.** This involves parents' monitoring and Structuring their child's daily activity or routine for studies, sports, screen time, etc. Stating clear expectations and rules; maintaining discipline via mechanisms as taking out time and explaining the mistake and motivating him / her to correct and using punishment as a last resort can be termed as Structuring by Parents. Adolescents were asked to rate their Parental Involvement for Structuring at home through questions like "My parents keep a tab on my daily usage of TV / internet", etc.
4. **School & Studies.** It includes Parental Involvement in their child's studies and school activities, their organised and unorganised interaction with teachers and guidance at home for studies. Adolescents rated parents for their help and guidance to improve their grades and accomplishments in school activities through questions such as "My parents take out time to teach me and help me in my assignments", etc.
5. **Friends.** Friends being a very crucial element of being an adolescent can't be ignored. Adolescents tend to get affected by how their parents treat their friends. Involvement of Parents in The present research study includes parents' interaction with

their child's friends, organising events and activities with them, knowing them personally or guiding their child about whom to be friends with. Adolescents perceived their Parental Involvement with their friends through questions like "My parents get involved in all the activities with my friends like movie, picnic, etc", etc.

3.18.2 **Impact of Parental Involvement on 'Behaviour Adjustment'**

Adjustment can be described as the process by which living organisms maintain a balance between the needs and the circumstances Shaffer L.F(1961). Kulshrestha S.P. (1979) explained that the Adjustment process is a way for individuals to deal with tensions, stress, conflicts, etc., that come along the way to meet his or her needs. In this process, the individual also attempts to maintain a harmonious relationship with the environment. UNICEF (2011) report estimated that around 20 percent of the world's adolescents have mental health or Behaviour problems. To understand 'Behaviour Adjustment' in adolescents, problem Behaviour and social competence are important criteria. Social competence can be measured in school through participation in class discussions, cooperation with classmates, completion of work, etc. while at home the parameters could be spending time with family, discussing personal issues and following instructions, etc. Problem Behaviour in class can be assessed though analysing items such as anxiety, disruption in class and difficulty following directions. Similarly, at home, lack of socialising, tantrums and aloofness can be signs of problem Behaviour.

In the present research study, 'Behaviour Adjustment' has been considered as the extent to which the adolescents are able to cope up to ever changing environment at home, outside and school.

Adolescents' perception of Parental' Involvement and its impact on Behaviour was observed through constructs like supportive emotional environment at home that made adolescents comfortable to ask questions or share their personal problems, improvement in Behaviour due to parents' intervention, discipline and rules for life.

Perceived impact on 'Behaviour Adjustment' was measured through questions like "My problems get solved whenever I approach my parents", etc.

3.18.3 **Impact of Parental Involvement on 'Academic Achievement'**

'Academic Achievement' has been explained as measured performance of a present level of Student knowledge through a series of standardised educational tests held in school. More frequently the term is used to depict performance in the curriculum subjects. 'Academic Achievement' or performance can be described as the degree to which a Student, teacher or the institution has accomplished their short or long-term educational goals. It is also an indicator of mental wellness of an adolescent and unexpected fall in the performance could be a precursor of mental stress owing to some external factors. Numerous methods are useful in measuring the Academic performance including standardised Achievement test scores, report cards, grades and teacher ratings. In the present research study, the researcher has considered 'Academic Achievement' as the extent to which students achieve their short or long term educational goals. Cumulative marks or grades are also representative of 'Academic Achievement'.

students' descriptions of Parental' involvement and maintaining a supportive environment, that help and guide them to perform better academically and / or help them achieve their short term and long term goals for 'Academic Achievement', were used to measure impact of Parental' involvement on 'Academic Achievement'. Perceived impact on 'Academic Achievement' was measured through grades in previous exams along with questions like "My parents monitoring of my grades motivates me to perform better academically", etc.

3.18.4 **Process of Analysis of Questionnaires**

3.18.4.1 **Adolescents' Questionnaire**

The response set for all the questions utilised a 5-Point Likert Type Scale in order to match the previous items and be easier for students to use with choices ranging from 'Never' to 'Very Often'. The negatively worded items were reverse coded for scoring purposes.

The items in the section of the adolescents' questionnaire asked adolescents to react to various statements regarding 'My parents' wherein they were instructed to consider about either of the Parent or both, as applicable, for individual questions before they started marking the answers.

3.18.4.2 **Parents' Questionnaire**

Parents' questionnaire carried same questions but worded from parents' point of view to compare the perception of parents and adolescents for Parental Involvement in all sub groups namely emotional, aspiration, structure, school & studies and friends.

3.18.5 **'Teacher's Involvement'**

In the present research study, the researcher has considered 'Teacher's Involvement' as activities including motivating, monitoring and influencing a child's activities in school during adolescent years. She further classified Teacher's Involvement into following constructs :-

1. **Emotional Involvement.** 'Emotional Involvement' involves teacher's support and interest in students' wellbeing along with their Academic progress. Teachers spending time, showing interest in students' life, their sense of caring and emotional support are some parameters which exceeds the 'required' teaching Behaviours and is reflected in students' perception of teacher's attempts to connect on an emotional level. Students were requested to rate their teacher's care for their wellbeing via questions like "My class teacher gives personal attention to every Student in the class", etc.
2. **Interaction with Parents.** 'Interaction with Parents' includes communication of teachers with parents in the form of feedbacks, counselling session, PTMs, etc. It also includes whether the teacher is able to recognise students' Academic and / or emotional distress. Students' perception about the interaction was measured using questions like "My class teacher keeps my parents updated about my performance in school", etc.
3. **Instrumental Support.** 'Instrumental Support' involves teaching practices which teachers incorporate to impart Academic concepts to the entire class and individual students, using diverse strategies (e.g. smart boards, group discussions, etc.) to provide additional learning experience. Students rated teachers for their help and guidance to improve their classroom grades and accomplishments through questions like "My class teacher uses teaching aids and innovative techniques (e.g. smart board, quiz, crossword, etc.) while teaching in class", etc.
4. **Structure Support.** 'Structure by Teacher's involves stating clear expectations, providing rewards, fair treatment and consequences, feedback for mistakes and ways for improvement, maintain discipline via mechanisms as taking out time and explaining the wrongdoer his / her mistake and motivate him / her to correct it and using punishment only as a last resort. Questions were asked to measure the perceived Structure support by Teachers as "My class teacher separately counsels me when I make any mistake", etc.

3.18.6 Impact of Teacher's Involvement on 'Behaviour Adjustment'

In the present research study, the researcher has considered as 'Behaviour Adjustment' as the extent to which the adolescents are able to cope up to ever changing environment at home, outside and school.

students' descriptions of Teacher's Involvement and creation of supportive emotional environment that made them comfortable to share their personal problems, ask questions, adjust their Behaviour as per rules, lead disciplined life, etc. were used to measure the impact of Teacher's Involvement on Behavioural Adjustment as perceived by adolescents. Perceived impact on Behavioural Adjustment was measured through questions like "I find my Teacher's instructions about the rules and its importance helpful to mould my Behaviour positively", etc.

3.18.7 Impact of Teacher's Involvement on 'Academic Achievement'

In the present research study, the researcher has considered 'Academic Achievement' as the extent to which students achieve their short or long term educational goals. Cumulative marks or grades are also representative of 'Academic Achievement'.

students' descriptions of Teacher's Involvement and creation of supportive environment, that help and guide them to perform better academically and / or help them achieve their short term and long term goals for 'Academic Achievement', were used to measure impact of Teacher's Involvement on 'Academic Achievement'. Perceived impact on 'Academic Achievement' was measured through grades in previous exams along with questions like "With constant monitoring of homework and assignment by my class teacher, I complete my homework and improve my assignments on time", etc.

3.18.8 Process of Analysis of Questionnaires

3.18.8.1 Adolescents' Questionnaire

The response set for all of the items utilised a 5-Point Likert Type Scale in order to match the previous items and be easier for students to use with choices ranging from 'Never' to 'Very Often'. The negatively worded items were reverse coded for scoring purposes. The questions in the section of the adolescents' questionnaire asked adolescents to react to various statements regarding "My teacher". However, since multiple teachers through the day taught participants, students assumed 'Class Teacher' as that teacher for marking the answers to avoid any confusion.

3.18.8.2 **Teacher's Questionnaire**

Teacher's questionnaire had same questions but worded from teacher's point of view to compare the perception of teachers and adolescent for Teacher's Involvement in all sub groups namely emotional, Interaction with Parents, Instrumental and structural support.

3.19 Limitations and Scope of the Study

The impact of Parental and Teacher Involvement was limited to adolescents' 'Academic Achievement' and Behaviour Adjustment only. The other variables like self concept, self esteem, creativity, study habits, stress, family dynamics and school type, etc. were not included This research was restricted to the students of standard 9th and did not include those studying at any other level of education in school or college. The present research study involved only the students studying through the CBSE Board and not ICSE, SSC, IGCSE or IE.

The variable 'Academic Achievement' was studied with respect to adolescents' 'Academic Achievement' in their previous exam along with responses from participants (parents, teachers and adolescents) related to increased interest / keenness to work towards 'Academic Achievement'. The 'Academic Achievement' under other existing cognitive domains was not under the scope of this study.

The variable 'Behaviour Adjustment' was studied with respect to adolescents' ability to adjust to their environment at home and school only, which could be confirmed by them or their parents and teachers. The Behaviour Adjustment included constructs as listed in the research definitions only. The unobserved 'Behaviour Adjustment', as well those that happened at places other than home and school were not under the scope of the present research study.

The sample includes students from public and private schools of the CBSE Board. Schools situated in Greater Mumbai were only included for the present research study. The schools coming under the jurisdiction of Navi Mumbai and Thane were not included. The present research study was conducted in English medium schools and it excluded schools with other mediums of instruction such as Marathi, Hindi.

The present research study includes gender difference of adolescents response with respect to parents' and teacher's involvement and its' impact. No other constrains like financial status, parents' education level, parental style, home environment, social stress of the students, gender difference of parents & teachers, etc. were considered for the present research study. The present research study focused only on impact of parental and teacher's involvement on 'Behaviour Adjustment' and 'Academic Achievement' of adolescents. It purposefully did not include involvement by others and their impact, nor did it include variables other than 'Academic Achievement' and 'Behaviour Adjustment' which may have also got affected by Parental and Teacher's Involvement.

3.20 Significance of the Study

Adolescents are the bearers of humanity for the future generations of the free world. With such onerous responsibility lined up for their delicate shoulders, it becomes vital that they are raised as healthy, happy individuals and to achieve this it is imperative they get appropriate support from parents and teachers.

Over time, parental involvement and teacher involvement have proved very pertinent, keeping both practitioners and theoreticians in the field of education busy. The researcher observed that many national and international literature claimed that everyone concerned – students, parents, teachers, schools, society as a whole – will benefit if parents and teachers are convinced to get involved in their children's education.

The present research study advocates that, in spite of the popularity of the concept, parental involvement and teacher involvement concepts are still vague, and their impact is rather unclear. This research study shall prove beneficial in understanding the scope of parental involvement and teacher involvement and also their impact on behaviour adjustment and academic achievement in adolescents. Parents are willing to give their support to their adolescent child at home and at school too but are often apprehensive or clueless as to how they could participate in their child's life. This research study helps them to not only understand their role but also how to guide their adolescent child to gain maximum benefit.

The research study also provides teachers with a framework to aid their students to improve their academic performance and interpersonal interactions. The significance of the present study is to facilitate all round development of adolescents with focus on 'Behaviour Adjustment' and 'Academic Achievement'. The researcher emphasises that parents and teachers should shoulder responsibility to show adolescents the right direction to improve themselves and this research helps in the same.

The present research study focuses on parental and teacher's involvement on adolescents studying in class 9th and its impact on adolescents' 'Behaviour Adjustment' as well as 'Academic Achievement'. Since scarcely any studies have been done in the past on this topic and it is the gap in the existing body of knowledge, the present research study is beneficial in filling these gaps.

The present research study is helpful to the schools, parents, teachers and students as it gives an understanding about how exactly the parental and teacher involvement in adolescent years can help in quantifiably improving the 'Academic Achievement' and 'Behaviour Adjustment'.

This research study throws light upon various constructs of parental and teacher involvement which facilitates in recommending parental and teachers involvement procedures beneficial for the 'Academic Performance' and 'Behaviour Adjustment' of adolescents, with collaboration of all stakeholders in the field of education like students, parents, teachers and school.

The present research study is especially significant in bringing to the fore the relatively lesser addressed inter-dependent variables, and in turn the multiple constructs, which cumulatively have a cascading effect in the shaping of adolescents as robust and capable citizens of the future world.

CHAPTER 4

DESCRIPTIVE DATA ANALYSIS

4.1 Descriptive Analysis

Descriptive Analysis are utilised to present quantitative descriptions in a manageable Structure. Raw data if simply presented is hard to visualise and comprehend, especially if it's a large data. Descriptive analysis thus enables us a more meaningful presentation of the data along with an easier interpretation.

4.1.1 Importance of Descriptive Analysis of Data

Descriptive analysis of data is limited to generalising a particular group of individuals observed. Conclusions are not extended beyond this group, and no assumption can be made of any similarity to those outside the group. The data describes one and only one group. The descriptive analysis of data provides the following :-

1. The first summaries and estimates arranged in tables and graphs.
2. Information regarding the variability or uncertainty in the data.
3. Signs and indication of unexpected patterns and observations that need consideration while doing formal analysis.

Descriptive statistics describes the basic features of the data in the study. They present simple summaries as regards to the sample and the measures. Collectively with simple graphics analysis, they outline the basis of virtual quantitative analysis of data. With descriptive analysis, one can basically describe what is or what the data shows.

4.1.2 Procedure for Descriptive Analysis

According to Garrett and Woodworth (1958) "Data collected from test and experiment may have little meaning to the investigator until they have been arranged or classified in some systematic way." The data once grouped, is analysed using different statistical measures to draw out conclusions. The diverse statistical measures used for descriptive analysis of the data in the present study are as follows :-

1. Measures of central tendency.
2. Measures of spread or dispersion.
3. Measures of divergence from normality.
4. Graphical representations.

4. 2 Variables of the Study

The major variables in the present research study were as follows :-

1. **Outcome Variable.**

(a) Academic Achievement.

(b) Behaviour Adjustment.

2. **Predictor Variable.**

(a) Parental Involvement.

(b) Teacher's Involvement.

3. **Control Variables.**

(a) IQ.

(b) Socio Economic Status.

(c) Gender and Educational Qualification of parents and teachers.

4.3 Descriptive Analysis of Variables in the Study

The data was collected from adolescents, teachers and parents through individual questionnaires.(Appx A, Appx B and Appx C). The data was further classified into following three categories:-

1. As perceived by Adolescents.
2. As perceived by Parents.
3. As perceived by Teachers.

The collected data after tabulation was analysed through statistical tools namely mean Standard Deviation (SD), coefficient of variance, etc. Normalcy of collected data was checked through skeweness and kurtosis while variable constructs were analysed through tabulation and graphical representation.

4.4 Descriptive Analysis of Academic Achievement (AA)

4.4.1. Descriptive Analysis of AA as Perceived by Adolescents

Table 15 shows the measures of central tendency and measures of variability of the AA as perceived by Adolescents.

Table 15 : Descriptive Statistics of AA as Perceived by Adolescents

Sample	Mean	S.D.	Coefficient of Variance (S.D / Mean*100)	Skew	Kurtosis
250	3.28	0.482	14.70%	- 0.209	- 0.588

Interpretation

According to George & Mallery (2010) variables with skew values between +1 and -1 and kurtosis values between +2 and -2 indicate normalcy. Here both skew value (-0.209) and kurtosis value (- 0.588) are in acceptable range so it can be concluded that 'Normalcy' is supported. Since coefficient of variance (14.70%) is less than 33%, there is less disparity in data and hence, Mean is more stable and meaningful. Since skew is negative, the curve is left skewed and data is piled on the right side. As kurtosis is negative, the curve is flat and short (Platykurtic) as can be seen in figure 22. skew and kurtosis further confirm the meaningfulness of Mean.

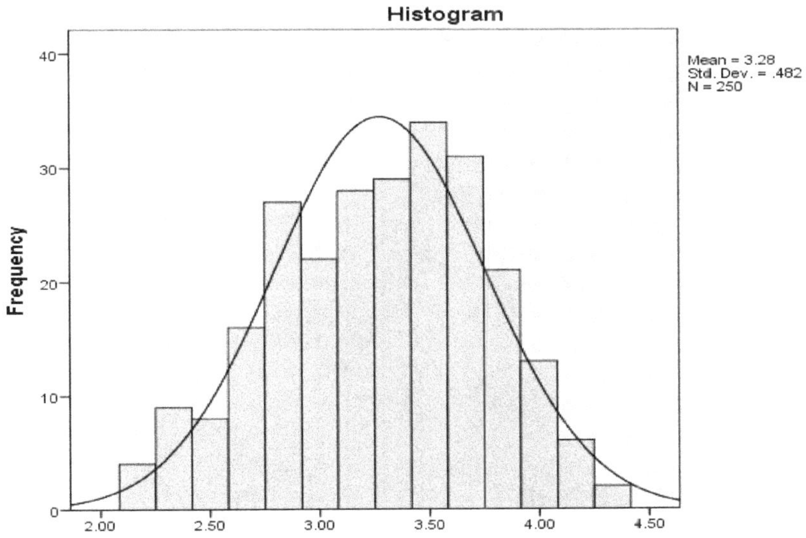

Figure 22 : AA as Perceived by Adolescents

4.4.2 Descriptive Analysis of AA as Perceived by Parents

Table 16 shows the measures of central tendency and measures of variability of the AA as perceived by parents.

Table 16 : Descriptive Statistics of AA as Perceived by Parents

Sample	Mean	S.D.	Coefficient of Variance (S.D / Mean*100)	Skew	Kurtosis
40	3.26	0.607	18.62%	- 0.547	1.220

Interpretation

According to George & Mallery (2010) variables with skew values between +1 and -1 and kurtosis values between +2 and -2 indicate normalcy. Here both skew value (-0.547) and kurtosis value (1.220) are in acceptable range so it can be concluded that 'Normalcy' is supported. Since coefficient of variance (18.62%) is less than 33%, there is less disparity in data and hence, Mean is more stable and meaningful. Since skew is negative, the curve is left skewed and data is piled on the right side. As kurtosis is positive, the curve is tall and narrow (Leptokurtic) as can be seen in figure 23. Skew and kurtosis further confirm the meaningfulness of Mean.

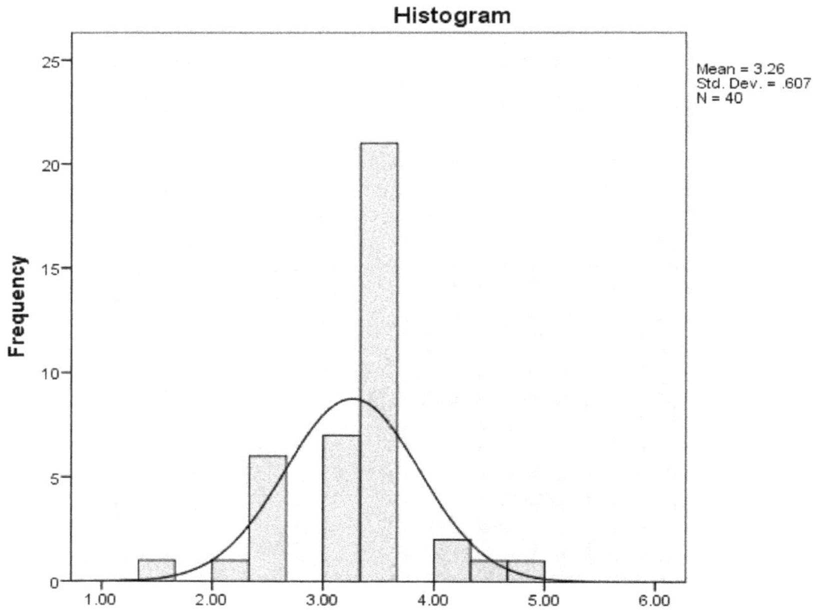

Figure 23 : AA as Perceived by Parents

4.4.3 Descriptive Analysis of AA as Perceived by Teachers

Table 17 shows the measures of central tendency and measures of variability of the AA as perceived by Teachers.

Table 17 : Descriptive Statistics of AA as Perceived by Teachers

Sample	Mean	S.D.	Coefficient of Variance (S.D / Mean*100)	Skew	Kurtosis
40	3.18	0.446	14.03%	0.422	0.703

Interpretation

According to George & Mallery (2010) variables with skew values between +1 and -1 and kurtosis values between +2 and -2 indicate normalcy. Here both skew value (0.422) and kurtosis value (0.703) are in acceptable range so it can be concluded that 'Normalcy' is supported. Since coefficient of variance (14.03%) is less than 33%, there is less disparity in data and hence, Mean is more stable and meaningful. Since skew is positive, the curve is right skewed and data is piled on the left side. As kurtosis is positive, the curve is tall and narrow (Leptokurtic) as can be seen in figure 24. Skew and kurtosis further confirm the meaningfulness of Mean.

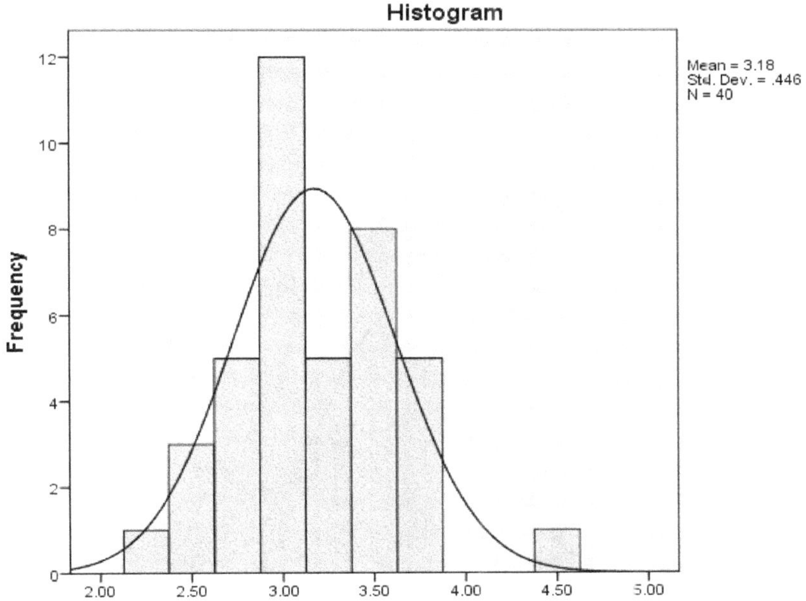

Figure 24 : AA as Perceived by Teachers

4.5 Descriptive Analysis of Behaviour Adjustment (BA)

4.5.1 Descriptive Analysis of BA as Perceived by Adolescents

Table 18 shows the measures of central tendency and measures of variability of the BA as perceived by Adolescents.

Table 18 : Descriptive Statistics of BA as Perceived by Adolescents

Sample	Mean	S.D.	Coefficient of Variance (S.D / Mean*100)	Skew	Kurtosis
250	3.07	0.359	11.69%	0.292	0.218

Interpretation

According to George & Mallery (2010) values between +1 and -1 and kurtosis values between +2 and -2 indicate normalcy. Here both skew value (0.292) and kurtosis value (0.218) are in acceptable range so it can be concluded that 'Normalcy' is supported. Since coefficient of variance (11.69%) is less than 33%, there is less disparity in data and hence, Mean is more stable and meaningful. Since skew is positive, the curve is right skewed and data is piled on the left side. As kurtosis is positive, the curve is tall and narrow (Leptokurtic) as can be seen in figure 25. Skew and kurtosis further confirm the meaningfulness of Mean.

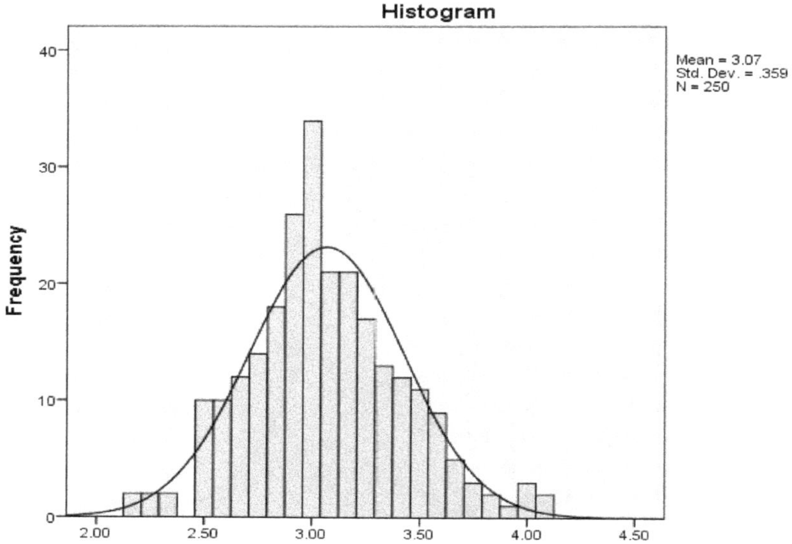

Figure 25 : BA as Perceived by Adolescents

4.5.2 Descriptive Analysis of BA as Perceived by Parents

Table 19 shows the measures of central tendency and measures of variability of the BA as perceived by parents.

Table 19 : Descriptive Statistics of BA as Perceived by Parents

Sample	Mean	S.D.	Coefficient of Variance (S.D / Mean*100)	Skew	Kurtosis
40	2.76	0.374	13.55%	0.863	1.20

Interpretation

According to George & Mallery (2010) variables with skew values between +1 and -1 and kurtosis values between +2 and -2 indicate normalcy. Here both skew value (0.863) and kurtosis value (1.20) are in acceptable range so it can be concluded that 'Normalcy' is supported. Since coefficient of variance (13.55%) is less than 33%, there is less disparity in data and hence, Mean is more stable and meaningful. Since skew is positive, the curve is right skewed and data is piled on the left side. As kurtosis is positive, the curve is tall and narrow (Leptokurtic) as can be seen in figure 26. Skew and kurtosis further confirm the meaningfulness of Mean.

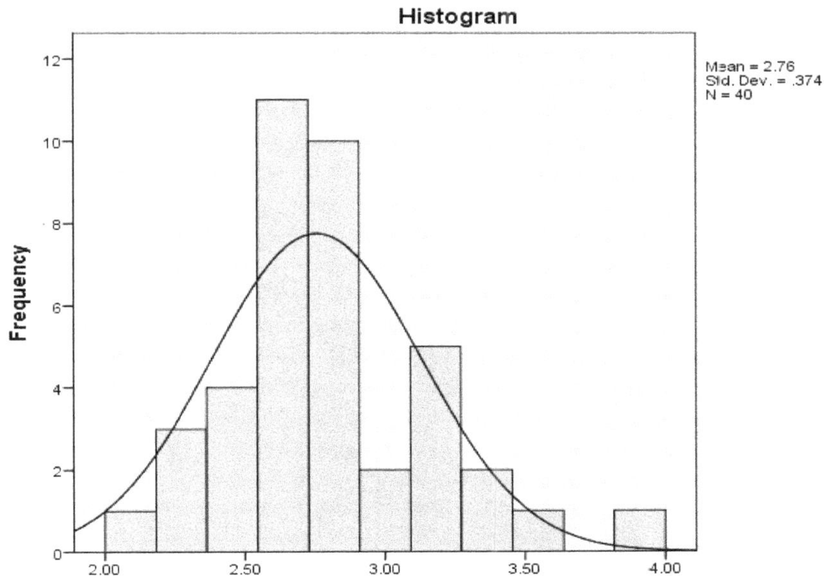

Figure 26 : BA as Perceived by Parents

4.5.3 Descriptive Analysis of BA as Perceived by Teachers

Table 20 shows the measures of central tendency and measures of variability of the BA as perceived by Teachers.

Table 20 : Descriptive Statistics of BA as Perceived by Teachers

Sample	Mean	S.D.	Coefficient of Variance (S.D / Mean*100)	Skew	Kurtosis
40	3.90	0.483	12.38%	- 0.003	- 0.726

Interpretation

According to George & Mallery (2010) variables with skew values between +1 and -1 and kurtosis values between +2 and -2 indicate normalcy. Here both skew value (- 0.003) and kurtosis value (- 0.726) are in acceptable range so it can be concluded that 'Normalcy' is supported. Since coefficient of variance (12.38%) is less than 33%, there is less disparity in data and hence, Mean is more stable and meaningful. Since skew is negative, the curve is left skewed and data is piled on the right side. As kurtosis is negative, the curve is flat and short (Platykurtic) as can be seen in figure 27. Skew and kurtosis further confirm the meaningfulness of Mean.

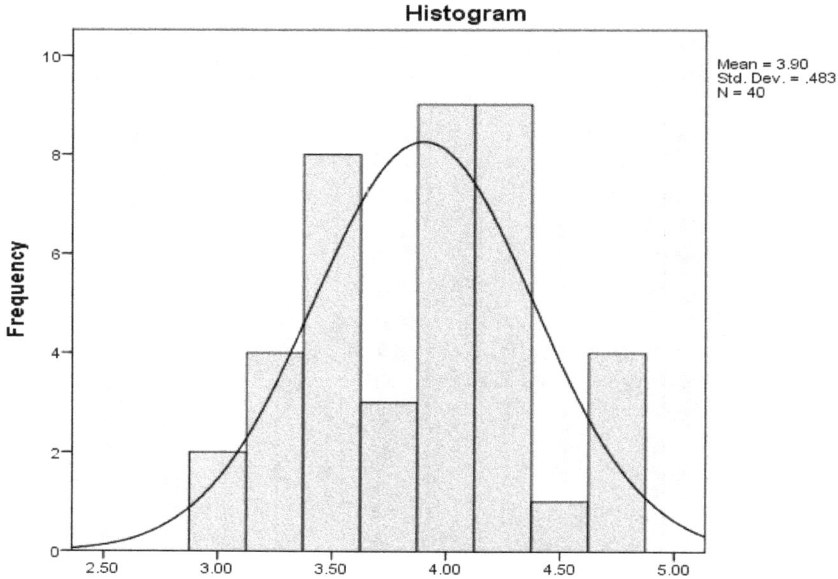

Figure 27 : BA as Perceived by Teachers

4.6 Descriptive Analysis of Parental Involvement (PI)

4.6.1 Descriptive Analysis of PI as Perceived by Adolescents

Table 21 shows the measures of central tendency and measures of variability of the PI as perceived by Adolescents.

Table 21 : Descriptive Statistics of PI as Perceived by Adolescents

Sample	Mean	S.D.	Coefficient of Variance (S.D / Mean*100)	Skew	Kurtosis
250	3.28	0.363	11.07%	0.130	1.073

Interpretation

According to George & Mallery (2010) variables with skew values between +1 and -1 and kurtosis values between +2 and -2 indicate normalcy. Here both skew value (0.130) and kurtosis value (1.073) are in acceptable range so it can be concluded that 'Normalcy' is supported. Since coefficient of variance (11.07%) is less than 33%, there is less disparity in data and hence, Mean is more stable and meaningful. Since skew is positive, the curve is right skewed and data is piled on the left side. As kurtosis is positive, the curve is tall and narrow (Leptokurtic) as can be seen in figure 28. Skew and kurtosis further confirms the meaningfulness of Mean.

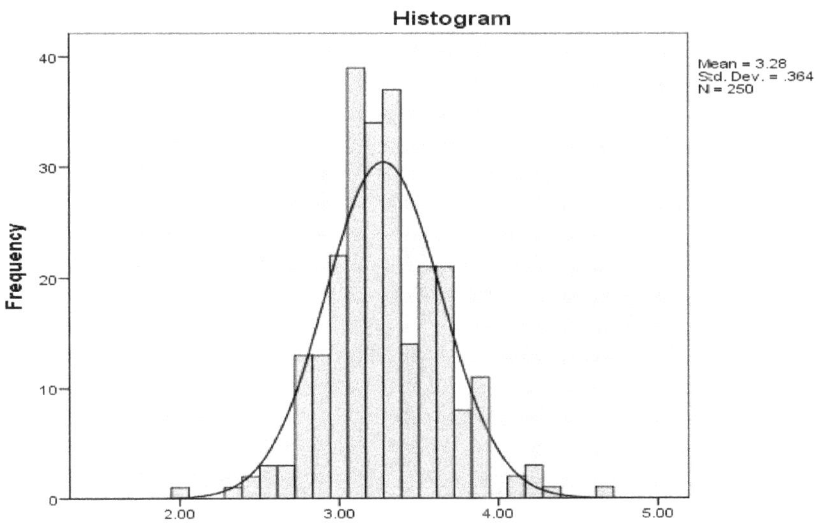

Figure 28 : PI as Perceived by Adolescents

4.6.2 Descriptive Analysis of PI as Perceived by Parents

Table 22 shows the measures of central tendency and measures of variability of the PI as perceived by parents.

Table 22 : Descriptive Statistics of PI as Perceived by Parents

Sample	Mean	S.D.	Coefficient of Variance (S.D / Mean*100)	Skew	Kurtosis
40	3.41	0.240	7.04%	- 0.368	- 0.030

Interpretation

According to George & Mallery (2010) variables with skew values between +1 and -1 and kurtosis values between +2 and -2 indicate normalcy. Here both skew value (- 0.368) and kurtosis value (- 0.030) are in acceptable range so it can be concluded that 'Normalcy' is supported. Since coefficient of variance (7.04%) is less than 33%, there is less disparity in data and hence, Mean is more stable and meaningful. Since skew is negative, the curve is left skewed and data is piled on the right side. As kurtosis is negative, the curve is flat and short (Platykurtic) as can be seen in figure 29.Skew and kurtosis further confirm the meaningfulness of Mean.

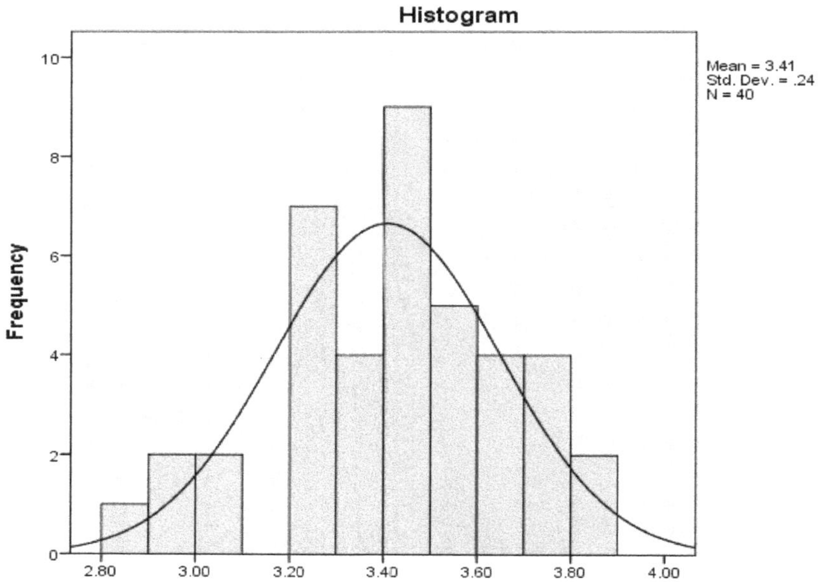

Figure 29 : PI as Perceived by Parents

4.6.3 Descriptive Analysis of PI as Perceived by Teachers

Table 23 shows the measures of central tendency and measures of variability of the PI as perceived by Teachers.

Table 23 : Descriptive Statistics of PI as Perceived by Teachers

Sample	Mean	S.D.	Coefficient of Variance (S.D / Mean*100)	Skew	Kurtosis
40	2.78	0.389	13.99%	0.599	0.597

Interpretation

According to George & Mallery (2010) variables with skew values between +1 and -1 and kurtosis values between +2 and -2 indicate normalcy. Here both skew value (0.599) and kurtosis value (0.597) are in acceptable range so it can be concluded that 'Normalcy' is supported. Since coefficient of variance (13.99%) is less than 33%, there is less disparity in data and hence, Mean is more stable and meaningful. Since skew is positive, the curve is right skewed and data is piled on the left side. As kurtosis is positive, the curve is tall and narrow (Leptokurtic) as can be seen in figure 30. Skew and kurtosis further confirm the meaningfulness of Mean.

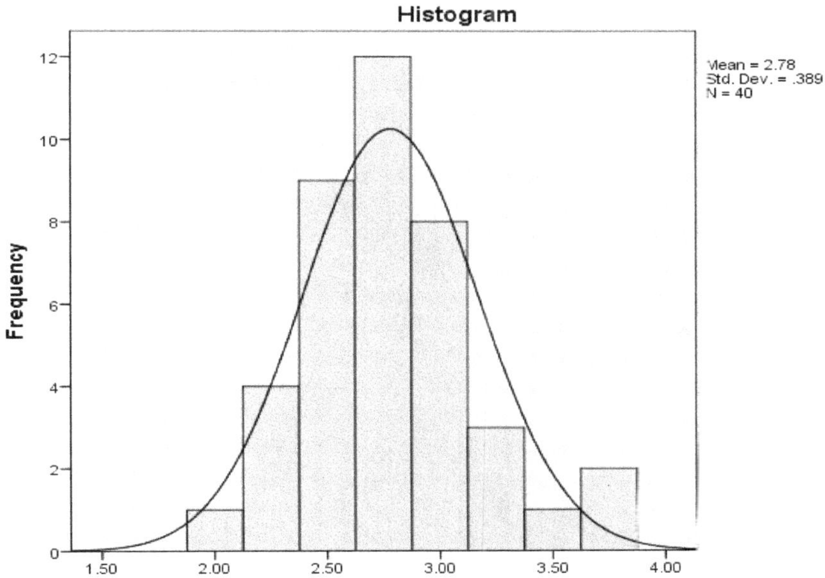

Figure 30 : PI as Perceived by Teachers

4.7 Descriptive Analysis of Teacher's Involvement (TI)

4.7.1 Descriptive Analysis of TI as Perceived by Adolescents

Table 24 shows the measures of central tendency and measures of variability of the TI as perceived by Adolescents.

Table 24 : Descriptive Statistics of TI as Perceived by Adolescents

Sample	Mean	S.D.	Coefficient of Variance (S.D / Mean*100)	Skew	Kurtosis
250	3.06	0.358	11.07%	0.203	0.032

Interpretation

According to George & Mallery (2010) variables with skew values between +1 and -1 and kurtosis values between +2 and -2 indicate normalcy. Here both skew value (0.203) and kurtosis value (0.032) are in acceptable range so it can be concluded that 'Normalcy' is supported. Since coefficient of variance (11.70%) is less than 33%, there is less disparity in data and hence, Mean is more stable and meaningful. Since skew is positive, the curve is right skewed and data is piled on the left side. As kurtosis is positive, the curve is tall and narrow (Leptokurtic) as can be seen in figure 31.Skew and kurtosis further confirm the meaningfulness of Mean.

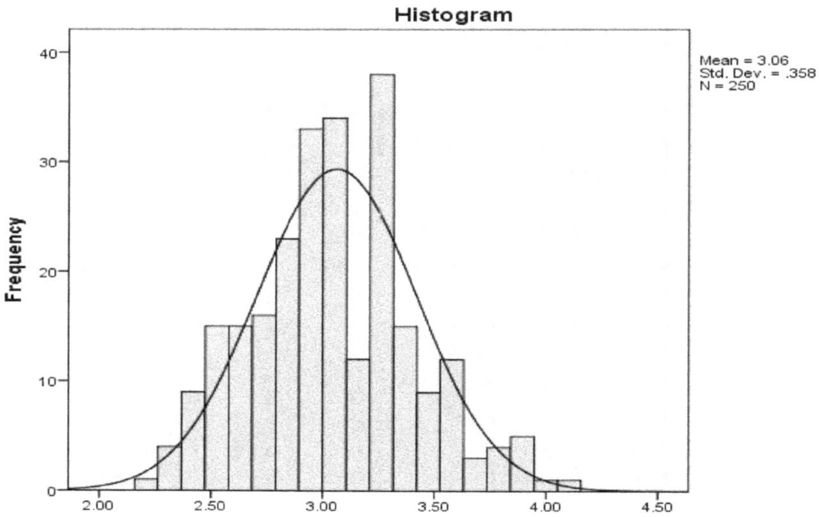

Figure 31 : TI as Perceived by Adolescents

4.7.2 Descriptive Analysis of TI as Perceived by Parents

Table 25 shows the measures of central tendency and measures of variability of the TI as perceived by parents.

Table 25 : Descriptive Statistics of TI as Perceived by Parents

Sample	Mean	S.D.	Coefficient of Variance (S.D / Mean*100)	Skew	Kurtosis
40	3.66	0.472	12.90%	0.704	0.223

Interpretation

According to George & Mallery (2010) variables with skew values between +1 and -1 and kurtosis values between +2 and -2 indicate normalcy. Here both skew value (0.704) and kurtosis value (0.223) are in acceptable range so it can be concluded that 'Normalcy' is supported. Since coefficient of variance (12.90%) is less than 33%, there is less disparity in data and hence, Mean is more stable and meaningful. Since skew is positive, the curve is right skewed and data is piled on the left side. As kurtosis is positive, the curve is tall and narrow (Leptokurtic) as can be seen in figure 32.Skew and kurtosis further confirm the meaningfulness of Mean.

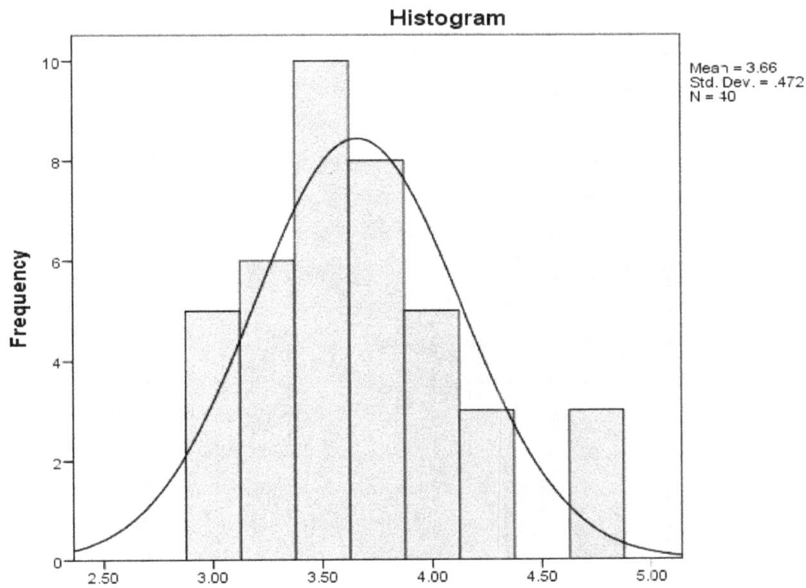

Figure 32 : TI as Perceived by Parents

4.7.3 Descriptive Analysis of TI as Perceived by Teachers

Table 26 shows the measures of central tendency and measures of variability of the TI as perceived by Teachers.

Table 26 : Descriptive Statistics of TI as Perceived by Teachers

Sample	Mean	S.D.	Coefficient of Variance (S.D / Mean*100)	Skew	Kurtosis
40	3.52	0.262	7.44%	- 0.390	- 0.616

Interpretation

According to George & Mallery (2010) variables with skew values between +1 and -1 and kurtosis values between +2 and -2 indicate normalcy. Here both skew value (-0.390) and kurtosis value (- 0.616) are in acceptable range so it can be concluded that 'Normalcy' is supported. Since coefficient of variance (7.44%) is less than 33%, there is less disparity in data and hence, Mean is more stable and meaningful. Since skew is negative, the curve is left skewed and data is piled on the right side. As kurtosis is negative, the curve is flat and short (Platykurtic) as can be seen in figure 33. Skew and kurtosis further confirm the meaningfulness of Mean.

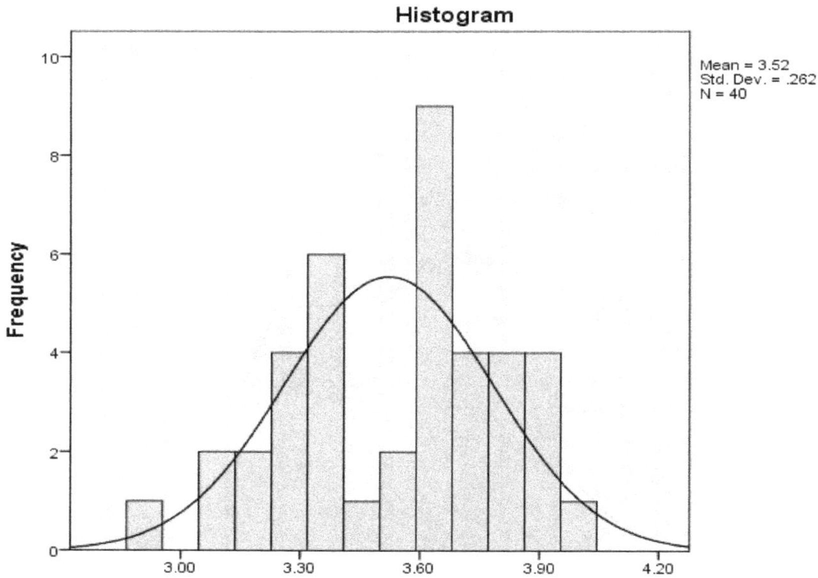

Figure 33 : TI as Perceived by Teachers

4.8 Analysis of Adolescents Feedback

Following is the analysis of responses from Adolescents that were taken through individual questionnaire (Appx A).

4.8.1 Gender wise Classification

Table 27 shows frequency distribution for Adolescents with respect to gender of Total Sample Size (TSS).

Table 27 : Gender Wise Classification of TSS

Gender	Frequency	Percent (%)
Girls	90	36%
Boys	160	64%

Interpretation

From the above table, it can be concluded that from the participant Adolescents, 64% were boys while 36% were girls as can be seen in Figure 34.

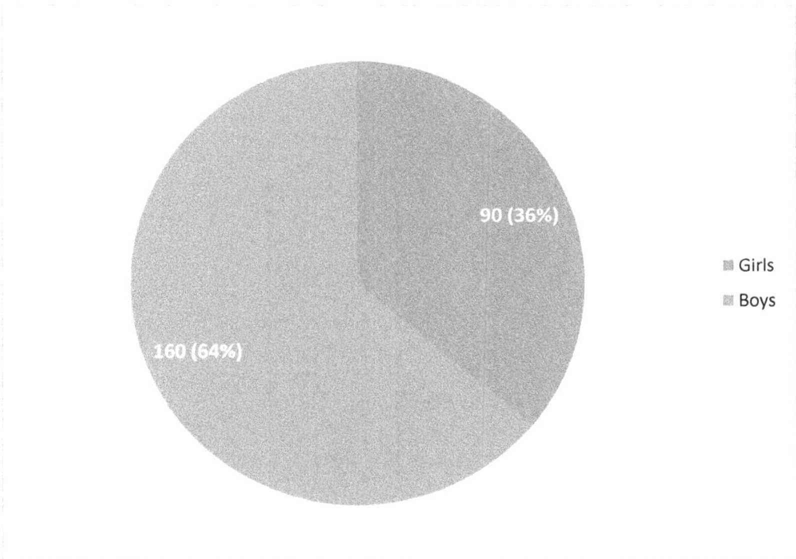

Figure 34 : Gender Wise Participation of Adolescents

4.8.2 Frequency Distribution of Grades

Table 28 shows frequency distribution of grades scored by Adolescents of Total Sample Size (TSS).

Table 28 : Frequency Distribution of Grades of TSS

Grades Scored %	Frequency	% of Adolescents
40-50 %	15	6%
50-60 %	58	23.2%
60 – 70 %	69	27.6%
70-80 %	46	18.4%
80 % and above	62	24.8%
Total	**250**	**100%**

Interpretation

The above table shows that majority Adolescents scored marks in the range of 60% to 70% while the least number of Adolescents scored marks in the range of 40% to 50% as can also be seen in Figure 35.

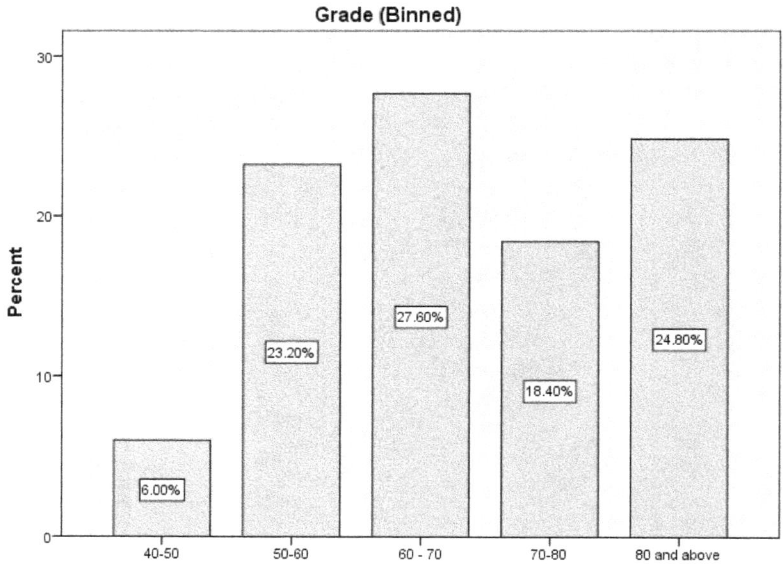

Figure 35 : Grades Scored by Adolescents

4.8.3 Frequency Distribution for Closeness with Parents and Others

The following variables were used to measure closeness of children with parents and others using a nominal scale :-

1. Closeness with respect to 'Discussion about Marks'.
2. Closeness with relation to 'Sharing Personal Problems'.
3. Closeness with respect to 'Appreciation of Performance in school'.
4. Closeness with respect to 'Attending Parent Teachers Meet in school'.
5. Closeness with respect to 'Approaching for Difficulties in Studies'.

4.8.3.1 Closeness with respect to 'Discussion about Marks'.

Table 29 shows the measurement of closeness with Parents and others with respect to discussion about marks of Total Sample Size (TSS).

Table 29 : Closeness with Respect to Discussion about Marks

Response Option	Frequency	Percentage
Mother	83	33.2%
Father	37	14.8%
Teachers	15	6%
Friends	115	46%
Total	**250**	**100%**

Interpretation

When adolescents were requested to tell "With whom are they comfortable in discussing when they get less marks in exams", 33.2% said 'Mother', 14.8% said 'Father', 6% said 'Teacher's and 46% said 'Friends'. Majority of adolescents felt comfortable discussing about their marks with 'Friends' followed by their 'Mother'. Figure 36 shows closeness with respect to discussion about marks.

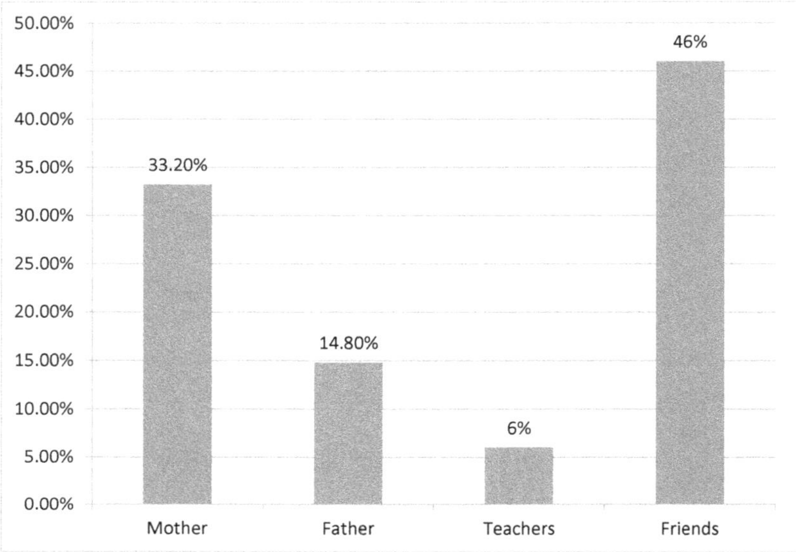

Figure 36: Closeness with Respect to Discussion about Marks

Interpretation

Maximum of the adolescents were found to be more close to their 'Friends' when they got less marks and wanted to discuss. This might be because they think their friends will understand them better and empathise with them while they might be afraid of parents and teachers judging them or scolding them.

4.8.3.2 **Closeness with relation to 'Sharing Personal Problems'.**

Table 30 shows the measurement of closeness with Parents and others with respect to sharing personal problems of Total Sample Size (TSS).

Table 30 : Closeness with Respect to Sharing Personal Problems

Response Option	Frequency	Percentage
Mother	111	44.4%
Father	23	9.2%
Teacher	4	1.6%
Friends	112	44.8%
Total	**250**	**100%**

Interpretation

When adolescents were asked "With whom are they comfortable in sharing personals problems", 44.4% said 'Mother', 9.2% said ' Father', 1.6% said 'Teacher's and 44.8% said 'Friends'. Majority of adolescents felt comfortable in sharing their personal problems with 'Mother' and 'Friends'.

Figure 37 shows closeness with relation to sharing personal problems.

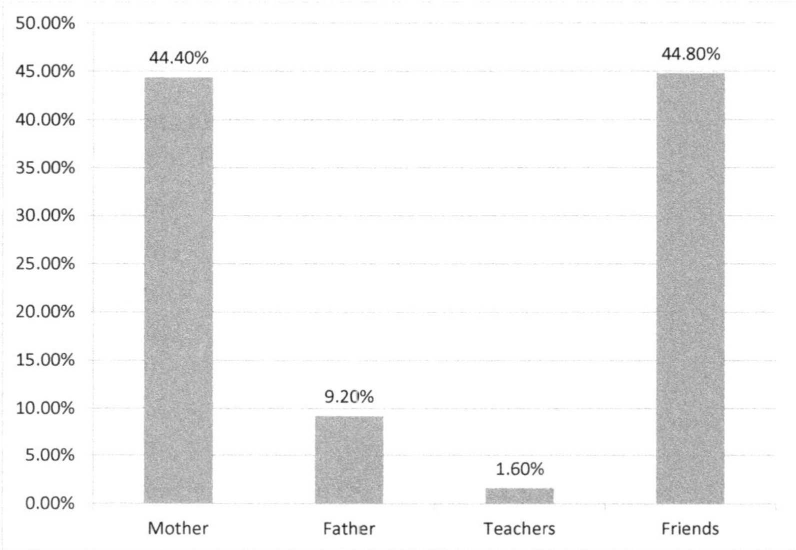

Figure 37 : Closeness with Relation to Sharing Personal Problems

Interpretation

Maximum of the adolescents were found to be more close to their 'Friends' and 'Mothers' when they wanted to share their personal problems. This might be because they think their friends being in the same age will understand their problems better while mothers might be more patient and understanding to their problems.

4.8.3.3 **Closeness with respect to 'Appreciation of Performance in school'.**

Table 31 shows the measurement of closeness with Parents and others with respect to appreciation of performance in school of Total Sample Size (TSS).

Table 31 : Closeness with Respect to Appreciation of Performance in school

Response Option	Frequency	Percentage
Mother	60	24%
Father	76	30.4%
Teacher	57	22.8%
Friends	57	22.8%
Total	**250**	**100%**

Interpretation

When adolescents were requested to tell "who appreciates them more for their performance in school ", 24% said 'Mother', 30.4% said ' Father', 22.8% said 'Teacher's and 22.8% said 'Friends'. Majority of adolescents felt that their 'Father' appreciated more for their school performance.

Figure 38 shows closeness with relation to appreciation of performance in school.

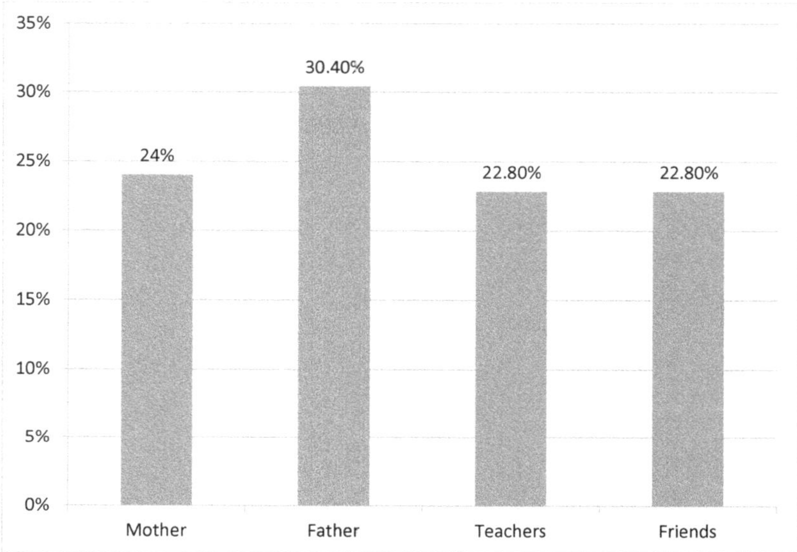

Figure 38 : Closeness with Relation to Appreciation of Performance in school

Interpretation

Maximum of the adolescents disclosed that they got more appreciation by their 'Fathers' for their performance in school. This might be because fathers are probably more concerned about marks and Academic performance of the children.

4.8.3.4 **Closeness with respect to 'Attending Parents Teachers Meet in school'.**

Table 32 shows measurement of closeness with Parents and others with respect to attending Parents Teachers Meet (PTM) in school of Total Sample Size (TSS).

Table 32 : Closeness with Respect to Attending PTM Held in school

Response Option	Frequency	Percentage
Mother	140	56%
Father	92	36.8%
Grandparents	4	1.6%
No one	14	5.6%
Total	**250**	**100%**

Interpretation

When adolescents were requested to tell "who mostly attended the Parents Teachers Meet held in school", 56% said 'Mother', 36.8% said 'Father', 1.6% said 'Grandparents' and 5.6% said 'No one'. Majority of adolescents confided that their 'Mother' mostly attended the Parents Teacher's Meet.

Figure 39 shows closeness with relation to attending PTM in school.

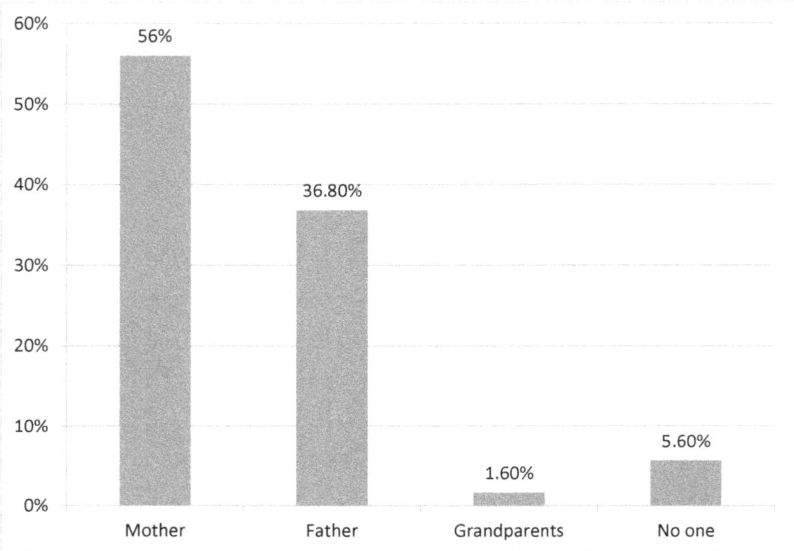

Figure 39 : Closeness with Relation to Attending PTM in school

Interpretation

Maximum of the adolescents found their 'Mothers' to be usually attending PTM held in school. This might be because mothers are probably able to take out time during working hours to attend the PTM.

4.8.3.5 **Closeness with respect to 'Approaching for Difficulties in Studies'.**

Table 33 shows the measurement of closeness with Parents and others with respect to approaching for difficulties in studies of Total Sample Size (TSS).

Table 33 : Closeness with Respect to Approaching for Difficulties in Studies

Response Option	Frequency	Percentage
Mother	27	10.8%
Father	48	19.2%
Teacher	128	51.2%
Friends	47	18.8%
Total	**250**	**100%**

Interpretation

When adolescents were requested to tell "to whom do they approach when they face difficulties in studies," 10.8% said 'Mother', 19.2% said 'Father', 51 2% said 'Teacher' and 18.8% said 'Friends'. Majority of adolescents approached their 'Teacher' when they faced difficulties in studies.

Figure 40 shows closeness with relation to approaching for difficulties in studies.

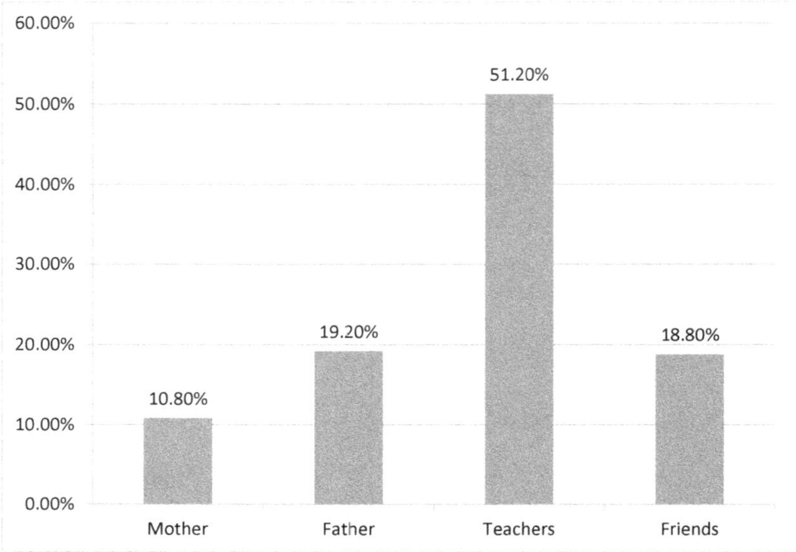

Figure 40 : Closeness with Relation to Approaching for Difficulty in Study

Interpretation

Maximum of the adolescents usually approached their 'Teacher's when they faced difficulties in studies. This might be because adolescents find their teachers to be probably most suitable to solve their problems in studies.

4.8.3.6 Overall Closeness of Adolescents with Parents and Others

Table 34 shows the measurement of overall closeness of Adolescents with Parents and others.

Table 34 : Measurement of Overall Closeness with Parents and Others

Closeness With	If I Get Less Marks in Exams, I am Comfort-able in Discussing about it with	I am Comfort-able in Sharing Personal Problem with	I am Appreciated Of Performance in school More by	Parents Teachers Meet Held in school is Mostly Attended by	Whenever I Face Difficulties in Studies, I Usually Approach	Total	Percent (%)
Mother	83	111 .	60	140	27	421	33.68%
Father	37	23	76	92	48	276	22.08%
Teachers	15	4	57	4	128	208	16.64%
Friends	115	112	57	14	47	345	27.6%
Total	**250**	**250**	**250**	**250**	**250**	**1250**	**100%**

Interpretation

When adolescents were requested to tell about their overall closeness with Parents and others, 33.68% said 'Mother', 22.08% said ' Father', 16.64% said 'Teacher's and 27.6% said 'Friends' as can be seen in Figure 41.

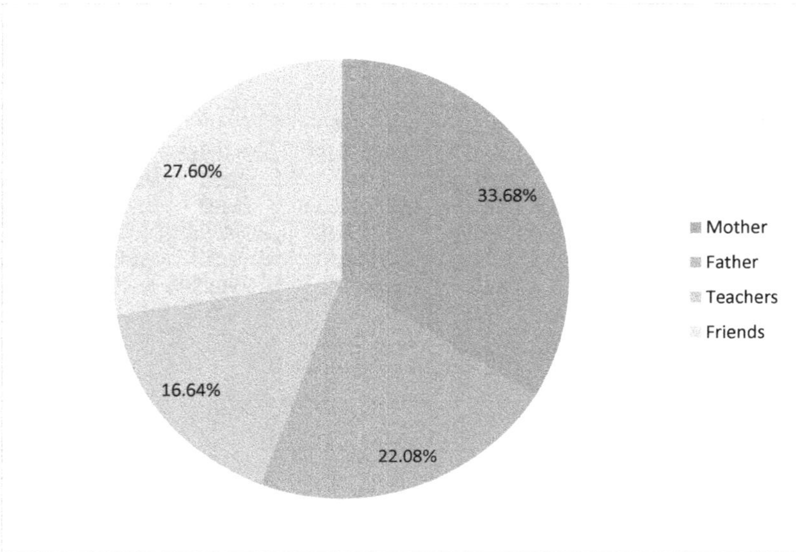

Figure 41 Overall Closeness with Parents and Others

Interpretation

Maximum of the adolescents were found to be close to their 'Friends' followed by their 'Mother'. This might be because at this stage of life, adolescents spend more time with friends than anyone else and feel comfortable with them the most. As for closeness with mothers, the reason maybe that the mothers probably are more compassionate and caring in nature which in turn makes the children trust them more.

4.8.4 **Frequency Distribution and Descriptive Statistics for 'Parental Involvement' as Perceived by Adolescents**

'Parental Involvement' was measured through the following five constructs :-

1. Emotional Involvement.
2. Aspiration of Parents.
3. Structure by Parents.
4. School & Studies Involvement.
5. Involvement with Friends.

4.8.4.1 **Emotional Involvement.**

'Emotional Involvement' is measured using the following four measured indicators where each measured indicator is scaled on 5-point rating scale (5 = Very Often, 4 = Often, 3 = Sometimes, 2 = Rarely and 1 = Never).

(a) EM1: My parents have time for me whenever I approach them.

(b) EM2 : If I do not behave as per my parents expectations, they never reprimand me.

(c) EM3 : If I make a mistake, my parents do not ridicule me.

(d) EM4 : My parents take out time and sit with me whenever I have faltered.

Table 35 shows analysis of emotional involvement of parents as perceived by Adolescents.

Table 35 : Emotional Involvement of Parents as Perceived by Adolescents

Variable Code	Very Often		Often		Sometimes		Rarely		Never		Mean	Std. Deviation
	F	%	F	%	F	%	F	%	F	%		
EM1	29	11.6	37	14.8	131	52.4	35	14.0	18	7.2	3.10	1.017
EM2	27	10.8	28	11.2	151	60.4	30	12.0	14	5.6	3.1	0.939
EM3	36	14.4	33	13.2	143	57.2	26	10.4	12	4.8	3.2	0.98
EM4	53	21.2	59	23.6	111	44.4	14	5.6	13	5.2	3.5	1.05
Grand Mean											**3.23**	

Interpretation

When adolescents were asked "if their parents have time for them whenever they approach them", 11.6% said 'Very Often', 14.8% said 'Often', 52.4% said 'Sometimes', 14% said 'Rarely' and 7.2% said 'Never'. Majority of the adolescents felt that their parents 'Sometimes' have time when they approach them.

When adolescents were asked "if their parents did not reprimand them for not behaving as per their expectations", 10.8% said 'Very Often', 11.2% said 'Often', 60.4% said 'Sometimes', 12% said 'Rarely' and 5.6% said 'Never'.

Majority of the adolescents felt that their parents 'Sometimes' did not reprimand them when they do not behave as per their expectations.

When adolescents were asked "if their parents did not ridicule them if they made a mistake", 14.4% said 'Very Often', 13.2% said 'Often', 57.2% said 'Sometimes', 10.4% said 'Rarely' and 4.8% said 'Never'. Majority of the adolescents felt that their parents 'Sometimes' did not ridicule them if they did a mistake.

When adolescents were asked 'if their parents sit with them if they have faltered' 21.2% said 'Very Often', 23.6% said 'Often', 44.4% said 'Sometimes', 5.6% said 'Rarely' and 5.2% said 'Never'. Majority of the adolescents felt that their parents 'Sometimes' sat with them if they have faltered.

On the basis of grand mean (3.23), it can be concluded that 'Emotional Involvement' as a parameter of 'Parental Involvement' with adolescents is 'Moderate'.

4.8.4.2 **Aspiration of Parents.**

'Aspiration of Parents' is measured using the following three measured indicators where each measured indicator is scaled on 5-point rating scale (5 = Very Often, 4 = Often, 3 = Sometimes, 2 = Rarely and 1 = Never).

(a) ASP1 : My parents discuss with me my job aspirations.

(b) ASP2 : My parents discuss with me my career options.

(c) ASP3 : During dinners or outings, my parents tell me inspiring stories of successful people to motivate me.

Table 36 shows analysis of Aspiration of parents as perceived by Adolescents.

Table 36 : Aspiration of Parents as Perceived by Adolescents

Variable Code	Very Often		Often		Sometimes		Rarely		Never		Mean	Std. Deviation
	F	%	F	%	F	%	F	%	F	%		
ASP1	58	23.2	59	23.6	93	37.2	26	10.4	14	5.6	3.48	1.124
ASP2	62	24.8	66	26.4	92	36.8	14	5.6	16	6.4	3.58	1.114
ASP3	59	23.6	56	22.4	101	40.4	12	4.8	22	8.8	3.47	1.162
Grand Mean											**3.51**	

Interpretation

When adolescents were asked "if their parents discussed their job aspirations with them"' 23.2% said 'Very Often', 23.6% said 'Often', 37.2% said 'Sometimes', 10.4% said 'Rarely' and 5.6% said 'Never'. Majority of the adolescents felt that their parents 'Sometimes' discusses with them their job aspirations.

When adolescents were asked "if their parents discuss career options with them", 24.8% said 'Very Often', 26.4% said 'Often', 36.8% said 'Sometimes', 5.6% said 'Rarely' and 6.4% said 'Never'. Majority of the adolescents felt that their parents 'Sometimes' discussed career options with them.

When adolescents were asked "if their parents told them inspiring stories of successful people to motivate them during dinners or outings", 23.6% said 'Very Often', 22.4% said 'Often', 40.4% said 'Sometimes', 4.8% said 'Rarely' and 8.8% said 'Never'. Majority of the adolescents felt that their parents 'Sometimes' told inspiring stories of successful people to motivate them during dinners and outings.

On the basis of grand mean (3.51), it can be concluded that 'Aspiration of Parents' as a parameter of 'Parental Involvement' with adolescents is 'High'.

4.8.4.3 **Structure by Parents.**

'Structure by Parents' is measured using the following three measured indicators where each measured indicator is scaled on 5-point rating scale (5 = Very Often, 4 = Often, 3 = Sometimes, 2 = Rarely and 1 = Never).

(a) STR1 : My parents keep a tab on my daily usage of TV / Internet.

(b) STR2 : My parents decide on the clothes I wear.

(c) STR3 : On weekends we as a family make sure to spend one evening together, either going out or playing a board game.

Table 37 shows Analysis of Structure by parents as perceived by Adolescents.

Table 37 : Structure by Parents as Perceived by Adolescents

Variable Code	Very Often		Often		Sometimes		Rarely		Never		Mean	Std. Deviation
	F	%	F	%	F	%	F	%	F	%		
STR1	55	22.0	55	22.0	88	35.2	30	12.0	22	8.8	3.36	1.202
STR2	38	15.2	40	16.0	96	38.4	53	21.2	23	9.2	3.07	1.161
STR3	45	18.0	44	17.6	113	45.2	27	10.8	21	8.4	3.26	1.130
Grand Mean											**3.23**	

Interpretation

When adolescents were asked "if their parents kept tab on their usage of TV / Internet", 22% said 'Very Often', 22% said 'Often', 35.2% said 'Sometimes', 12% said 'Rarely' and 8.8% said 'Never'. Majority of the adolescents felt that their parents 'Sometimes' kept tab on their TV / Internet usage.

When adolescents were asked "if their parents decided on the clothes they wore", 15.2% said 'Very Often', 16% said 'Often', 38.4% said 'Sometimes', 21.2% said 'Rarely' and 9.2% said 'Never'. Majority of the adolescents felt that their parents 'Sometimes' decided on the clothes they wore.

When adolescents were asked "if they as a family spent one evening together either by going out or playing a board game", 18% said 'Very Often', 17.6% said 'Often',

45.2% said 'Sometimes', 10.8% said 'Rarely' and 8.4% said 'Never'. Majority of the adolescents felt that they as a family 'Sometimes' spent one evening together either by going out or playing a board game.

On the basis of grand mean (3.23), it can be concluded that 'Structure by Parents' as a parameter of 'Parental Involvement' with adolescents is 'Moderate'.

4.8.4.4 **School & Studies Involvement.**

'School & Studies Involvement' is measured using the following four measured indicators where each measured indicator is scaled on 5-point rating scale (5 = Very Often, 4 = Often, 3 = Sometimes, 2 = Rarely and 1 = Never).

(a) SSI1 : My parents take out time to teach me and help me in my assignments.

(b) SSI2 : My parents are concerned about my studies other than exams.

(c) SSI3 : My parents keep track of my marks and grades in class examination.

(d) SSI4 : Apart from PTMs, my parents are in constant touch with my teachers.

Table 38 shows analysis of school and studies involvement by parents as perceived by Adolescents.

Table 38 : School & Studies Involvement by Parents as Perceived by Adolescents

Variable Code	Very Often		Often		Sometimes		Rarely		Never		Mean	Std. Deviation
	F	%	F	%	F	%	F	%	F	%		
SSI1	56	22.4	47	18.8	111	44.4	23	9.2	13	5.2	3.44	1.093
SSI2	21	8.4	32	12.8	100	40.0	66	26.4	31	12.4	2.78	1.087
SSI3	79	31.6	79	31.6	61	24.4	13	5.2	18	7.2	3.75	1.166
SSI4	54	21.6	39	15.6	103	41.2	30	12.0	24	9.6	3.28	1.206
Grand Mean											**3.31**	

Interpretation

When adolescents were asked "if their parents took out time to teach them and helped them in their assignments", 22.4% said 'Very Often', 18.8% said 'Often', 44.4%

said 'Sometimes', 9.2% said 'Rarely' and 5.2 % said 'Never'. Majority of the adolescents felt that their parents 'Sometimes' took out time to teach them and helped them in their assignments.

When adolescents were asked "if their parents are concerned about their studies other than exams", 8.4% said 'Very Often', 12.8% said 'Often', 40% said 'Sometimes', 26.4% said 'Rarely' and 12.4% said 'Never'. Majority of the adolescents felt that their parents 'Sometimes' their parents are concerned about their studies other than exams.

When adolescents were asked "if their parents kept track of their marks and grades in class examination", 31.6% said 'Very Often', 31.6% said 'Often', 24.4% said 'Sometimes', 5.2% said 'Rarely' and 7.2% said 'Never'. Majority of the adolescents felt that their parents 'Very Often' and 'Often' kept track of their marks and grades in class examination.

When adolescents were asked "if their parents are in constant touch with their teachers apart from PTM", 21.6% said 'Very Often', 15.6% said 'Often', 41.2% said 'Sometimes', 12% said 'Rarely' and 9.6% said 'Never'. Majority of the adolescents felt that their parents 'Sometimes' are in constant touch with their teachers apart from PTM.

On the basis of grand mean (3.31), it can be concluded that 'school & Studies Involvement' as a parameter of 'Parental Involvement' with adolescents is 'Moderate'.

4.8.4.5 **Involvement with Friends.**

'Involvement with Friends' is measured using the following four measured indicators where each measured indicator is scaled on 5-point rating scale (5 = Very Often, 4 = Often, 3 = Sometimes, 2 = Rarely and 1 = Never).

(a) FI1 : My parents get involved in all the activities with my friends like movie, picnic, etc.

(b) FI2 : My parents give advice on whom to be friends with.

(c) FI3 : My parents do not compare me with other boys and girls of my age.

(d) FI4 : My parents invite my friends at home.

Table 39 shows analysis of involvement with friends by Parents as perceived by Adolescents.

Table 39 : Involvement with Friends by Parents as Perceived by Adolescents

Variable Code	Very Often		Often		Sometimes		Rarely		Never		Mean	Std. Deviation
	F	%	F	%	F	%	F	%	F	%		
FI1	29	11.6	30	12.0	85	34.0	54	21.6	52	20.8	2.72	1.249
FI2	48	19.2	60	24.0	85	34.0	25	10.0	32	12.8	3.27	1.247
FI3	41	16.4	44	17.6	85	34.0	46	18.4	34	13.6	3.05	1.251
FI4	59	23.6	62	24.8	77	30.8	24	9.6	28	11.2	3.40	1.258
Grand Mean											**3.11**	

Interpretation

When adolescents were asked "if their parents got involved in all the activities with their friends like movie, picnic, etc", 11.6% said 'Very Often', 12% said 'Often', 34% said 'Sometimes', 21.6% said 'Rarely' and 20.8 % said 'Never'. Majority of the adolescents felt that their parents 'Sometimes' get involved in all the activities with their friends like movie, picnic, etc.

When adolescents were asked "if their parents gave advice on whom to be friends with", 19.2% said 'Very Often', 24% said 'Often', 34% said 'Sometimes', 10% said 'Rarely' and 12.8% said 'Never'. Majority of the adolescents felt that their parents 'Sometimes' gave advice on whom to be friends with.

When adolescents were asked "if their parents did not compare them with other boys and girls of their age", 16.4% said 'Very Often', 17.6% said 'Often', 34% said 'Sometimes', 18.4% said 'Rarely' and 13.6% said 'Never'. Majority of the adolescents felt that their parents 'Sometimes' did not compare them with other boys and girls of their age.

When adolescents were asked "if their parents invited their friends at home", 23.6% said 'Very Often', 24.8% said 'Often', 30.8% said 'Sometimes', 9.6% said 'Rarely' and 11.2% said 'Never'. Majority of the adolescents felt that their parents 'Sometimes' invited their friends at home.

On the basis of grand mean (3.11), it can be concluded that 'Involvement with Friends' as a parameter of 'Parental Involvement' with adolescents is 'Moderate'.

4.8.5 Frequency Distribution and Descriptive Statistics for impact of Parental Involvement on Adolescents' Behaviour Adjustment as Perceived by Adolescents

Impact on 'Behaviour Adjustment' was measured using the following twelve measured indicators where each measured indicator is scaled on 5-point rating scale (5 = Very Often, 4 = Often, 3 = Sometimes, 2 = Rarely and 1 = Never).

(a) IBA1 : My problems get solved whenever I approach my parents.

(b) IBA2 : I feel relaxed when I share my thoughts with my parents.

(c) IBA3 : I don't get stressed out because of continuous guidance from parents and teachers in academics.

(d) IBA4 : I take parents reprimand / counselling positively and change my Behaviour accordingly.

(e) IBA5 : I find my parents preaching important.

(f) IBA6 : I consider the suggestions given by my parents for my clothes, friends and eating preferences.

(g) IBA7 : I do not mind when my parents express their choices for clothes, friends and food.

(h) IBA8 : When any guests come to my house and my parents insist on meeting them, I do not get annoyed.

(i) IBA9 : When my parents ask for my help in entertaining the guests, I keep aside all my work to help them.

(j) IBA10 : Disagreements with my parents do not make me upset.

(k) IBA11 : I do not get upset when my parents do not listen to my point of view.

(l) IBA12 : When I go out with my family I do not get bored.

Table 40 shows analysis of impact of Parental Involvement on Behaviour Adjustment.

Table 40 : Impact of Parental Involvement on Behaviour Adjustment as Perceived by Adolescents

Variable Code	Very Often		Often		Sometimes		Rarely		Never		Mean	Std. Deviation
	F	%	F	%	F	%	F	%	F	%		
IBA1	73	29.2	69	27.6	86	34.4	8	3.2	14	5.6	3.72	1.092
IBA2	75	30.0	71	28.4	64	25.6	18	7.2	22	8.8	3.64	1.229
IBA3	33	13.2	33	13.2	125	50.0	27	10.8	32	12.8	3.03	1.133
IBA4	55	22.0	49	19.6	117	46.8	13	5.2	16	6.4	3.45	1.087
IBA5	48	19.2	46	18.4	119	47.6	16	6.4	21	8.4	3.34	1.115
IBA6	47	18.8	38	15.2	109	43.6	29	11.6	27	10.8	3.20	1.191
IBA7	46	18.4	44	17.6	114	45.6	22	8.8	24	9.6	3.25	1.149
IBA8	52	20.8	52	20.8	95	38.0	26	10.4	25	10.0	3.32	1.203
IBA9	46	18.4	43	17.2	108	43.2	26	10.4	27	10.8	3.22	1.184
IBA10	41	16.4	41	16.4	101	40.4	34	13.6	33	13.2	3.09	1.217
IBA11	41	16.4	39	15.6	124	49.6	25	10.0	21	8.4	3.22	1.098
IBA12	53	21.2	53	21.2	92	36.8	23	9.2	29	11.6	3.31	1.235

Interpretation

When adolescents were asked "if their problems get solved when they approach parents' 29.2% said 'Very Often', 27.6% said 'Often', 34.4% said 'Sometimes', 3.2% said 'Rarely' and 5.6 % said 'Never'. Majority of adolescents felt that 'Sometimes' their problems got solved when they approached parents.

When adolescents were asked "if they felt relaxed when they shared their thoughts with their parents", 30% said 'Very Often', 28.4% said 'Often', 25.6% said 'Sometimes', 7.2% said 'Rarely' and 8.8% said 'Never'. Majority of adolescents 'Very Often' felt relaxed when they shared their thoughts with parents.

When adolescents were asked "if they didn't get stressed out because of continuous guidance from parents and teachers in academics", 13.2% said 'Very Often', 13.2% said 'Often', 50% said 'Sometimes', 10.8% said 'Rarely' and 12.8% said 'Never'. Majority of adolescents felt that they 'Sometimes' didn't get stressed out because of continuous guidance from parents and teachers in academics.

When adolescents were asked "if they took parents reprimand / counselling positively and changed their Behaviour accordingly", 22% said 'Very Often', 19.6% said 'Often', 46.8% said 'Sometimes', 5.2% said 'Rarely' and 6.4 % said 'Never'. Majority of adolescents felt that they took parents reprimand / counselling positively and changed their Behaviour accordingly.

When adolescents were asked "if they found their parents preaching important", 19.2% said 'Very Often', 18.4% said 'Often', 47.6% said 'Sometimes', 6.4% said 'Rarely' and 8.4% said 'Never'. Majority of adolescents felt that they 'Sometimes' found their parents' preaching important.

When adolescents were asked "if they considered the suggestions given by their parents for their clothes, friends and eating preferences", 18.8% said 'Very Often', 15.2% said 'Often', 43.6% said 'Sometimes', 11.6% said 'Rarely' and 10.8% said 'Never'. Majority of adolescents felt that they 'Sometimes' considered suggestions given by their parents for their clothes, friends and eating preferences.

When adolescents were asked "if they didn't mind when their parents expressed their choices for clothes, friends and food", 18.4% said 'Very Often', 17.6% said 'Often', 45.6% said 'Sometimes', 8.8% said 'Rarely' and 9.6% said 'Never'. Majority of adolescents felt that they 'Sometimes' didn't mind when their parents expressed their choices of clothes, friends and food.

When adolescents were asked "if they do not get annoyed when guests come to their house and their parents insist on meeting them", 20.8% said 'Very Often', 20.8% said 'Often', 38% said 'Sometimes', 10.4% said 'Rarely' and 10 % said 'Never'. Majority of adolescents felt that 'Sometimes' they didn't get annoyed when guests come to their house and their parents insist on meeting them.

When adolescents were asked "if they kept aside all their work when asked to help in entertaining the guests", 18.4% said 'Very Often', 17.2% said 'Often', 43.2% said 'Sometimes', 10.4% said 'Rarely' and 10.8% said 'Never'. Majority of adolescents felt that they 'Sometimes' kept aside all their work when asked to help in entertaining the guests.

When adolescents were asked "if they didn't get upset by disagreements with their parents", 16.4% said 'Very Often', 16.4% said 'Often',40.4% said 'Sometimes', 13.6% said 'Rarely' and 13.2% said 'Never'. Majority of adolescents felt that they 'Sometimes' didn't get upset by disagreements with their parents.

When adolescents were asked "if they didn't get upset when their parents did not listen to their point of view", 16.4% said 'Very Often', 15.6% said 'Often', 49.6% said 'Sometimes', 10% said 'Rarely' and 8.4% said 'Never'. Majority of adolescents felt that they 'Sometimes' didn't t get upset when their parents did not listen to their point of view.

When adolescents were asked "if they didn't get bored when they went out with their family", 21.2% said 'Very Often', 21.2% said 'Often', 36.8% said 'Sometimes', 9.2% said 'Rarely' and 11.6% said 'Never'. Majority of adolescents felt that they 'Sometimes' didn't get bored when they went out with their family.

4.8.6 **Frequency Distribution and Descriptive Statistics for impact of Parental Involvement on Adolescents' Academic Achievement as Perceived by Adolescents**

'Impact on Academic Achievement' is measured using the following five measured indicators where each measured indicator is scaled on 5-point rating scale (5 = Very Often, 4 = Often, 3 = Sometimes, 2 = Rarely and 1 = Never).

(a) IAA1 : Discussion with my parents has helped me realise my inclination towards future career option.

(b) IAA2 : As I have limited access to TV / internet, I have more time to focus on my studies.

(c) IAA3 : My parents monitoring of my grades motivates me to perform better academically.

(d) IAA4 : With my parents help I am able to perform better in my academics.

(e) IAA5 : The regular interaction of my parents and teachers guides me to improve myself academically.

Table 41 shows impact of Parental Involvement on Academic Achievement.

Table 41 : Impact of Parental Involvement on Academic Achievement as Perceived by Adolescents

Variable Code	Very Often		Often		Sometimes		Rarely		Never		Mean	Std. Deviation
	F	%	F	%	F	%	F	%	F	%		
IAA1	70	28.0	67	26.8	87	34.8	9	3.6	17	6.8	3.66	1.127
IAA2	61	24.4	63	25.2	91	36.4	15	6.0	20	8.0	3.52	1.159
IAA3	59	23.6	84	33.6	60	24.0	31	12.4	16	6.4	3.44	1.165
IAA4	80	32.0	72	28.8	69	27.6	8	3.2	21	8.4	3.64	1.164
IAA5	68	27.2	80	32.0	60	24.0	18	7.2	24	9.6	3.72	1.229

Interpretation

When adolescents were asked "if discussion with parents helped them in realising their inclination towards future career option.", 28% said 'Very Often', 26.8% said 'Often', 34.8% said 'Sometimes', 3.6% said 'Rarely' and 6.8% said 'Never'. Majority of the adolescents felt that discussion with parents 'Sometimes' helped them in realising their inclination towards future career option.

When adolescents were asked "if limited access to TV/ internet gave them more time to focus on studies", 24.4% said 'Very Often', 25.2% said 'Often', 36.4% said 'Sometimes', 6% said 'Rarely' and 8% said 'Never'. Majority of the adolescents 'Very Often' felt limited access to TV/ internet gave them more time to focus on studies.

When adolescents were asked "if monitoring of grades by parents motivated them to perform better in academics", 23.6% said 'very Often', 33.6% said 'Often', 24% said 'Sometimes', 12.4% said 'Rarely' and 6.4% said 'Never'. Majority of the adolescents felt that they 'Sometimes' got motivated to perform better in academics when parents monitored the grades".

When adolescents were asked "if they performed better in academics with help from parents", 32% said 'very Often', 28.8% said 'Often', 27.6% said 'Sometimes', 3.2% said 'Rarely' and 8.4% said 'Never'. Majority of the adolescents felt that they 'Sometimes' performed better in academics with help from parents.

When adolescents were asked "if regular interaction of parents and teachers guided them to improve themselves in academics", 27.2% said 'Very Often', 32% said 'Often', 24% said 'Sometimes', 7.2% said 'Rarely' and 9.6% said 'Never'. Majority of the adolescents felt that regular Interaction with parents and teachers 'Sometimes' guided them to improve themselves in academics.

4.8.7 **Frequency Distribution and Descriptive Statistics for Teacher's Involvement as Perceived by Adolescents**

'Teacher's Involvement' was measured through following five constructs :-

1. Emotional Involvement.
2. Interaction with Parents.
3. Instrumental Support.
4. Structure by Teachers.

4.8.7.1 **Emotional Involvement.**

'Emotional Involvement' is measured using the following five measured indicators where each measured indicator is scaled on 5-point rating scale (5 = Very Often, 4 = Often, 3 = Sometimes, 2 = Rarely and 1 = Never).

(a) EMT1 : My class teacher gives personal attention to every Student in the class.

(b) EMT2 : My class teacher discusses about my likes and interests.

(c) EMT3 : My class teacher does not get confused with my name.

(d) EMT4 : My class teacher can immediately find out whenever I am upset or disturbed.

(e) EMT5 : My class teacher involves me in all class activities.

Table 42 shows analysis of emotional involvement of Teachers.

Table 42 : Emotional Involvement of Teachers as Perceived by Adolescents

Variable Code	Very Often		Often		Sometimes		Rarely		Never		Mean	Std. Deviation
	F	%	F	%	F	%	F	%	F	%		
EMT1	57	22.8	56	22.4	87	34.8	20	8.0	30	12.0	3.36	1.254
EMT2	32	12.8	32	12.8	121	48.4	31	12.4	34	13.6	2.99	1.146
EMT3	50	20.0	52	20.8	95	38.0	27	10.8	26	10.4	3.29	1.205
EMT4	33	13.2	38	15.2	134	53.6	23	9.2	22	8.8	3.15	1.052
EMT5	49	19.6	52	20.8	112	44.8	13	5.2	24	9.6	3.36	1.143
Grand Mean											**3.30**	

Interpretation

When adolescents were asked "if their class teacher gave personal attention to every adolescent in the class", 22.8% said 'Very Often', 22.4% said 'Often', 34.8% said 'Sometimes', 8.0% said 'Rarely' and 12% said 'Never'. Majority of the adolescents felt that their class teacher 'Sometimes' gave personal attention to every adolescent in the class.

When adolescents were asked "if their teacher discussed about their likes and interests", 12.8% said 'Very Often', 12.8% said 'Often', 48.4% said 'Sometimes', 12.4% said 'Rarely' and 13.6% said 'Never'. Majority of the adolescents felt that their class teacher 'Sometimes' discussed about their likes and interests.

When adolescents were asked "if their class teacher did not get confused with their name", 20% said 'Very Often', 20.8% said 'Often', 38% said 'Sometimes', 10.8% said 'Rarely' and 10.4% said 'Never'. Majority of the adolescents felt that their class teacher 'Sometimes' did not get confused with their name.

When adolescents were asked "if their class teacher can immediately find out whenever they are upset or disturbed", 13.2% said 'Very Often', 15.2% said 'Often', 53.6% said 'Sometimes', 9.2% said 'Rarely' and 8.8% said 'Never'. Majority of the adolescents felt that their class teacher 'Sometimes' finds out when they are upset or disturbed.

When adolescents were asked "if their class teacher involved them in all class activities", 19.6% said 'Very Often', 20.8% said 'Often', 44.8% said 'Sometimes', 5.2% said 'Rarely' and 9.6% said 'Never'. Majority of the adolescents felt that their class teacher 'Sometimes' involved them in all class activities.

On the basis of grand mean (3.30) it can be concluded that 'Emotional Involvement' as a parameter of 'Teacher's Involvement' with adolescents is 'Moderate'.

4.8.7.2 **Interaction with Parents.**

'Interaction with Parents' is measured using the following four measured indicators where each measured indicator is scaled on 5-point rating scale (5 = Very Often, 4 = Often, 3 = Sometimes, 2 = Rarely and 1 = Never).

(a) IP1 : My class teacher keeps my parents updated about my performance in school.

(b) IP2 : Whenever I am upset, my class teacher discusses with my parents.

(c) IP3 : My class teacher does not avoid interaction with my parents.

(d) IP4 : My class teacher shares my achievements with my parents.

Table 43 shows analysis of Interaction with Parents by Teachers.

Table 43 : Interaction with Parents by Teachers as Perceived by Adolescents

Variable Code	Very Often		Often		Sometimes		Rarely		Never		Mean	Std. Deviation
	F	%	F	%	F	%	F	%	F	%		
IP1	45	18.0	51	20.4	108	43.2	19	7.6	27	10.8	3.27	1.168
IP2	32	12.8	19	7.6	116	46.4	43	17.2	40	16.0	2.84	1.175
IP3	70	28.0	66	26.4	64	25.6	25	10.0	25	10.0	3.52	1.271
IP4	50	20.0	53	21.2	93	37.2	25	10.0	29	11.6	3.28	1.226
Grand Mean											**3.23**	

Interpretation

When adolescents were asked "if their class teacher kept their parents updated about their performance in school", 18% said 'Very Often', 20.4% said 'Often', 43.2% said 'Sometimes', 7.6% said 'Rarely' and 10.8% said 'Never'. Majority of the adolescents felt that their class teacher 'Sometimes' kept their parents updated about their performance in school.

When adolescents were asked "if their teacher discussed with their parents when they are upset", 12.8% said 'Very Often', 7.6% said 'Often', 46.4% said 'Sometimes', 17.2% said 'Rarely' and 16% said 'Never'. Majority of the adolescents felt that their class teacher 'Sometimes' discussed with their parents when they are upset.

When adolescents were asked "if their class teacher did not avoid interaction with their Parent", 28% said 'Very Often', 26.4% said 'Often', 25.6% said 'Sometimes', 10% said 'Rarely' and 10% said 'Never'. Majority of the adolescents felt that their class teacher 'Very Often' did not avoid interaction with their parents.

When adolescents were asked "if their class teacher shared their achievements with their parents", 20% said 'Very Often', 21.2% said 'Often', 37.2% said 'Sometimes', 10% said 'Rarely' and 11.6% said 'Never'. Majority of the adolescents felt that their class teacher 'Sometimes' shared their achievements with their parents.

On the basis of grand mean (3.23) it can be concluded that 'Interaction with Parents' as a parameter of 'Teacher's Involvement' with adolescents is 'Moderate'.

4.8.7.3 **Instrumental Support.**

'Instrumental Support' is measured using the following five measured indicators where each measured indicator is scaled on 5-point rating scale (5 = Very Often, 4 = Often, 3 = Sometimes, 2 = Rarely and 1 = Never).

(a) IS1 : My class teacher regularly checks the assignment and homework given.

(b) IS2 : My class teacher appreciates my asking doubts and questions in class.

(c) IS3 : My class teacher is concerned about difficulties faced in other subjects.

(d) IS4 : My class teacher uses teaching aids and innovative techniques (e.g. smart board, quiz, crossword, etc.) while teaching in class.

(e) IS5 : My class teacher does not make fun of me or scolds me if I do not understand any particular topic.

Table 44 shows analysis of Instrumental Support by Teachers.

Table 44 : Instrumental Support by Teachers as Perceived by Adolescents

Variable Code	Very Often		Often		Sometimes		Rarely		Never		Mean	Std. Deviation
	F	%	F	%	F	%	F	%	F	%		
IS1	77	30.8	65	26.0	73	29.2	17	6.8	18	7.2	3.56	1.189
IS2	66	26.4	66	26.4	62	24.8	27	10.8	29	11.6	3.45	1.302
IS3	39	15.6	36	14.4	125	50.0	21	8.4	29	11.6	3.14	1.141
IS4	37	14.8	36	14.4	108	43.2	30	12.0	39	15.6	3.01	1.219
IS5	54	21.6	76	30.4	67	26.8	19	7.6	34	13.6	3.35	1.279
Grand Mean											**3.32**	

Interpretation

When adolescents were asked "if their class teacher regularly checks the assignment and homework given", 30.8% said 'Very Often', 26% said 'Often', 29.2% said 'Sometimes', 6.8% said 'Rarely' and 7.2% said 'Never'. Majority of the adolescents felt that their class teacher 'Very Often' regularly checks the assignment and homework given.

When adolescents were asked "if their teacher appreciated them for asking doubts and questions in class", 26.4% said 'Very Often', 26.4% said 'Often', 24.8% said 'Sometimes', 10.8% said 'Rarely' and 11.6% said 'Never'. Majority of the adolescents felt that their class teacher 'Very Often' and 'Often' appreciated them for asking doubts and questions in class.

When adolescents were asked "if their class teacher is concerned about difficulties faced in other subjects", 15.6% said 'Very Often', 14.4% said 'Often', 50% said 'Sometimes', 8.4% said 'Rarely' and 11.6% said 'Never'. Majority of the adolescents felt that their class teacher is 'Sometimes' concerned about difficulties faced in other subjects.

When adolescents were asked "if their class teacher used teaching aids and innovative techniques (e.g. smart board, quiz, crossword, etc.) while teaching in class", 14.8% said 'Very Often', 14.4% said 'Often', 43.2% said 'Sometimes', 12% said 'Rarely' and 15.6% said 'Never'. Majority of the adolescents felt that their class teacher 'Sometimes' used teaching aids and innovative techniques while teaching in class.

When adolescents were asked "if their class teacher did not make fun of them or scolded if they did not understand any particular topic", 21.6% said 'Very Often', 30.4% said 'Often', 26.8% said 'Sometimes', 7.6% said 'Rarely' and 13.6% said 'Never'. Majority of the adolescents felt that their class teacher 'Often' did not make fun of them or scolded if they did not understand any particular topic.

On the basis of grand mean (3.32) it can be concluded that 'Instrumental Support' as a parameter of 'Teacher's Involvement' with adolescents is 'Moderate'.

4.8.7.4 **Structure by Teachers.**

'Structure by Teacher's is measured using the following five measured indicators where each measured indicator is scaled on 5-point rating scale (5 = Very Often, 4 = Often, 3 = Sometimes, 2 = Rarely and 1 = Never).

(a) ST1 : My class teacher understands the mood of the class and accordingly plans activities.

(b) ST2 : My class teacher does not reprimand me when I misbehave in class.

(c) ST3 : My class teacher appreciates me when I perform well in curricular and / or co-curricular activities.

(d) ST4 : My class teacher separately counsels me when I make any mistake-.

(e) ST5 : My class teacher organises fun activities (school trips, picnic, role play, etc.).

Table 45 shows analysis of Structure by Teachers.

Table 45 : Structure by Teachers as Perceived by Adolescents

Variable Code	Very Often		Often		Sometimes		Rarely		Never		Mean	Std. Deviation
	F	%	F	%	F	%	F	%	F	%		
ST1	39	15.6	41	16.4	123	49.2	21	8.4	26	10.4	3.18	1.122
ST2	24	9.6	27	10.8	110	44.0	49	19.6	40	16.0	2.78	1.134
ST3	61	24.4	66	26.4	85	34.0	15	6.0	23	9.2	3 51	1.190
ST4	42	16.8	35	14.0	130	52.0	19	7.6	24	9.6	3 21	1.111
ST5	37	14.8	34	13.6	119	47.6	32	12.8	28	11.2	3.08	1.141
Grand Mean											**3.15**	

Interpretation

When adolescents were asked "if their class teacher understood the mood of the class and accordingly planned activities", 15.6% said 'Very Often', 16.4% said 'Often', 49.2% said 'Sometimes', 8.4% said 'Rarely' and 10.4% said 'Never'. Majority of the adolescents felt that their class teacher 'Sometimes' understood the mood of the class and accordingly planned activities.

When adolescents were asked '"if their teacher did not reprimand them when they misbehaved in class", 9.6% said 'Very Often', 10.8% said 'Often', 44% said 'Sometimes', 19.6% said 'Rarely' and 16% said 'Never'. Majority of the adolescents felt that their class teacher 'Sometimes' did not reprimand them when they misbehaved in class.

When adolescents were asked "if their class teacher appreciated them when they performed well in curricular and / or co-curricular activities", 24 4% said 'Very Often', 26.4% said 'Often', 34% said 'Sometimes', 6% said 'Rarely' and 9.2% said 'Never'. Majority of the adolescents felt that their class teacher 'Sometimes' appreciated them when they performed well in curricular and / or co-curricular activities.

When adolescents were asked "if their class teacher separately counselled them when they made any mistake", 16.8% said 'Very Often', 14% said 'Often', 52% said 'Sometimes', 7.6% said 'Rarely' and 9.6% said 'Never'. Majority of the adolescents felt that their class teacher 'Sometimes' counselled them separately when they made any mistake.

When adolescents were asked "if their class teacher organised fun activities (school trips, picnic, role play, etc.)", 14.8% said 'Very Often', 13.6% said 'Often', 47.6% said 'Sometimes', 12.8% said 'Rarely' and 11.2% said 'Never'. Majority of the adolescents felt that their class teacher 'Sometimes' organised fun activities (school trips, picnic, role play, etc.).

On the basis of grand mean (3.15) it can be concluded that 'Structure' as a parameter of 'Teacher's Involvement' with Adolescents is 'Moderate'.

4.8.8 **Frequency Distribution and Descriptive Statistics for impact of Teacher's Involvement on 'Academic Achievement' as Perceived by Adolescents**

Impact of Teacher's Involvement on 'Academic Achievement' is measured using the following six measured indicators where each measured indicator is scaled on 5-point rating scale (5 = Very Often, 4 = Often, 3 = Sometimes, 2 = Rarely and 1 = Never).

1. ITA1 : I am comfortable to approach my teacher regarding the difficulties I face in any subject.
2. ITA2 : Remedial classes arranged by my class teacher helps me in coping up.
3. ITA3 : With constant monitoring of homework and assignment by my class teacher, I complete my homework and improve my assignments on time.
4. ITA4 : I do not get stressed out due to constant vigilance of my teacher on my studies.
5. ITA5 : Due to usage of teaching aids and innovative techniques by my class teacher, it is easier for me to understand complex topics.
6. ITA6 : I enjoy going to school due to fun activities organised by my class teacher.

Table 46 shows analysis of impact of Teacher's Involvement on 'Academic Achievement'.

Table 46 : Impact of Teacher's Involvement on Academic Achievement

Variable Code	Very Often		Often		Sometimes		Rarely		Never		Mean	Std. Deviation
	F	%	F	%	F	%	F	%	F	%		
ITA1	45	18.0	51	20.4	108	43.2	19	7.6	27	10.8	3.27	1.168
ITA 2	32	12.8	19	7.6	116	46.4	43	17.2	40	16.0	2.84	1.175
ITA 3	70	28.0	66	26.4	64	25.6	25	10.0	25	10.0	3.52	1.271
ITA 4	50	20.0	53	21.2	93	37.2	25	10.0	29	11.6	3.28	1.226

Interpretation

When adolescents were asked "if they felt comfortable to approach their teacher regarding the difficulties they faced in any subject", 24.8% said 'Very Often', 18.8% said 'Often', 32.8% said 'Sometimes', 10.4% said 'Rarely' and 13.2% said 'Never'. Majority of the adolescents felt that they 'Sometimes' felt comfortable to approach their teacher regarding the difficulties they faced in any subject.

When adolescents were asked "if the remedial classes arranged by their class teacher helped them in coping up", 8.4% said 'Very Often', 13.2% said 'Often', 41.6% said 'Sometimes', 17.6% said 'Rarely' and 19.2% said 'Never'. Majority of the adolescents felt that 'Sometimes' the remedial classes arranged by their class teacher helped them in coping up.

When adolescents were asked "if with the constant monitoring of homework and assignment by their class teacher, did they complete their homework and improve their assignments on time", 26% said 'Very Often', 28% said 'Often', 24.8% said 'Sometimes', 8.8% said 'Rarely' and 12.4% said 'Never'. Majority of the adolescents felt that the constant monitoring of homework and assignment by their class teacher 'Often' helped them to complete their homework and improve their assignments on time.

When adolescents were asked "if they did not get stressed out due to constant vigilance of their teacher on their studies", 13.6% said 'Very Often', 13.2% said 'Often', 53.6% said 'Sometimes', 9.6% said 'Rarely' and 10% said 'Never'. Majority of the adolescents felt that they 'Sometimes' did not get stressed out due to constant vigilance of their teacher on their studies.

When adolescents were asked "if they enjoyed going to school due to fun activities organised by their class teacher", 22.4% said 'Very Often', 24.8% said 'Often', 35.6% said 'Sometimes', 7.2% said 'Rarely' and 10% said 'Never'. Majority of the adolescents felt that they 'Sometimes' enjoyed going to school due to fun activities organised by their class teacher.

4.8.9 **Frequency Distribution and Descriptive Statistics for impact of Teacher's Involvement on 'Behaviour Adjustment' as Perceived by Adolescents**

Impact of Teacher's Involvement on 'Behaviour Adjustment' is measured using the following six measured indicators where each measured indicator is scaled on 5-point rating scale (5 = Very Often, 4 = Often, 3 = Sometimes, 2 = Rarely and 1 = Never).

1. ITB1 : I can comfortably discuss my personal problems with my class teacher as she gives a patient hearing.
2. ITB2 : I appreciate my class teacher for giving advice on my friends and other personal issue.
3. ITB3 : I find my class teacher's instructions about the rules and its importance helpful to mould my Behaviour positively.
4. ITB4 : I like my class teacher as she doesn't ridicule me.
5. ITB5 : My class teacher's concern for me motivates me to attend school regularly.

Table 47 shows analysis of impact of Teacher's Involvement on 'Behaviour Adjustment'.

Table 47 : Impact of Teacher's Involvement on Behaviour Adjustment as Perceived by Adolescents

Variable Code	Very Often		Often		Sometimes		Rarely		Never		Mean	Std. Deviation
	F	%	F	%	F	%	F	%	F	%		
ITB1	49	19.6	37	14.8	96	38.4	30	12.0	38	15.2	3.12	1.286
ITB2	50	20.0	55	22.0	77	30.8	32	12.8	36	14.4	3.20	1.300
ITB3	57	22.8	59	23.6	92	36.8	13	5.2	29	11.6	3.41	1.226
ITB4	46	18.4	44	17.6	99	39.6	29	11.6	32	12.8	3.17	1.231
ITB5	73	29.2	69	27.6	61	24.4	19	7.6	28	11.2	3.56	1.289

Interpretation

When adolescents were asked "if they felt comfortable in discussing their personal problems with their class teacher as she gives a patient hearing", 19.6% said 'Very Often', 14.8% said 'Often', 38.4% said 'Sometimes', 12% said 'Rarely' and 15.2% said 'Never'. Majority of the adolescents felt that they 'Sometimes' felt comfortable discussing their personal problems with their class Teacher as she gives a patient hearing.

When adolescents were asked "if they appreciated their class teacher for giving advice on their friends and other personal issue", 20% said 'Very Often', 22% said 'Often', 30.8% said 'Sometimes', 12.8% said 'Rarely' and 14.4% said 'Never'. Majority of the adolescents felt that they 'Sometimes' appreciated their class teacher for giving advice on their friends and other personal issue.

When adolescents were asked "if they felt that the instructions about the rules and its importance by their class teacher was helpful to mould their Behaviour positively", 22.8% said 'Very Often', 23.6% said 'Often', 36.8% said 'Sometimes',5.2% said 'Rarely' and 11.6% said 'Never'. Majority of the adolescents felt that they

'Sometimes' felt that the instructions about the rules and its importance by their class teacher was helpful to mould their Behaviour positively.

When adolescents were asked "if they liked their class Teacher as she doesn't ridicule them", 18.4% said 'Very Often', 17.6% said 'Often', 39.6% said 'Sometimes', 11.6% said 'Rarely' and 12.8% said 'Sometimes'. Majority of the adolescents felt that they 'Very Often' liked their class teacher as she / he doesn't ridicule them.

When adolescents were asked "if their class teacher's concern for them motivated them to attend school regularly", 29.2% said 'Very Often', 27.6% said 'Often', 24.4% said 'Sometimes', 7.6% said 'Rarely' and 11.2% said 'Never'. Majority of the adolescents felt that 'Very Often' their class teacher's concern for them motivated them to attend school regularly.

4.9 Analysis of Parents Feedback

Responses from parents were taken through individual questionnaire (Appx B).

4.9.1 Gender wise Relationship

Table 48 : Gender wise Relationship

Relationship	Frequency	Percent
Mother	20	50%
Father	20	50%
Total	**40**	**100%**

Figure 42 shows gender wise relationship.

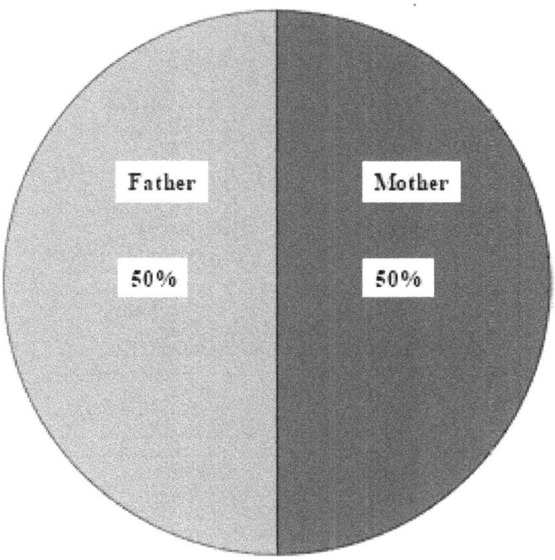

Figure 42 Gender wise Relationship

From the above graph it can be concluded that from the participant parents, 50% were mothers while 50% were fathers.

4.9.2 **Frequency Distribution for Closeness with Parents and Others as Perceived by Parents**

The following variables were used to measure closeness of children with parents and others using a nominal scale.

Table 49 shows measurement of closeness with Parents and others.

Table 49 : Measurement of Closeness with Parents and Others

Variable	Response Option	Frequency	Percentage
1. My child is friendly with	Mother	30	75%
	Father	10	25%
	Relatives	0	0
	Friends	0	0
	Total		**100%**
2. My child is more fearful of	Mother	11	27.5%
	Father	29	72.5%
	Relatives	0	0
	Friends	0	0
	Total		**100%**
3. My child confides his secrets and problems with	Mother	33	82.5%
	Father	5	12.5%
	Relatives	0	0
	Friends	2	5%
	Total		**100%**
4. My child is taught at home by	Mother	8	20%
	Father	18	45%
	Relatives	2	5%
	Friends	12	30%
	Total		**100%**
5. Parents Teachers Meet is mostly attended by	Mother	22	55%
	Father	17	42.5%
	Relatives	0	0
	No one	1	2.5%
	Total		**100%**

Interpretation

When parents were requested to tell "with whom their child is friendly with", 75% said 'Mother', 25% said 'Father'. Majority of parents felt that their child is friendly with their 'Mother'.

When parents were requested to tell "from whom their child is more fearful of", 27.5% said 'Mother', 72.5% said 'Father'. Majority of parents felt that their child is more fearful of their 'Father'.

When parents were requested to tell "with whom their child confides his secrets and problems with", 82.5% said 'Mother', 12.5% said 'Father' and 5% said 'Friends'. Majority of parents felt that their child confides his secrets and problems with their 'Mother'.

When parents were requested to tell "by whom is their child taught at home", 20% said 'Mother', 45% said 'Father', 5% said 'Relatives' and 30% said 'Friends'. Majority of parents felt that their child is taught at home by their 'Father'.

When parents were requested to tell "by whom is the Parents Teachers Meet mostly attended", 55% said 'Mother', 42.5% said 'Father' and 2.5% said 'None'. Majority of parents felt that the Parents Teachers Meet is mostly attended by their 'Mother'.

4.9.3 **Frequency Distribution and Descriptive Statistics for 'Parental Involvement' as Perceived by Parents**

'Parents' Involvement' was measured through following five constructs :-

1. Emotional Involvement.
2. Aspiration of Parents.
3. Structure by Parents.
4. School & Studies Involvement.
5. Involvement with Friends.

4.9.3.1 **Emotional Involvement.**

'Emotional Involvement' is measured using the following six measured indicators where each measured indicator is scaled on 5-point rating scale (5 = Very Often, 4 = Often, 3 = Sometimes, 2 = Rarely and 1 = Never).

(a) EIP1 : I do not reprimand child when they don't behave as expected.

(b) EIP2 : I endeavour to explain consequences to child when he falters.

(c) EIP3 : I can make out if my child is upset or disturbed.

(d) EIP4 : My child tells me if he / she gets scolded or punished in school.

(e) EIP5 : My child confides in me about fights or any other incident.

(f) EIP6 : I understand problem shared by my child & guide accordingly.

Table 50 shows analysis of Emotional Involvement of Parents.

Table 50 : Emotional Involvement as Perceived by Parents

Variable Code	Very Often		Often		Sometimes		Rarely		Never		Mean	Std. Deviation
	F	%	F	%	F	%	F	%	F	%		
EIP1	1	2.5	5	12.5	18	45.0	11	27.5	5	12.5	2.65	0.949
EIP2	11	27.5	17	42.5	12	30.0	0	0	0	0	3.85	0.834
EIP3	17	42.5	16	40.0	3	7.5	2	5.0	2	5.0	4.10	1.081
EIP4	3	7.5	3	7.5	18	45.0	3	7.5	13	32.5	2.50	1.240
EIP5	8	20.0	9	22.5	16	40.0	3	7.5	4	10.0	3.35	1.189
EIP6	18	45.0	16	40.0	6	15.0	0	0	0	0	4.30	0.723
Grand Mean											**3.46**	

Interpretation

When parents were asked "if they did not reprimand their child when he / she did not behave as per their expectations", 2.5% said 'Very Often', 12.5% said 'Often', 45% said 'Sometimes', 27.5% said 'Rarely' and 12.5% said 'Never'. Majority of the parents felt that they 'Sometimes' did not reprimand their child when he / she did not behave as per their expectations.

When parents were asked "if they made an effort to explain the consequences to their child whenever he / she faltered", 27.5% said 'Very Often', 42.5% said 'Often', 30% said 'Sometimes'. Majority of the parents felt that they 'Often' made an effort to explain the consequences to their child whenever he / she faltered.

When parents were asked "if they could make out if their child is upset or disturbed"' 42.5% said 'Very Often', 40% said 'Often', 7.5% said 'Sometimes', 5% said 'Rarely' and 5% said 'Never'. Majority of the parents felt that they 'Very Often' could make out if their child is upset or disturbed.

When parents were asked "if their child told them if they got scolded or punished in school", 7.5% said 'Very Often', 7.5% said 'Often', 45% said 'Sometimes', 7.5% said 'Rarely' and 32.5% said 'Never'. Majority of the parents felt that their child 'Sometimes' told them if they got scolded or punished in school.

When parents were asked "if their child confided in them about fights or any other incident", 20% said 'Very Often', 22.5% said 'Often', 40% said 'Sometimes', 7.5% said 'Rarely' and 10% said 'Never'. Majority of the parents felt that 'Sometimes' their child confided in them about fights or any other incident.

When parents were asked "if they tried to understand the problem shared by their child and guided accordingly", 45% said 'Very Often', 40% said 'Often', 15% said 'Sometimes'. Majority of the parents felt that they 'Very Often' tried to understand the problem shared by their child and guided accordingly.

On the basis of grand mean (3.46) it can be concluded that 'Emotional Involvement' as a parameter for 'Parental Involvement' with Adolescents as perceived by parents is 'Moderate'.

4.9.3.2 **Aspiration of Parents.**

'Parents' Aspiration' is measured using the following five measured indicators where each measured indicator is scaled on 5-point rating scale (5 = Very Often, 4 = Often, 3 = Sometimes, 2 = Rarely and 1 = Never).

(a) PAP1 : I discuss with my child to know about his / her inclination for future career aspirations.

(b) PAP2 : I want my child to make his own career decision.

(c) PAP3 : I discuss in a casual manner about importance of achieving goals during dinner or outing to motivate my child to achieve his / her goals \

(d) PAP4 : I have career related discussions with my child.

(e) PAP5 : I think it's right time to discuss about future with my child.

Table 51 shows analysis of Parents' Aspiration.

Table 51 : Parents' Aspirations as Perceived by Parents

Variable Code	Very Often		Often		Sometimes		Rarely		Never		Mean	Std. Deviation
	F	%	F	%	F	%	F	%	F	%		
PAP1	12	30.0	12	30.0	16	40.0	0	0	0	0	3.90	0.841
PAP2	16	40.0	15	37.5	9	22.5	0	0	0	0	4.18	0.781
PAP3	4	10.0	8	20.0	26	65.0	1	2.5	1	2.5	3.33	0.797
PAP4	3	7.5	3	7.5	20	50.0	8	20.0	6	15.0	2.73	1.062
PAP5	2	5.0	3	7.5	24	60.0	6	15.0	5	12.5	2.78	0.947
Grand Mean											**3.38**	

Interpretation

When parents were asked "if they 'discussed with their child to know about his / her inclination for future career aspirations", 30% said 'Very Often', 30% said 'Often', 40% said 'Sometimes'. Majority of the parents felt that they 'Sometimes' discussed with their child to know about his / her inclination for future career aspirations.

When parents were asked "if they wanted their child to make his / her own career decision", 40% said 'Very Often', 37.5% said 'Often', 22.5% said 'Sometimes'. Majority of the parents felt that they 'Very Often' wanted their child to make his / her own career decision.

When parents were asked "if they discussed in a casual manner about importance of achieving goals during dinner or outing to motivate their child to achieve his / her goals", 10% said 'Very Often', 20% said 'Often', 65% said 'Sometimes', 2.5% said 'Rarely' and 2.5% said 'Never'. Majority of the parents felt that they 'Sometimes' discussed in a casual manner about importance of achieving goals during dinner or outing to motivate their child to achieve his / her goals.

When parents were asked "if they had career related discussions with their child", 7.5% said 'Very Often', 7.5% said 'Often', 50% said 'Sometimes', 20% said 'Rarely' and 15% said 'Never'. Majority of the parents felt that they 'Sometimes' had career related discussions with their child.

When parents were asked "If they thought it's right time to discuss about future with their child", 5.0% said 'Very Often',7.5% said 'Often', 60% said 'Sometimes', 15% said 'Rarely' and 12.5% said 'Never'. Majority of the parents felt that they 'Sometimes' thought it's right time to discuss about future with their child.

On the basis of grand mean (3.38) it can be concluded that 'Parents' aspiration' as a parameter for 'Parental Involvement' with adolescents, as perceived by parents is 'Moderate'.

4.9.3.3 **Structure by Parents.**

'Structure by Parents' is measured using the following four measured indicators where each measured indicator is scaled on 5-point rating scale (5 = Very Often, 4 = Often, 3 = Sometimes, 2 = Rarely and 1 = Never).

(a) SPP1 : I keep a check on child's daily routine.

(b) SPP2 : I keep a tab on my child's daily usage of TV / internet.

(c) SPP3 : I prefer to choose clothes for my child.

(d) SPP4 : On weekends we as a family make sure to spend one evening together either going out or playing a board game.

Table 52 shows analysis of Structure by Parents.

Table 52 : Structure by Parents' as Perceived by Parents

Variable Code	Very Often		Often		Sometimes		Rarely		Never		Mean	Std. Deviation
	F	%	F	%	F	%	F	%	F	%		
SPP1	14	35.0	16	40.0	6	15.0	1	2.5	3	7.5	3.93	1.141
SPP2	13	32.5	13	32.5	8	20.0	3	7.5	3	7.5	3.75	1.214
SPP3	7	17.5	6	15.0	17	42.5	6	15.0	4	10.0	3.15	1.189
SPP4	10	25.0	10	25.0	20	50.0	0	0	0	0	3.75	0.840
Grand Mean											**3.65**	

Interpretation

When parents were asked "if they kept a check on their child's daily routine", 35% said 'Very Often', 40% said 'Often', 15% said 'Sometimes', 2.5% said 'Rarely' and 7.5% said 'Never'. Majority of the parents felt that they 'Often' kept a check on their child's daily routine.

When parents were asked "if they kept a tab on their child's daily usage of TV / internet", 32.5% said 'Very Often', 32.5% said 'Often', 20% said 'Sometimes', 7.5% said 'Rarely' and 7.5% said 'Never'. Majority of the parents felt that they 'Very Often' and 'Often' kept a tab on their child's daily usage of TV / internet.

When parents were asked "if they preferred to choose clothes for their child", 17.5% said 'Very Often', 15% said 'Often', 42.5% said 'Sometimes', 15% said 'Rarely' and 10% said 'Never'. Majority of the parents felt that they 'Sometimes' preferred to choose clothes for their child.

When parents were asked "if on weekends they as a family made sure to spend one evening together either going out or playing a board game", 25% said 'Very Often', 25% said 'Often', 50% said 'Sometimes'. Majority of the parents felt that on weekends they as a family 'Sometimes' made sure to spend one evening together either going out or playing a board game.

On the basis of grand mean (3.65) it can be concluded that 'Structure by Parents' as a parameter for 'Parental Involvement' with Adolescents, as perceived by parents is 'High'.

4.9.3.4 **School & Studies Involvement.**

'School & Studies Involvement' is measured using the following six measured indicators where each measured indicator is scaled on 5-point rating scale (5 = Very Often, 4 = Often, 3 = Sometimes, 2 = Rarely and 1 = Never).

(a) SSIP1 : I am appreciative of my child if he / she works hard but doesn't score good marks.

(b) SSIP2 : I am happy when my child works hard for exams irrespective of results.

(c) SSIP3 : I find time for attending Teachers Meet held in my child's school.

(d) SSIP4 : I keep myself available to help solve my child's difficulties in studies and help in assignments / projects.

(e) SSIP5 : I make effort to help my child in studies and assignments.

(f) SSIP6 : I keep track of my child's marks and grades in class examination.

Table 53 shows analysis of Parents' school and studies involvement.

Table 53 : Parents' school & Studies Involvement as Perceived by Parents

Variable Code	Very Often		Often		Sometimes		Rarely		Never		Mean	Std. Deviation
	F	%	F	%	F	%	F	%	F	%		
SSIP1	5	12.5	5	12.5	18	45.0	6	15.0	6	15.0	2.93	1.185
SSIP2	16	40.0	17	42.5	7	17.5	0	0	0	0	4.23	0.733
SSIP3	1	2.5	1	2.5	11	27.5	14	35.0	13	32.5	2.08	0.971
SSIP4	13	32.5	16	40.0	11	27.5	0	0	0	0	4.05	0.783
SSIP5	17	42.5	15	37.5	8	20.0	0	0	0	0	1.78	0.768
SSIP6	19	47.5	18	45.0	3	7.5	0	0	0	0	4.40	0.632
Grand Mean											**3.25**	

Interpretation

When parents were asked "if they are appreciative of their child if he / she works hard but doesn't score good marks", 12.5% said 'Very Often', 12.5% said 'Often', 45% said 'Sometimes', 15% said 'Rarely' and 15% said 'Never'. Majority of the parents felt that they 'Sometimes' are appreciative of their child if he / she works hard but doesn't score good marks.

When parents were asked "if they are happy when their child works hard for exams irrespective of results", 40% said 'Very Often', 42.5% said 'Often', 17.5% said 'Sometimes'. Majority of the parents felt that they 'Often' are happy when their child works hard for exams irrespective of results.

When parents were asked "if they took out time for attending Teachers Meet held in their child's school", 2.5% said 'Very Often', 2.5% said 'Often', 27.5% said 'Sometimes', 35% said 'Rarely' and 32. 5% said 'Never'. Majority of the parents felt that they 'Rarely' took out time for attending Teachers Meet held in their child's school.

When parents were asked "if they kept themselves available to help solve their child's difficulties in studies and help in assignments / projects", 32.5% said 'Very Often', 40% said 'Often', 27.5% said 'Sometimes'. Majority of the parents felt that they 'Often' kept themselves available to help solve their child's difficulties in studies and help in assignments / projects.

When parents were asked "if they made effort to help their child in studies and assignments", 42.5% said 'Very Often', 37.5% said 'Often', 20% said 'Sometimes'. Majority of the parents felt that they 'Very Often' made effort to help their child in studies and assignments.

When parents were asked "if they kept track of their child's marks and grades in class examination", 47.5% said 'Very Often', 45% said 'Often' and 7.5% said 'Sometimes'. Majority of the parents felt that they 'Very Often' kept track of their child's marks and grades in class examination.

On the basis of grand mean (3.25) it can be concluded that 'School & Studies Involvement' as a parameter for 'Parental Involvement' with Adolescents, as perceived by parents is 'Moderate'.

4.9.3.5 **Involvement with Friends.**

'Involvement with Friends' is measured using the following four measured indicators where each measured indicator is scaled on 5-point rating scale (5 = Very Often, 4 = Often, 3 = Sometimes, 2 = Rarely and 1 = Never).

(a) IFP1 : I know my child's friends.

(b) IFP2 : I invite my child's friends at home.

(c) IFP3 : I give advice to my child on whom to be friends with so as to avoid wrong influence.

(d) IFP4 : I do not give examples of my child's friends who have performed well in academics and / or Behaviour.

Table shows 54 analysis of involvement with friends.

Table 54 : Involvement with Friends as Perceived by Parents

Variable Code	Very Often		Often		Sometimes		Rarely		Never		Mean	Std. Deviation
	F	%	F	%	F	%	F	%	F	%		
IFP1	11	27.5	15	37.5	14	35	0	0	0	0	3.98	0.800
IFP2	4	10.0	4	10.0	26	65.0	1	2.5	5	12.5	3.03	1.025
IFP3	9	22.5	10	25	17	42.5	2	5	2	5	3.51	1.048
IFP4	5	12.5	5	12.5	19	47.5	6	15	5	12.5	3.00	1.155
Grand Mean											**3.38**	

Interpretation

When parents were asked "if they 'knew their child's friends", 27.5% said 'Very Often', 37.5% said 'Often', 35% said 'Sometimes'. Majority of the parents felt that they 'Often' knew their child's friends.

When parents were asked "if they invited their child's friends at home", 10% said 'Very Often', 10% said 'Often', 65% said 'Sometimes', 2.5% said 'Rarely' and 12.5% said 'Never'. Majority of the parents felt that they 'Sometimes' invited their child's friends at home.

When parents were asked "if they gave advice to their child on whom to be friends with, so as to avoid wrong influence", 22.5% said 'Very Often', 25% said 'Often', 42.5% said 'Sometimes', 5% said 'Rarely' and 5% said 'Never'. Majority of the parents felt that they 'Sometimes' gave advice to their child on whom to be friends with, so as to avoid wrong influence.

When parents were asked "if they did not give examples of their child's friends who have performed well in academics and / or Behaviour", 12.5% said 'Very Often', 12.5% said 'Often', 47.5% said 'Sometimes', 15% said 'Rarely' and 12.5% said 'Never'. Majority of the parents felt that they 'Sometimes' did not give examples of their child's friends who have performed well in academics and / or Behaviour.

On the basis of grand mean (3.38) it can be concluded that 'Involvement with Friends' as a parameter for 'Parental Involvement' with Adolescents as perceived by parents is 'Moderate'.

4.9.4 **Frequency Distribution and Descriptive Statistics for impact of Parental Involvement on Behaviour Adjustment of Adolescents as Perceived by Parents**

Impact of 'Parental Involvement' on 'Behaviour Adjustment of Adolescents' is measured using the following eleven measured indicators where each measured indicator is scaled on 5-point rating scale (5 = Very Often, 4 = Often, 3 = Sometimes, 2 = Rarely and 1 = Never).

(a) IBP1 : My child prefers to study more than playing or spending time on TV / internet / mobile games.

(b) IBP2 : I find my child getting irritated with my constant interaction with his / her teachers.

(c) IBP3 : My child seems to be happy when I interact with his / her teachers.

(d) IBP4 : My child gets irritated when I suggest him / her about clothes, friends and food choices.

(e) IBP5: My child keeps aside whatever he is doing at that particular time whenever he / she is asked to help in entertaining the guests.

(f) IBP6 : Discussion with my child leads to argument.

(g) IBP7 : My child is attentive whenever I try to give our perspective towards life.

(h) IBP8 : My child does not get upset and does not throw a tantrum when I do not fulfil his demands.

(j) IBP9 : My child does the task when asked to do.

(k) IBP10 : When we go out as a family, my child does not get bored.

(l) IBP11 : My child happily interacts whenever any guests come to our house.

Table 55 shows analysis of impact of Parental Involvement on 'Behaviour Adjustment'.

Table 55 : Impact of Parental Involvement on Behaviour Adjustment as Perceived by Parents

Variable Code	Very Often		Often		Sometimes		Rarely		Never		Mean	Std. Deviation
	F	%	F	%	F	%	F	%	F	%		
IBP1	4	10.0	4	10.0	22	55.0	5	12.5	5	12.5	2.93	1.071
IBP2	2	5.0	1	2.5	11	27.5	13	32.5	13	32.5	2.15	1.075
IBP3	6	15.0	5	12.5	29	72.5	0	0	0	0	3.43	0.747
IBP4	1	2.5	2	5.0	9	22.5	16	40.0	12	30.0	2.10	0.982
IBP5	5	12.5	5	12.5	21	52.5	5	12.5	4	10.0	3.05	1.085
IBP6	3	7.5	4	10.0	14	35.0	9	22.5	10	25.0	2.53	1.198
IBP7	15	37.5	10	25.0	14	35.0	1	2.5	0	0	3.98	0.920
IBP8	1	2.5	3	7.5	19	47.5	7	17.5	10	25.0	2.45	1.037
IBP9	7	17.5	6	15.0	23	57.5	0	0	4	10.0	3.30	1.091
IBP10	2	5.0	2	5.0	9	22.5	14	35.0	13	32.5	2.15	1.099
IBP11	2	5.0	0	0	17	42.5	9	22.5	12	30.0	2.28	1.062

Interpretation

When parents were asked “if their child preferred to study more than playing or spending time on TV / internet / mobile games”, 10% said ‘Very Often’, 10% said ‘Often’, 55% said ‘Sometimes’, 12.5% said ‘Rarely’ and 12.5% said ‘Never’. Majority of the parents felt that their child ‘Sometimes’ preferred to study more than playing or spending time on TV / internet / mobile games.

When parents were asked “if they found their child getting irritated with their constant interaction with his / her teachers”, 5% said ‘Very Often’, 2.5% said ‘Often’, 27.5% said ‘Sometimes’, 32.5% said ‘Rarely’ and 32.5% said ‘Never’. Majority of the parents felt that they ‘Rarely’ or ‘Never’ found their child to get irritated with their constant interaction with his / her teachers.

When parents were asked “if their child seemed to be happy when they interacted with his / her teachers”, 15% said ‘Very Often’, 12.5% said ‘Often’ and 72.5% said ‘Sometimes. Majority of the parents felt that their child ‘Sometimes’ seemed to be happy when they interacted with his / her teachers.

When parents were asked “if their child got irritated when they suggested him / her about clothes, friends and food choices”, 2.5% said ‘Very Often’, 5% said ‘Often’, 22.5% said ‘Sometimes, 40% said ‘Rarely’, and 30% said ‘Never’. Majority of the parents felt that their child ‘Rarely’ got irritated when they suggested him / her about clothes, friends and food choices.

When parents were asked “if their child keeps aside whatever he is doing at that particular time whenever he / she is asked to help in entertaining the guests”, 12.5% said ‘Very Often’, 12.5% said ‘Often’, 52.5% said ‘Sometimes’, 12.5% said ‘Rarely’ and 10% said ‘Never’. Majority of the parents felt that their child ‘Sometimes’ keeps aside whatever he / she is doing at that particular time whenever he / she is asked to help in entertaining the guests.

When parents were asked “if they found discussion with their child leads to argument”, 7.5% said ‘Very Often’, 10% said ‘Often’, 35% said ‘Sometimes’, 22.5% said ‘Rarely’ and 25% said ‘Never’. Majority of the parents felt that they ‘Sometimes’ found discussion with their child leads to argument.

When parents were asked "if they find their child to be attentive whenever they try to give their perspective towards life", 37.5% said 'Very Often', 25% said 'Often', 35% said 'Sometimes' and 2.5% said 'Rarely'. Majority of the parents felt that they 'Very Often' find their child to be attentive whenever they try to give their perspective towards life.

When parents were asked "if their child did not get upset and did not throw a tantrum when they did not fulfil his / her demands", 2.5% said 'Very Often', 7.5% said 'Often', 47.5% said 'Sometimes, 17.5% said 'Rarely' and 25% said 'Never'. Majority of the parents felt that their child 'Sometimes' did not get upset and did not throw a tantrum when they did not fulfil his / her demands.

When parents were asked "if their child did the task when asked to do", 17.5% said 'Very Often', 15% said 'Often', 57.5% said 'Sometimes' and 10% said 'Never'. Majority of the parents felt that their child 'Sometimes' did the task when asked to do.

When parents were asked "if they felt their child did not get bored when they went out as a family", 5% said 'Very Often', 5% said 'Often', 22.5% said 'Sometimes', 35% said 'Rarely' and 32.5% said 'Never'. Majority of the parents felt that their child 'Rarely' did not get bored when they went out as a family.

When parents were asked "if they felt their child happily interacted when any guests came to their house", 5% said 'Very Often', 42.5% said 'Sometimes', 22.5% said 'Rarely' and 30% said 'Never'. Majority of the parents felt that their child 'Sometimes' happily interacted when any guests came to their house.

4.9.5 Frequency Distribution and Descriptive Statistics for impact of Parental Involvement on Academic Achievement of Adolescents as Perceived by Parents

Impact of 'Parental Involvement' on 'Academics of Adolescents' is measured using the following two measured indicators where each measured indicator is scaled on 5-point rating scale (5 = Very Often, 4 = Often, 3 = Sometimes, 2 = Rarely and 1 = Never).

(a) IAP1 : I find my child to be attentive and interested while we discuss about his / her future.

(b) IAP2 : My child is not distracted / casual when we discuss his future.

Table 56 shows analysis of impact of 'Parental Involvement' on 'Academic Achievement'.

Table 56 : Impact of Parental Involvement on Academic Achievement as Perceived by Parents

Variable Code	Very Often		Often		Sometimes		Rarely		Never		Mean	Std. Deviation
	F	%	F	%	F	%	F	%	F	%		
IAP1	13	32.5	9	22.5	17	42.5	1	2.5	0	0	3.90	0.882
IAP2	3	7.5	3	7.5	12	30.0	16	40.0	6	15.0	2.53	1.086

Interpretation

When parents were asked "if they found their child to be attentive and interested while they discussed about his / her future", 32.5% said 'Very Often', 22.5% said 'Often', 42.5% said 'Sometimes' and 2.5% said 'Rarely'. Majority of the parents felt their child 'Sometimes' was attentive / interested when they discussed about his future.

When parents were asked "if their child did not get distracted and was not casual when they discussed about his / her future", 7.5% said 'Very Often', 7.5% said 'Often', 30% said 'Sometimes', 40% said 'Rarely' and 15% said 'Never'. Majority of the parents felt that their child 'Rarely' did not get distracted and was not casual when they discussed about his / her future.

4.9.6 **Frequency Distribution and Descriptive Statistics for Teacher's Involvement and its impact on Adolescents as Perceived by Parents**

'Teacher's Involvement and its impact on Adolescents' is measured using the following four measured indicators where each measured indicator is scaled on 5-point rating scale (5 = Very Often, 4 = Often, 3 = Sometimes, 2 = Rarely and 1 = Never).

(a) ITP1 : I find teacher's support helpful in Academic improvement of child.

(b) ITP2 : I have seen changes in my child's Behaviour with teacher's support.

(c) ITP3 : I find Parents and teacher's interactive sessions helpful in understanding my child.

(d) ITP4 : My child's class teacher makes it a point to discuss about my child's performance or Behaviour with me.

Table 57 shows analysis of involvement and impact of teacher's Involvement on Adolescents.

Table 57 : Involvement & impact of Teacher's on Adolescents as Perceived by Parents

Variable Code	Very Often		Often		Sometimes		Rarely		Never		Mean	Std. Deviation
	F	%	F	%	F	%	F	%	F	%		
ITP1	13	32.5	15	37.5	12	30.0	0	0	0	0	4.03	0.800
ITP2	5	12.5	7	17.5	28	70.0	0	0	0	0	3.43	0.712
ITP3	11	27.5	10	25.0	18	45.0	1	2.5	0	0	3.82	0.854
ITP4	7	17.5	8	20.0	20	50.0	2	5.0	3	7.5	3.41	1.019
Grand Mean											**3.66**	

Interpretation

When parents were asked "if they found teacher's support to help in Academic improvement of their child", 32.5% said 'Very Often', 37.5% said 'Often' and 30% said 'Sometimes'. Majority of the parents felt that teachers support 'Often' helped in Academic improvement of their child.

When parents were asked "if they saw changes in their child's Behaviour with teacher's support", 12.5% said 'Very Often', 17.5% said 'Often' and 70% said 'Sometimes'. Majority of the parents felt that they 'Sometimes' saw changes in their child's Behaviour with teacher's support.

When parents were asked "if they found parents and teacher's interactive sessions helpful in understanding their child", 27.5% said 'Very Often', 25% said 'Often', 45% said 'Sometimes' and 2.5% said 'Rarely'. Majority of the parents felt that parents and teacher's interactive session 'Sometimes' helped in understanding their child.

When parents were asked "if their child's class teacher made it a point to discuss about their child's performance or Behaviour with them", 17.5% said 'Very Often', 20% said 'Often', 50% said 'Sometimes', 5% said 'Rarely' and 7.5% said 'Never'. Majority of the parents felt that their child's class teacher 'Sometimes' made it a point to discuss about their child's performance or Behaviour with them.

On the basis of grand mean (3.66) it can be concluded that 'Impact of Teacher's Involvement' on Adolescents' as perceived by parents is 'High'.

4.10 Analysis of Teachers Feedback

4.10.1 Gender wise Distribution

Table 58 shows the analysis of responses from Adolescents that were taken through individual questionnaire (Appx C).

Table 58 : Gender wise Distribution of Teachers

	Frequency	Percent
Male	12	30%
Female	28	70%
Total	40	100%

Figure 43 shows Gender wise distribution of Teachers.

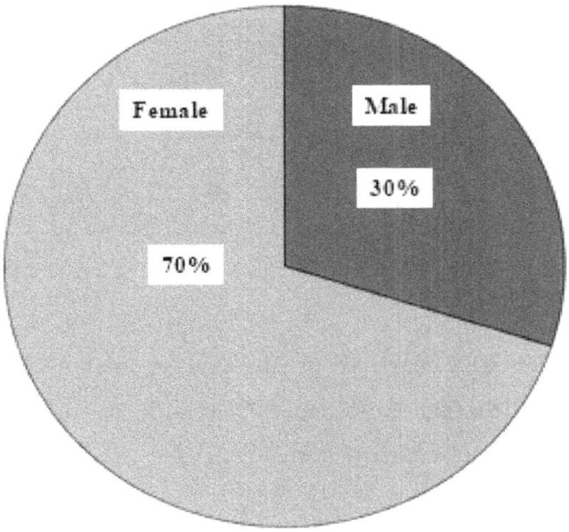

Figure 43 Gender wise distribution of Teachers

Interpretation

From the above graph it can be concluded that from the participant Teachers, 70% were female while 30% were male.

4.10.2 **Frequency Distribution for Traits of Adolescents as Perceived by Teachers**

The following variables were used to measure traits of Adolescents with respect to gender, using a nominal scale :-

Table 59 : Measurement of Traits of Adolescents

Variable	Response Option	Frequency	Percentage
1. In my opinion more restless and destructive are	Boys	28	70%
	Girls	0	0
	None	12	30%
	Total	**40**	**100%**
2. In my opinion more studious and hardworking are	Boys	12	30%
	Girls	24	60%
	None	4	10%
	Total	**40**	**100%**
3. In my opinion more talkative are	Boys	17	42.5%
	Girls	21	52.5%
	None	2	5%
	Total	**40**	**100%**
4. In my opinion more physically active are	Boys	20	50%
	Girls	17	42.5%
	None	3	7.5%
	Total	**40**	**100%**
5. In my opinion more forthcoming in discussing their personal problems are	Boys	11	27.5%
	Girls	29	72.5%
	None	0	0
	Total	**40**	**100%**

Interpretation

When teachers were requested to tell "In their opinion who was more restless and destructive", 70% said 'Boys' and 30% said 'None'. Majority of teachers felt that 'Boys' were more restless and destructive.

When teachers were requested to tell "In their opinion who was more studious and hardworking", 30% said 'Boys', 60% said 'Girls' and 10% said 'None'. Majority of teachers felt that 'Girls' were more studious and hardworking.

When teachers were requested to tell "In their opinion who was more talkative", 42.5% said 'Boys', 52.5% said 'Girls' and 5% said 'None'. Majority of teachers felt that 'Girls' were more talkative.

When teachers were requested to tell "In their opinion who was more physically active", 50% said 'Boys', 42.5% said 'Girls and 7.5% said 'None'. Majority of teachers felt that 'Boys' were more physically active.

When teachers were requested to tell "In their opinion who was more forthcoming in discussing their personal problems', 27.5% said 'Boys' and 72.5% said 'Girls'. Majority of teachers felt that 'Girls' were more forthcoming in discussing their personal problems.

4.10.3 **Frequency Distribution and Descriptive Statistics for 'Teacher's Involvement' as Perceived by Teachers**

'Teacher's Involvement' was measured through following five constructs :-

1. Emotional Involvement.
2. Interaction with Parents.
3. Instrumental Support.
4. Structure by Teachers.

4.10.3.1 **Emotional Involvement.**

'Emotional Involvement' is measured using the following five measured indicators where each measured indicator is scaled on 5-point rating scale (5 = Very Often, 4 = Often, 3 = Sometimes, 2 = Rarely and 1 = Never).

(a) EIT1 : I try to give personal attention to every Student in the class.

(b) EIT2 : I try to know about likes and interests of my students.

(c) EIT3 : I do not get confused with my students name.

(d) EIT4 : I can make out whenever any of my Student is upset or disturbed.

(e) EIT5 : I am concerned for my students' achievements and motivate them to attend school regularly.

Table 60 shows analysis of Teacher's emotional involvement.

Table 60 : Teacher's Emotional Involvement as Perceived by Teachers

Variable Code	Very Often		Often		Sometimes		Rarely		Never		Mean	Std. Deviation
	F	%	F	%	F	%	F	%	F	%		
EIT1	13	32.5	14	35.0	13	32.5	0	0	0	0	4.00	.816
EIT2	4	10.0	3	7.5	27	67.5	2	5.0	4	10.0	3.03	.974
EIT3	13	32.5	11	27.5	14	35.0	1	2.5	1	2.5	3.85	1.001
EIT4	16	40.0	17	42.5	7	17.5	0	0	0	0	4.23	.733
EIT5	13	32.5	17	42.5	10	25.0	0	0	0	0	4.08	.764
Grand Mean											**3.84**	

Interpretation

When teachers were asked "if they gave personal attention to every Student in the class", 32.5% said 'Very Often', 35% said 'Often' and 32.5% said 'Sometimes'. Majority of the teachers felt that they 'Often' gave personal attention to every Student in the class.

When teachers were asked "if they tried to know about likes and interests of their students", 10% said 'Very Often', 7.5% said 'Often', 67.5% said 'Sometimes', 5% said 'Rarely' and 10% said 'Never'. Majority of the teachers felt that they 'Sometimes' tried to know about likes and interests of their students.

When teachers were asked "if they did not get confused with their students' name", 32.5% said 'Very Often',27.5% said 'Often', 35% said 'Sometimes', 2.5% said 'Rarely' and 2.5% said 'Never'. Majority of the teachers felt that they 'Sometimes' did not get confused with their students' name.

When teachers were asked "if they could make out whenever any student is upset or disturbed, 40% said 'Very Often', 42.5% said 'Often' and 17.5% said 'Sometimes'. Majority of the teachers felt that they could 'Often' make out whenever any Student is upset or disturbed.

When teachers were asked "if they were concerned for their students' achievements and motivated them to attend school regularly", 32.5% said 'Very Often', 42.5% said 'Often' and 25% said 'Sometimes'. Majority of the teachers felt that they were 'Often' concerned for their students' achievements and motivated them to attend school regularly.

On the basis of grand mean (3.84) it can be concluded that 'Emotional Involvement' as a parameter for 'Teacher's Involvement' with Adolescents, as perceived by Teachers, is 'High'.

4.10.3.2 **Interaction with Parents.**

'Interaction with Parents' is measured using the following five measured indicators where each measured indicator is scaled on 5-point rating scale (5 = Very Often, 4 = Often, 3 = Sometimes, 2 = Rarely and 1 = Never).

(a) IPT1 : I make sure to inform and discuss with the parents IF I find anything unusual with their child.

(b) IPT2 : I keep parents updated about their performance in school.

(c) IPT3 : I conduct counselling for parents to help them deal with their adolescents.

(d) IPT4 : I find Interaction with parents helpful.

(e) IPT5 : I do not avoid Interaction with parents other than scheduled PTMs.

Table 61 shows analysis of Teacher's interaction with Parents'.

Table 61 : Teacher's Interaction with Parents as perceived by Teachers

Variable Code	Very Often		Often		Sometimes		Rarely		Never		Mean	Std. Deviation
	F	%	F	%	F	%	F	%	F	%		
IPT1	16	40.0	16	40.0	8	20.0	0	0	0	0	4.20	0.758
IPT2	10	25.0	13	32.5	17	42.5	0	0	0	0	3.83	0.813
IPT3	2	5.0	2	5.0	7	17.5	18	45.0	2	5.0	1.98	1.143
IPT4	2	5.0	1	2.5	6	15.0	15	37.5	16	40.0	1.95	1.061
IPT5	5	12.5	24	60.0	6	15.0	4	10.0	1	2.5	3.70	0.911
Grand Mean											**3.13**	

Interpretation

When teachers were asked "if they made sure to inform and discuss with the parents, if they found anything unusual with their child", 40% said 'Very Often', 40% said 'Often' and 20% said 'Sometimes'. Majority of the teachers felt that they 'Very Often' and 'Often' made sure to inform and discuss with the parents if they found anything unusual with their child.

When teachers were asked "if they kept their students' parents updated about their performance in school", 25% said 'Very Often', 32.5% said 'Often' and 42.5% said 'Sometimes'. Majority of the teachers felt that they 'Sometimes' kept their students' parents updated about their performance in school.

When teachers were asked "if they conducted counselling for parents to help them deal with their adolescents", 5% said 'Very Often', 5% said 'Often', 17.5% said 'Sometimes', 45% said 'Rarely' and 5% said 'Never'. Majority of the teachers felt that they 'Rarely' conducted counselling for parents to help them deal with their adolescents.

When teachers were asked "if they found Interaction with parents helpful", 5% said 'Very Often', 2.5% said 'Often', 15% said 'Sometimes', 37.5% said 'Rarely' and 40% said 'Never'. Majority of the teachers felt that they 'Never' found Interaction with parents helpful.

When teachers were asked "if they did not avoid Interaction with parents other than scheduled PTMs", 12.5% said 'Very Often', 60% said 'Often', 15% said 'Sometimes', 10% said 'Rarely' and 2.5% said 'Never'. Majority of the teachers felt that they 'Often' did not avoid Interaction with parents other than scheduled PTMs.

On the basis of grand mean (3.13) it can be concluded that 'Interaction with Parents' as a parameter for 'Teacher's Involvement' with Adolescents, as perceived by Teachers, is 'Moderate'.

4.10.3.3 **Instrumental Support.**

'Instrumental Support' is measured using the following seven measured indicators where each measured indicator is scaled on 5-point rating scale (5 = Very Often, 4 = Often, 3 = Sometimes, 2 = Rarely and 1 = Never).

(a) IST1 : I involve all students equally in all class activities.

(b) IST2 : I motivate my students to ask doubts and questions in class.

(c) IST3 : I try and arrange for remedial classes for other subjects my students are weak in.

(d) IST4 : I think that organising career guidance programs are my responsibility.

(e) IST5 : I check the assignment and homework given to my students.

(f) IST6 : I use teaching aids and innovative techniques (e.g. smart board, quiz, crossword, etc.) while teaching in class.

(g) IST7 : I do not ignore those students who do not understand any particular topic.

Table 62 shows analysis of Teacher's Instrumental Support .

Table 62 : Teacher's Instrumental Support as Perceived by Teachers

Variable Code	Very Often		Often		Sometimes		Rarely		Never		Mean	Std. Deviation
	F	%	F	%	F	%	F	%	F	%		
IST1	17	42.5	20	50.0	3	7.5	0	0	0	0	4.35	0.622
IST2	10	25.0	12	30.0	18	45.0	0	0	0	0	3.80	0.823
IST3	2	5.0	4	10.0	8	20.0	12	30.0	14	35.0	2.20	1.181
IST4	13	32.5	12	30.0	8	20.0	2	5.0	5	12.5	3.65	1.331
IST5	14	35.0	18	45.0	8	20.0	0	0	0	0	4.15	0.736
IST6	3	7.5	1	2.5	8	20.0	16	40.0	12	30.0	2.18	1.130
IST7	6	15.0	9	22.5	16	40.0	5	12.5	4	10.0	3.20	1.159
Grand Mean											**3.36**	

Interpretation

When teachers were asked "if they involved all students equally in all class activities", 42.5% said 'Very Often', 50% said 'Often' and 7.5% said 'Sometimes'. Majority of the teachers felt that they 'Often' involved all students equally in all class activities.

When teachers were asked "if they motivated their students to ask doubts and questions in class", 25% said 'Very Often', 30% said 'Often' and 45% said 'Sometimes'. Majority of the teachers felt that they 'Sometimes' motivated their students to ask doubts and questions in class.

When teachers were asked "if they tried and arranged for remedial classes for other subjects that their students were weak in', 5% said 'Very Often', 10% said 'Often', 20% said 'Sometimes', 30% said 'Rarely' and 35% said 'Never'. Majority of the teachers felt that they 'Never' arranged for remedial classes for other subjects their students are weak in.

When teachers were asked "if they thought organising career guidance programs are their responsibility", 32.5% said 'Very Often', 30% said 'Often', 20% said 'Sometimes', 5% said 'Rarely' and 12.5% said 'Never'. Majority of the teachers felt that they 'Very Often' thought organising career guidance programs are their responsibility.

When teachers were asked "if they checked the assignment and homework given to their students", 35% said 'Very Often', 45% said 'Often' and 20% said 'Sometimes'. Majority of the teachers felt that they 'Sometimes' checked the assignment and homework given to their students.

When teachers were asked "if they used teaching aids and innovative techniques (e.g. smart board, quiz, crossword, etc.) while teaching in class", 7.5% said 'Very Often', 2,5% said 'Often', 20% said 'Sometimes', 40% said 'Rarely' and 30% said 'Never'. Majority of the teachers felt that they 'Rarely' used teaching aids and innovative techniques while teaching in class.

When teachers were asked "if they did not ignore those students who did not understand any particular topic", 15% said 'Very Often', 22.5% said 'Often', 40% said 'Sometimes', 12.5% said 'Rarely' and 10% said 'Never'. Majority of the teachers felt that they 'Sometimes' did not ignore those students who did not understand any particular topic.

On the basis of grand mean (3.36) it can be concluded that 'Instrumental Support' as a parameter for 'Teacher's Involvement' with Adolescents, as perceived by Teachers, is 'Moderate'.

4.10.3.4 **Structure by Teachers.**

'Structure by Teacher's is measured using the following five measured indicators where each measured indicator is scaled on 5-point rating scale (5 = Very Often, 4 = Often, 3 = Sometimes, 2 = Rarely and 1 = Never).

(a) STT1 : I plan activities according to the mood of the class.

(b) STT2 : To make my class comfortable I make efforts to organise fun activities (school trips, picnic, role play, etc.) for my class.

(c) STT3 : I make effort to make the children understand if they misbehave.

(d) ST4 : I make sure that I appreciate the students if they perform well in their curricular and / or co-curricular activities.

(e) STT5 : I sit and counsel students when they make a mistake.

Table 63 shows analysis of Structure by Teachers.

Table 63 : Structure by Teachers as Perceived by Teachers

Variable Code	Very Often		Often		Sometimes		Rarely		Never		Mean	Std. Deviation
	F	%	F	%	F	%	F	%	F	%		
STT1	8	20.0	11	27.5	21	52.5	0	0	0	0	3.68	0.797
STT2	6	15.0	5	12.5	24	60.0	2	5.0	3	7.5	3.23	1.025
IST3	13	32.5	15	37.5	11	27.5	0	0	1	2.5	3.98	0.920
STT4	15	37.5	18	45.0	7	17.5	0	0	0	0	4.20	0.723
STT5	15	37.5	12	30.0	13	32.5	0	0	0	0	4.05	0.846
Grand Mean											**3.83**	

Interpretation

When teachers were asked "if they planned activities according to the mood of the class", 20% said 'Very Often', 27.5% said 'Often' and 52.5% said 'Sometimes'. Majority of the teachers felt that they 'Sometimes' planned activities according to the mood of the class.

When teachers were asked "if they made efforts to organise fun activities (school trips, picnic, role play, etc.) for their class to make them comfortable", 15% said 'Very Often', 12.5% said 'Often', 60% said 'Sometimes', 5% said 'Rarely' and 7.5% said 'Never'. Majority of the teachers felt that they 'Sometimes' made efforts to organise fun activities (school trips, picnic, role play, etc.) for their class to make them comfortable.

When teachers were asked "if they made effort to make the children understand when they misbehaved in class", 32.5% said 'Very Often', 37.5% said 'Often', 27.5% said 'Sometimes' and 2.5% said 'Never'. Majority of the teachers felt that they 'Very Often' made effort to make the children understand when they misbehaved in class.

When teachers were asked "if they made sure to appreciate the students if they performed well in their curricular and / or co-curricular activities", 37.5% said 'Very Often', 45% said 'Often' and 17.5% said 'Sometimes'. Majority of the teachers felt that they 'Often' made sure to appreciate the students if they performed well in their curricular and / or co-curricular activities.

When teachers were asked "if they sat and counselled students when they made a mistake", 37.5% said 'Very Often', 30% said 'Often' and 32.5% said 'Sometimes'. Majority of the teachers felt that they 'Very Often' sat and counselled students when they made a mistake.

On the basis of grand mean (3.83) it can be concluded that 'Structure by Teachers' as a parameter for 'Teacher's Involvement' with Adolescents, as perceived by Teachers, is 'High'.

4.10.4 **Frequency Distribution and Descriptive Statistics for impact of Teacher's Involvement on Behaviour Adjustment of Adolescents as Perceived by Teachers**

'Impact of Teacher's Involvement' on Behaviour Adjustment' of Adolescents' is measured using the following four measured indicators where each measured indicator is scaled on 5-point rating scale (5 = Very Often, 4 = Often, 3 = Sometimes, 2 = Rarely and 1 = Never).

(a) IBT1 : My students find me trustworthy so they can comfortably discuss their personal problems with me.

(b) IBT2 : My students do not ignore when I try to give advice on their friends and other personal issues.

(c) IBT3 : I find positive improvement in my student's Behaviour after my counselling.

(d) IBT4 : My class happiness quotient increases due to fun activities organised by me.

Table 64 shows analysis of impact of Teacher's Involvement on 'Behaviour Adjustment'.

Table 64 : Impact of Teacher's Involvement on Behaviour Adjustment as Perceived by Teachers

Variable Code	Very Often		Often		Sometimes		Rarely		Never		Mean	Std. Deviation
	F	%	F	%	F	%	F	%	F	%		
IBT1	12	30.0	13	32.5	12	30.0	1	2.5	2	5.0	3.78	1.074
IBT2	12	30.0	13	32.5	15	37.5	0	0	0	0	3.93	0.829
IBT3	13	32.5	12	30.0	15	37.5	0	0	0	0	3.95	0.846
IBT4	13	32.5	15	37.5	12	30.0	0	0	0	0	3.95	0.846

Interpretation

When teachers were asked "if their students found them trustworthy so they can comfortably discuss their personal problems with them", 30% said 'Very Often', 32.5% said 'Often', 30% said 'Sometimes', 2.5% said 'Rarely' and 5% said 'Never'.

Majority of the teachers felt that their students 'Often' found them trustworthy so they can comfortably discuss their personal problems with them.

When teachers were asked "if their students did not ignore when they tried to give advice on their friends and other personal issues", 30% said 'Very Often', 32.5% said 'Often' and 37.5% said 'Sometimes'. Majority of the teachers felt that their students 'Sometimes' did not ignore when they tried to give advice on their friends and other personal issues.

When teachers were asked "if they found positive improvement in their student's Behaviour after their counselling", 32.5% said 'Very Often', 30% said 'Often' and 37.5% said 'Sometimes'. Majority of the teachers felt that they 'Sometimes' found positive improvement in their student's Behaviour after their counselling.

When teachers were asked "if their class happiness quotient increased due to fun activities organised by them", 32.5% said 'Very Often', 37.5% said 'Often' and 30% said 'Sometimes'. Majority of the teachers felt that the class happiness quotient 'Often' increased due to fun activities organised by them.

4.10.5 **Frequency Distribution and Descriptive Statistics for impact of Teacher's Involvement on Academic Achievements of Adolescents as Perceived by Teachers**

'Impact of Teacher's Involvement on Academic Achievement' of Adolescents' is measured using the following four measured indicators where each measured indicator is scaled on 5-point rating scale (5 = Very Often, 4 = Often, 3 = Sometimes, 2 = Rarely and 1 = Never).

(a) IAT1 : My students approach me regarding the difficulties they face in any subject.

(b) IAT2 : I find my students to complete homework and assignments on time with my constant monitoring.

(c) IAT3 : I observe students to get them perform better due to my constant vigilance.

(d) IAT4 : My students enjoy and appreciate my class when I use teaching aids and innovative techniques.

Table 65 shows analysis of impact of Teacher's Involvement on 'Academic Achievement'.

Table 65 : Impact of Teacher's Involvement on Academic Achievement as Perceived by Teachers

Variable Code	Very Often		Often		Sometimes		Rarely		Never		Mean	Std. Deviation
	F	%	F	%	F	%	F	%	F	%		
IAT1	11	27.5	12	30.0	14	35.0	0	0	3	7.5	3.70	1.114
IAT2	6	15.0	4	10.0	20	50.0	4	10.0	6	15.0	3.00	1.198
IAT3	20	50.0	9	22.5	6	15.0	2	5.0	3	7.5	4.03	1.250
IAT4	1	2.5	0	0	8	20.0	19	47.5	12	30.0	4.13	0.704

Interpretation

When teachers were asked "if their students approached them regarding the difficulties they faced in any subject", 27.5% said 'Very Often', 30% said 'Often', 35% said 'Sometimes' and 7.5% said 'Never'. Majority of the teachers felt that their students 'Sometimes' approached them regarding the difficulties they faced in any subject.

When teachers were asked "if they found their students to complete homework and assignments on time with their constant monitoring", 15% said 'Very Often', 10% said 'Often', 50% said 'Sometimes', 10% said 'Rarely' and 15% said 'Never'. Majority of the teachers felt that they 'Sometimes' found their students to complete homework and assignments on time with their constant monitoring.

When teachers were asked "if they observed students performing better due to teacher's constant vigilance", 50% said 'Very Often', 22.5% said 'Often', 15% said 'Sometimes', 5% said 'Rarely' and 7.5% said 'Never'. Majority of the teachers felt that they 'Sometimes' did not get confused with their students name.

When teachers were asked "if their students enjoyed and appreciated their class when they use teaching aids and innovative techniques", 2.5% said 'Very Often', 20% said 'Sometimes', 47.5% said 'Rarely' and 30% said 'Never'. Majority of the teachers felt that their students 'Rarely' enjoyed and appreciated their class when they used teaching aids and innovative techniques.

4.10.6 **Frequency Distribution and Descriptive Statistics for Involvement and impact of Parental Involvement on Adolescents as Perceived by Teachers**

'Involvement and impact of Parents' on Adolescents' is measured using the following four measured indicators where each measured indicator is scaled on 5-point rating scale (5 = Very Often, 4 = Often, 3 = Sometimes, 2 = Rarely and 1 = Never).

(a) IPT1 : Parents of my class attend all scheduled events and are always ready for interaction.

(b) IPT2 : Parents of my class are interested to interact over and above the scheduled PTMs.

(c) IPT3 : I conduct sessions to educate parents about dealing with their adolescents.

(d) IPT4 : I feel frequency of parents and Teacher's interactive sessions should be increased.

Table 66 shows analysis of involvement and impact of Parents' on adolescents.

Table 66 : Involvement & impact of Parents' on Adolescents as Perceived by Teachers

Variable Code	Very Often		Often		Sometimes		Rarely		Never		Mean	Std. Deviation
	F	%	F	%	F	%	F	%	F	%		
ITP1	4	10.0	5	12.5	7	17.5	12	30.0	12	30.0	2.43	1.318
ITP2	1	2.5	1	2.5	24	60.0	8	20.0	6	15.0	2.58	0.874
ITP3	0	0	2	5.0	35	87.5	1	2.5	2	5.0	2.93	0.526
ITP4	3	7.5	2	5.0	35	87.5	2	5.0	3	7.5	3.20	0.564
Grand Mean											**2.48**	

Interpretation

When teachers were asked "if parents of their class attended all scheduled events and are always ready for interaction", 10% said 'Very Often', 12.5% said 'Often', 17.5% 'Sometimes', 30% said 'Rarely' and 30% said 'Never'. Majority of the teachers felt that parents of their class 'Rarely' and 'Never' attended all scheduled events and are always ready for interaction.

When teachers were asked "if parents of their class are interested to interact over and above the scheduled PTMs", 2.5% said 'Very Often', 2.5% said 'Often', 60% 'Sometimes', 20% said 'Rarely' and 15% said 'Never' . Majority of the teachers felt that parents of their class are 'Sometimes' interested to interact over and above the scheduled PTMs.

When teachers were asked "if they conducted sessions to educate parents about dealing with their adolescents", 5% said 'Often', 87.5% 'Sometimes', 2.5% said 'Rarely' and 5% said 'Never'. Majority of the teachers felt that they 'Sometimes' conducted sessions to educate parents about dealing with their adolescents.

When teachers were asked "if they felt frequency of parents and teacher's interactive sessions should be increased", 7.5% said 'Very Often', 5% said 'Often', 87.5% 'Sometimes', 5% said 'Rarely' and 7.5% said 'Never' . Majority of the teachers felt that 'Sometimes' the frequency of parents and teacher's interactive sessions should be increased.

On the basis of grand mean (2.48) it can be concluded that 'Involvement of Parents' with adolescents', as perceived by Teachers, is 'Low'.

CHAPTER 5

INFERENTIAL DATA ANALYSIS

5.1 Inferential Analysis

The most important purpose of research is finding the principles on the basis of observed relationships between the variables. Statistical analysis helps in achieving this purpose. On one hand, descriptive analysis describes the characteristics of specifics while inferential analysis makes generalisations regarding the population from which the sample is drawn. Descriptive analysis simply describes what's going on in the data while inferential analysis makes inferences from the data to more general conditions. The analysis process, followed by the description of data, with the aim of providing conclusive results is called Inferential Analysis.

Oxford Dictionary of English defines 'Statistical Inference' as "The theory, methods and practice of forming judgments about the parameters of a population and the reliability of statistical relationships, typically on the basis of random sampling". It is the process of data analysis used to infer properties of an underlying distribution of probability. Inferential statistical analysis deduces properties of a population by means of testing the hypotheses and drawing estimate. The assumption being that the observed data set is sampled from a larger population.

Inferential Analysis permits to make predictions ('inferences') from that data. It helps in making generalisations about a population through analysis of data from samples. With inferential analysis, sample data from a small number of people is collected and is analysed to reach to a conclusion for the larger population. It is useful in experimental and quasi-experimental research design or in program outcome evaluation. It uses statistical models to help compare the sample data to other samples or to previous research. Researchers use statistical models known as the 'Generalised Linear Model' and include 'Student's t-Tests', 'Analysis of Variance' (ANOVA), 'Analysis of Co-variance' (ANCOVA), regression analysis and range of other multivariate methods like factor analysis, multidimensional scaling, cluster analysis, discriminant function analysis that result in linear probabilities and results.

There are two main areas of inferential analysis :-

1. **Estimating Parameters.** It means taking a statistic from the sample data and using it to deduce something about a population parameter. For example the sample mean can be used to infer about the population mean.

2. **Hypothesis Tests**. This uses the sample data to answer various research questions. For example parents' discipline help children perform better in schools.

Inferential statistical techniques are useful in testing the hypothesis considered in the research, and on the basis of test results it is decided whether the hypothesis are accepted or rejected.

5.2 Hypothesis

A hypothesis is a specific proposition or statement that predicts exact relationship among multiple variables and which is stated in a testable form. Hypothesis in other words is an explicit statement of prediction. It is a tentative assumption elucidating a scientific problem, observation, or a phenomenon which can be tested by further observation, investigation and/ or experimentation. It is the postulation assumed to be true for the purpose of argument or investigation.

Hypothesis etymologically is made of two words, "hypo" (less than) and "research study" (less certain than). Hypothesis as defined by *Lunberg* is "A tentative generalisation, the validity of which remains to be tested. In its most elementary stages, the hypothesis may be any hunch, guess, imaginative idea or intuition whatsoever which the basis for action or investigation becomes".

The hypothesis is powerful tool in research process to achieve dependable knowledge. It helps researcher to relate theory to observation and observation to theory.

5.2.1 Types of Hypothesis

1. **Research Hypothesis.** Research hypothesis is a perspective statement which has the capability of being tested which states a probable relationship or dissimilarity between two variables.

2. **Directional Hypothesis.** It states the nature of relationship between variables or dissimilarity between groups.

3. **Non Directional Hypothesis.** It states whether any relationship or dissimilarity exists, but does not offer any indication of the course of these

relationship or dissimilarity. The example of a non directional hypothesis is null hypothesis.

5.2.2 Null Hypothesis

Null Hypothesis is denoted by (H0). It relates to the statistical method of deducing conclusions about characteristics of population inferred from collected data from samples. It affirms that there is no significant difference in relationship between two or more parameters. It states contrary of what the experimenter expected or predicted. The researcher aims to reject, nullify or disprove the null hypothesis.

5.2.3 Level of Significance

The level of significance might be 0.01 or at 0.05 level. Rejecting the null hypothesis at 0.01 is indicative that there is 99% probability that the differences are true and not due to a sampling error. Rejecting the null hypothesis at 0.05 level is indicative that there is 95% probability that the difference is a true one and not due to a sampling error. The hypotheses that are being tested in the present study are null hypotheses with level of significance as 0.05.

A null hypothesis is a statement assumed to be right all through the analysis and the analysis is based upon the null hypothesis. Hypothesis testing is the process of applying statistical analysis to establish whether the observed differences in the samples are caused due to a random chance or not. Based on the result of statistical analysis, a null hypothesis is either accepted or rejected.

In the present study, null hypotheses were formulated to study the "impact of 'Parental Involvement' and 'Teacher's Involvement' on Adolescents' 'Academic Achievement' and 'Behaviour Adjustment'".

5.3 Techniques for Testing the Hypothesis

There are two types of statistical techniques which are used for testing the hypothesis. They are :-

1. **Non Parametric Techniques.** The techniques enabling us to compare samples in order to make inferences or tests of significance without assuring the normality in the population are known as 'Non Parametric Technique'.
2. **Parametric Techniques.** 'Parametric Techniques' are useful to test the hypothesis in the study where randomly selected sample is large in size ($N > 30$) and

the data is in the interval scale, following a normal or near normal distribution, with independent observations having equal or nearly equal variances of various sub groups. The followings are the preconditions that are considered before using the parametric techniques :-

(a) Normal or near normal distribution of data.

(b) Random selection of the sample size.

(c) Large sample size i.e. N > 30.

(d) Equal or near equal variance of data.

(e) The data are in ratio or interval scale.

(f) The observations are independent in nature.

In the present study, the sample size is 250 for adolescents, 40 for teachers and parents, which is a large sample. The sample has been selected randomly where data are in the interval scale with independent observations. On the basis of descriptive analysis of data depicted in chapter 4, it might be said that the data have been mostly normally distributed. Hence, for the intention of testing the hypothesis in the present study, parametric techniques are used.

5.4 Techniques Used for Testing the Hypotheses in the Study

Following is the explanation of statistical techniques used for testing of hypotheses in the present study. The researcher in this study has endeavoured to find impact of Parental and Teacher's Involvement on Adolescents' 'Behaviour Adjustment' and 'Academic Achievement' on the basis of perceived involvement and perceived impact on 'Behaviour Adjustment' and 'Academic Achievement' by Adolescents, parents and teachers. The researcher has also attempted to compare the impact of Parental and Teacher's Involvement on Adolescents' 'Behaviour Adjustment' and 'Academic Achievement' on the basis of gender.

In the present study, following statistical techniques were employed for the purpose of testing the null hypothesis :-

1. Independent Sample t-Test.
2. Pearson Correlation.
3. Path Analysis of the model.

5.4.1 The independent Samples t-Test.

The Independent Samples t-Test is a parametric test which compares the 'Mean' of two independent groups so as to determine whether there is statistical evidence that 'Mean' of two unrelated groups are significantly different. In the present study, t-Test was used in comparing following means :-

(a) 'Parental Involvement' (PI) as perceived by Adolescents and Parents.

(b) 'Teacher's Involvement' (TI) as perceived by Adolescents and Teachers.

(c) 'Parental Involvement' (PI) as perceived by Parents and Teachers.

(d) 'Teacher's Involvement' (TI) as perceived by Parents and Teachers.

(e) Impact of PI on AA as perceived by Adolescents and Parents.

(f) Impact of PI on BA as perceived by Adolescents and Parents.

(g) Impact of TI on AA as perceived by Adolescents and Teachers.

(h) Impact of TI on BA as perceived by Adolescents and Teachers.

(j) Gender wise comparison of PI, TI, impact of PI on AA, impact of PI on BA, impact of TI on AA and impact of TI on BA.

The formula used by the researcher is as follows :-

$$t = \frac{M_1 - M_2}{\sqrt{\frac{(\sigma_1)^2}{N_1} + \frac{(\sigma_2)^2}{N_2}}}$$

Where :-

M1 = Mean of the first group

M2 = Mean of the second group

σ_1 = Standard deviation of first group

σ_2= Standard deviation of second group

N1 = Sample size of first group

N2 = Sample size of second group

Interpretation of t

The calculated *t* value is compared to the critical *t* value from the *t* distribution table with degrees of freedom $df = n_1 + n_2 - 2$ and chosen significance level. If the calculated *t* value is greater than the critical *t* value, then the null hypothesis is rejected. Here for N- 2 degree of freedom, the critical ratio of t is read at significance level 0.05 i.e. $\alpha = 0.05$. P value is the sig. (2-tailed) value corresponding to the test statistic. When obtained P value is greater than the significance level (α) the null hypothesis is rejected and while null hypothesis is accepted when the obtained value is lesser than the significance level.

Table 67 : Interpretation of Value of P when Tested for N-2 Degrees of Freedom at $\alpha =$ 0.05

Value of P	Result
Less than 0.05	Not Significant
More than 0.05	Significant

Table 68 : Interpretation of Mean Values

Mean Value	Result
Less than 2.5	Low
More than 2.5 and Less than 3.5	Moderate
More than 3.5	High

5.4.2 Pearson Correlation.

Pearson correlation is the test statistics that measures the statistical relationship or association between two continuous variables through the method of co-variance thus making it the best method of measuring the association between variables. It measures the linear correlation between two variables X and Y and is also referred to as Pearson's r, or the bi-variate correlation. In the present study, Pearson Correlation is used to find relation between following variables as perceived by adolescents, parents and teachers :-

(a) Parental Involvement (PI) and Academic Achievement (AA).

(b) Parental Involvement (PI) and Behaviour Adjustment (BA).

(c) Teacher's Involvement (TI) and Academic Achievement (AA).

(d) Teacher's Involvement (TI) and Behaviour Adjustment (BA).

(f) Parental Involvement and Teacher's Involvement (PI & TI) and Academic Achievement (AA).

(g) Parental Involvement and Teacher's Involvement (PI & TI) and Behaviour Adjustment (BA).

For a given a pair of random variables (x, y), the formula for correlation used by the researcher is as follows :-

$$Correlation = \frac{Cov\ (x, y)}{\sigma x * \sigma y}$$

Where :-

Cov = Co-variance

σx = Standard deviation of first group

σy = Standard deviation of second group

Interpretation of *r*

A Pearson Correlation is a number between -1 and +1 that indicates the extent to which two variables are linearly related. Value of +1 means that a linear equation describes the relationship between *X* and *Y* perfectly where all data points lie on a line in which *Y* increases as *X* increases. A value of -1 indicates that all data points lie on a line where *Y* decreases as *X* increases. Where as a 0 value implies that there is no linear correlation between the variables. The obtained value of r is tested for N-2 degrees of freedom at 0.05 and 0.01 level of significance.

Table 69 : Description of r Value

Coefficient (r)	Relationship
Less than 0.20	Low
0.20 to0 0.40	Moderate
More than 0.40	High

5.4.3 **Path Analysis of the Model.**

Path analysis is a minor version of Structural Equation Model (SEM) developed by Sewall Wright, a geneticist in 1918. With time, it is now widely used in other areas in physical science, social science and sociology. Path analysis can be conducted using statistical programs including SPSS, STATA, etc. The method is also known as Causal Modelling, analysis of co-variance structures and latent variables models. It is an advanced statistical tool used to establish relationship between several variables simultaneously. It is a form of multiple regression analysis used to evaluate causal models which examines the relationship between dependent variable with two or more independent variables. This method can estimate both magnitude and significance of causal connections between the variables. Path analysis has following major benefits over other predictive models :-

(a) It can fit theoretical model to sample data.

(b) It can study direct, indirect and total impact.

(c) Use of maximum probable techniques to compute path analysis.

(d) Better understanding of causal relationship between independent variables and dependent variables.

(e) Useful to evaluate causal hypothesis.

(f) Clarifies correlation.

(g) Indicates the strength of causal hypothesis.

Usage and Interpretation of Path Analysis

In Path Analysis, a path diagram is constructed where relationship between variables and causal direction between them are laid out. Before conducting a path analysis, an input path diagram is constructed which illustrates the hypothesised relationships where the researcher uses arrows to show relationships between variables. For instance, if an arrow points from A variable to B, it implies that A variable is hypothesised to influence variable B. Data is then fed into the variables and hypothesis testing is done on them. The path coefficients, standard errors and P values are calculated with statistical software (the researcher used SPSS Statistical Software) with P values; frequently the criterion $P < 0.05$ is used instead $P \leq 0.05$ for accepting a hypothesis.

The P value for each term tests the null hypothesis. If the coefficient is equal to zero, it indicates no impact. A low P value (< 0.05) indicates that the null hypothesis can be rejected while a higher P value (> 0.05) indicates that the null hypothesis can be accepted.

In the present study, Path Analysis was used to find relationship between following variables :-

(a) Impact of various constructs of Parental Involvement (PI) namely Emotional, Aspiration, Structure, School & Studies and friends on Academic Achievement of Adolescents (AA).

(b) Impact of various constructs of Parental Involvement (PI) namely Emotional, Aspiration, Structure, School & Studies and friends on Behaviour Adjustment of Adolescents (BA).

(c) Impact of various constructs of Teacher's Involvement (TI) namely Emotional, Interaction with Parents, Instrumental and Structure on Academic Achievement of Adolescents (AA).

(d) Impact of various constructs of Teacher's Involvement (TI) namely Emotional, Interaction with Parents, Instrumental and Structure on Behaviour Adjustment of Adolescents (BA).

In the present study, the researcher has used SPSS for statistical computations.

5.5 Acronyms in the study

The acronyms used in the present research study are tabulated below.

Table 70 : List Of Acronyms

Name of Variable	Acronym
Parental Involvement	PI
Teacher's Involvement	TI
Behaviour Adjustment	BA
Academic Achievement	AA
Total Sample Size	TSS

5.6 Testing of Hypothesis 1

$H1_0$: There is no significant impact of 'Parental Involvement' on 'Academic Achievement' for total Adolescent sample.

The Null Hypothesis was tested using Pearson Correlation where level of significance is a = 0.05.

Table 71 shows the impact of 'Parental Involvement' (PI) on 'Academic Achievement' (AA), as perceived by Adolescents.

Table 71 : Impact of PI on AA as Perceived by Adolescents

Relationship	Coefficient(r)	P Value	Correlation
Perceived PI and AA by Adolescents	0.310	0.000	Moderate

The above table reveals that the *p* value is less than the level of significance (0.05) ***hence the Null Hypothesis is rejected*** and it is concluded that there is a 'Significant' relationship between PI and AA as perceived by Adolescents.

Based on the *r* value (.310), it can be further concluded that there is a positive and '***Moderate***' relationship between PI and AA as perceived by Adolescents.

Interpretation of Result

For the total adolescent sample, it was observed that they perceived positive impact of 'Parental Involvement' (PI) on 'Academic Achievement' (AA), as can be seen from above analysis (Table 71).

As observed from the above analysis, the impact of PI on AA, as perceived by Adolescents is positive and ***'Moderate'***.

Perceptions and expectations of Adolescents as reflected in the questionnaire (Appx A), might be the reasons for the same :-

1. Parents discuss about career options.

2. With parents help adolescents able to perform better.

3. Parents & teachers interaction guides adolescents academically.

4. Structuring TV/internet, adolescents have more time for studies.

Thus, it may be inferred from the above analysis that adolescents might be comfortable with whatever time and help their parents are able to provide them to improve their Academic performance, leading them to their positive perception of impact of PI on AA.

However, reasons for impact to be '***Moderate***' may be due to a) Difference in expectations or expectations being met partially, b) Parents' lack of understanding for the novel education system, c) their level of education or stream of qualification, d) Different expectation and perception of individual adolescent.

5.7 Testing of Hypothesis 2

$H2_0$: There is no significant impact of 'Parental Involvement' on 'Behaviour Adjustment' of total adolescent sample.

The Null Hypothesis was tested using Pearson Correlation where level of significance is a = 0.05.

Table 72 shows the impact of 'Parental Involvement' (PI) on 'Behaviour Adjustment' (BA) as perceived by Adolescents.

Table 72 : Impact of PI on BA as Perceived by Adolescents

Relationship	Coefficient(r)	P Value	Correlation
Perceived PI and BA by Adolescents	0.166	0.008	Low

The above table reveals that the *p* value is less than the level of significance (0.05) ***hence the Null Hypothesis is rejected*** and it is concluded that there is a 'Significant' relationship between PI and BA as perceived by adolescents.

Based on the *r* value (.166), it can be further concluded that there is a positive but ***'Low'*** relationship between PI and BA as perceived by Adolescents.

Interpretation of Result

For the total adolescent sample, it was observed that they perceived positive impact of 'Parental Involvement' (PI) on 'Behaviour Adjustment' (BA), as can be seen from the above analysis (Table 72).

As can be observed, the impact of PI on BA, as perceived by Adolescents is positive but '***Low***'.

Perceptions and expectations of Adolescents for the following items, as reflected in the questionnaire (Appx A), might be the reason for the same :-

1. Parents reprimanding or ridiculing when they falter.

2. Parents deciding on the clothes/food choices.

3. Parents constantly compare with other boys and girls.

4. Adolescents may find parents preaching needless and tend to ignore.

Thus, it can be inferred that adolescents' acceptance of their parents' intention for their betterment leads them for positive impact of PI on BA.

However, reasons for impact to be '***Low***' may be due to a) involvement perceived to be overbearing or excessive, b) Parents' busy routine might not be allowing them to spend constructive time with adolescents so as to help them in 'Behaviour Adjustment', c) the difference in opinion and expectations due to generation gap, d) Different expectation and perception of individual adolescent.

5.8 Testing of Hypothesis 3

$H3_0$: There is no significant impact of Teacher's Involvement on 'Academic Achievement' of total adolescent sample.

The Null Hypothesis was tested using Pearson Correlation where level of significance is a = 0.05.

Table 73 shows the impact of 'Teacher's Involvement' (TI) on 'Academic Achievement' (AA), as perceived by Adolescents.

Table 73 : Impact of TI on AA as Perceived by Adolescents

Relationship	Coefficient(r)	P Value	Correlation
Perceived TI and AA by Adolescents	0.361	0.000	Moderate

The above table reveals that the *p* value is less than the level of significance (0.05) ***hence the Null Hypothesis is rejected*** and it is concluded that there is a 'Significant' relationship between TI and AA as perceived by Adolescents.

Based on the *r* value (.361), it can be further concluded that there is a positive and '***Moderate***' relationship between TI and AA as perceived by Adolescents.

Interpretation of Result

For the total adolescent sample, it was observed that they perceived positive impact of 'Teacher's Involvement' (TI) on 'Academic Achievement' (AA), as can be seen from above analysis (Table 73).

As can be observed, the impact of TI on AA, as perceived by adolescents is positive but '***Moderate***'.

Perceptions and expectations of adolescents for the following items, as reflected in the questionnaire (Appx A), might be the reason for the same :-

1. Class teacher give personal attention to every Student in the class.

2. Class teacher share adolescents' achievements with their parents.

3. Class teacher arranges for remedial classes for the subjects adolescents are weak in, which help them in coping up.

4. Class teacher uses teaching aids and innovative techniques (e.g. Smart board, quiz, crossword, etc.) while teaching in class.

Thus it can be inferred that adolescents spend lot of time with teachers and look up to them for Academic guidance. Teacher's knowledge prowess, sincerity and ways of teaching might be the reasons for perceived positive relationship between TI and AA by adolescents.

However, reasons for impact to be '***Moderate***' may be due to a) Lack of time adolescents spend with the class teacher, b) Excessive syllabus and busy timetable, c) Inability of teachers to explain few topics or solve doubts, d) Different expectation and perception of individual adolescent.

5.9 Testing of Hypothesis 4

$H4_0$: There is no significant impact of Teacher's Involvement on 'Behaviour Adjustment' of total Adolescent sample.

The Null Hypothesis was tested using Pearson Correlation where level of significance is a = 0.05.

Table 74 shows the impact of 'Teacher's Involvement' (TI) on 'Behaviour Adjustment' (BA), as perceived by Adolescents.

Table 74 : Impact of TI on BA as Perceived by Adolescents

Relationship	Coefficient(r)	P Value	Correlation
Perceived TI and BA by Adolescents	0.389	0.000	Moderate

The above table reveals that the *p* value is less than the level of significance (0.05) ***hence the Null Hypothesis is rejected*** and it is concluded that there is a 'Significant' relationship between TI and BA as perceived by adolescents.

Based on the *r* value (.389), it can be further concluded that there is a positive and '***Moderate***' relationship between TI and BA as perceived by adolescents.

Interpretation of Result

For the total adolescent sample, it was observed that they perceived positive relationship impact of 'Teacher's Involvement' (TI) on 'Behaviour Adjustment' (BA), as can be seen from above analysis (Table 74).

As can be observed, the impact of TI on BA, as perceived by adolescents is positive and '***Moderate***'.

Perception of adolescents for following items, as reflected in the questionnaire (Appx A), might be the reasons for the same :-

1. Class teacher discusses about their likes and interests.

2. Class teacher involves all children in all class activities.

3. Adolescents find teacher's instructions about the rules and its importance helpful to mould their Behaviour positively.

4. Adolescents comfortably discuss personal problems with teacher.

Thus it can be inferred that teacher's counselling to make adolescents understand rules and their importance, explanation of virtues to become a perfect individual and / or friendly Behaviour might be the reasons for perceived positive relationship between TI and BA by both adolescent boys and girls. school being a second home to adolescents offers them many lessons of life, while teachers are adults whom adolescents idolise and look up for inspiration.

However, reasons for impact to be ***'Moderate'*** may be due to a) Lack of time Adolescents spend with the class teacher, b) Limited trust , c) Apprehension of adolescents to discuss personal problems, d) Different point of view for accepted Behaviour.

5.10 Testing of Hypothesis 5

$H5_0$: There is no significant relationship in the mean scores of Adolescents' response and parents' response towards 'Parental Involvement'.

The Null Hypothesis was tested using Independent t-Test.

Table 75 shows the relationship of mean scores of Adolescents' response and parents' response towards 'Parental Involvement' (PI).

Table 75 : Adolescents & Parents' Response Towards PI

Group	N	Mean	Std. Deviation	P Value Sig. (2-tailed)	Result
Adolescents	250	3.31	0.314	0.341	Significant
Parents	40	3.26	0.267		

Since the P value (0.341) is more than 0.05, it can be concluded that relationship between mean scores of adolescents and Parents is ***'Significant'*** with respect to PI, ***hence the Null Hypothesis is rejected*** and it is concluded that there is a 'Significant' relationship between the mean scores of Adolescents' response and parents' response towards 'Parental Involvement'.

Based upon the mean values, it can be further concluded that both Adolescents (3.31) and Parents (3.26) have opined PI as ***'Moderate'***.

Interpretation of Result

For the total Adolescent and Parent sample it was observed that they have perceived same level of 'Parental Involvement' (PI), as can be seen from above analysis (Table 75).

The reason might be similar perception of following items, as reflected in the questionnaire (Appx A & B) :-

1. Parents discuss with their children to know about their inclination for future career Aspiration.

2. Parents ensure to spend one evening together, either going out or playing a board game.

3. Parents keep themselves available to help solve their child's difficulties in studies and help in assignments / projects.

4. Parents inviting their child's friends at home.

Thus it can be inferred that adolescence is a difficult stage for both parents and adolescents as there is rapid change in the adolescents' life where an individual grows physically, mentally and socially. Parents' sensitive and thoughtful Behaviour might be the reason for Adolescents' positive perception of PI, while parents' contentment for their efforts to get positively involved with their child may possibly be the reason for their positive perception.

However, reasons for PI to be ***'Moderate'*** by both may be due to a) limited time spent together, b) difference in opinion and perception.

5.11 Testing of Hypothesis 6

H6₀ : There is no significant relationship in the mean scores of Adolescents' and Teacher's response towards Teacher's Involvement.

The Null Hypothesis was tested using Independent t-Test.

Table 76 shows the relationship of mean scores of Adolescents' response and Teacher's response towards 'Teacher's Involvement' (TI).

Table 76 : Adolescents & Teacher's Response Towards TI

Group	N	Mean	Std. Deviation	P Value Sig. (2-Tailed)	Result
Adolescents	250	3.06	0.358	0.000	Not Significant
Teachers	40	3.52	0.262		

Since the P value (0.000) is less than 0.05 it can be concluded that relationship between mean scores of Adolescents and Teachers is ***'Not Significant'*** with respect to TI, ***hence the Null Hypothesis is accepted*** and it is concluded that there is no 'Significant' relationship in the mean scores of Adolescents' and Teacher's response towards Teacher's Involvement.

Based upon the mean values, it can be further concluded that Adolescents (3.06) perceived TI as ***'Moderate'*** while Teachers (3.52) have opined TI as ***'High'***.

Interpretation of Result

For the total adolescent and Teacher's sample it was observed that they have different responses for 'Teacher's Involvement' (TI), as can be seen from above analysis (Table 76).

The reason might be different perceptions and expectations of Teachers and Adolescents on following items, as reflected in the questionnaire (Appx A & C) :-

1. Class teacher discussing about likes and interests of the students.

2. Class teacher sharing achievements with parents.

3. Class teacher encourage for asking questions/doubts.

4. Appreciation by the class teacher when the students perform well in curricular and / or co-curricular activities.

Thus it can be inferred that there is a great change in teachers and Adolescents' Behaviour from a primary grade to being in middle school due to many reasons like a) Increase in syllabus, b) Lack of time, c) Change in temperament of adolescents. Adolescents' expectations not being met by their teachers due to above changes might be the reason for their lower perception of TI. On the other hand, teacher's satisfaction about their effort to get positively involved with their students may be the reason for teacher's higher level of perception of TI.

5.12 Testing of Hypothesis 7

$H7_0$: There is no significant relationship in the mean scores of parents' response and teacher's response towards 'Parental Involvement'.

The Null Hypothesis was tested using Independent t-Test.

Table 77 shows the relationship of mean scores of parents' response and Teacher's response towards 'Parental Involvement' (PI).

Table 77 : Parents & Teacher's Response Towards PI

Group	N	Mean	Std. Deviation	P Value Sig. (2-Tailed)	Result
Parents	40	3.41	0.240	0.000	Not Significant
Teachers	40	2.48	0.389		

Since the P value (0.000) is less than 0.05, it can be concluded that relationship between mean scores of Parents and Teachers is ***'Not Significant'*** with respect to 'Parental Involvement', ***hence the Null Hypothesis is accepted*** and it is concluded that there is no 'Significant' relationship in the mean scores of Parents' and Teacher's response towards 'Parental Involvement'.

Based upon the mean values, it can be further concluded that Parents (3.41) perceived PI as ***'Moderate'*** while Teachers (3.48) have opined PI as ***'Low'.***

Interpretation of Result

For the total Parents and Teachers sample it was observed that they have different responses for 'Parental Involvement' (PI), as can be seen from above analysis (Table 77).

The reason may be different perceptions of parents and teachers on following items, as reflected in the questionnaire (Appx B & C) :-

1. Parents' willingness to attend all scheduled events and their readiness for interaction with teachers.

2. Parents' approach for "Parents Teacher's Interactive Session".

3. Parents' participation in activities and projects of their child in school.

4. Parents' interest in child's performance in study, co-curricular activity.

Thus it can be inferred that teachers have certain expectations from parents for their involvement in adolescents' school and studies related activities, like attending PTMs, regular interaction with Teachers, participation in school activities, etc. The reason for teacher's perception maybe due to the above expectations not getting met either partially or fully. On the other hand, as the total parents' population is from an urban metropolitan city where parents have a busy lifestyle, which might cause them to miss few events in school, it could lead to different opinions by parents and teachers with regards to PI.

5.13 Testing of Hypothesis 8

$H8_0$: There is no significant relationship in the mean scores of parents' response and Teacher's response towards Teacher's Involvement.

The Null Hypothesis was tested using Independent t-Test.

Table 78 shows the relationship of mean scores of Parents' response and Teacher's response towards 'Teacher's Involvement' (TI).

Table 78 : Parents & Teacher's Response Towards TI

Group	N	Mean	Std. Deviation	P Value Sig. (2-Tailed)	Result
Teachers	40	3.52	0.262	0.103	Significant
Parents	40	3.66	0.472		

Since the P value (0.103) is more than 0.05, it can be concluded that relationship between mean scores of Parents and Teachers is ***'Significant'*** with respect to TI, ***hence the Null Hypothesis is rejected*** and it is concluded that there is a 'Significant' relationship in the mean scores of Parents' response and Teacher's response towards Teacher's Involvement.

Based upon the mean values, it can be further concluded that Teachers (3.52) and Parents (3.66) opined TI as ***'High'***.

Interpretation of Result

For the total parents & teachers sample it was observed that they have same responses for 'Teacher's Involvement' (TI) as can be seen from above analysis (Table 78).

The reason may be perception of parents and Teachers on following items, as reflected in the questionnaire (Appx B & Appx C) :-

1. Teacher's support may help in Academic improvement of adolescents.

2. Interaction with teacher may help Parents in understanding child.

3. Class teacher may be discussing about child's performance or Behaviour with their Parents.

4. Parents may see child's positive Behaviour with teacher's support.

Thus it can be inferred that teachers are a pillar of support to adolescents in their growing years and parents too feel comforted when their child is in care of supporting and caring teachers. Parents' confidence on their child's teacher for guiding their child to achieve his / her best in academics and Behaviour aspects might be the reason of their positive assessment of TI. They might have also observed positive changes attributing to teacher's counselling and guidance, strengthening their perception. Furthermore, teacher's satisfaction with their efforts of constructively helping their students in academics and Behaviour aspects along with observed affirmative changes in their students' Behaviour may be the reason for their positive perception.

5.14 Testing of Hypothesis 9

H9₀ : There is no significant relationship between the mean scores of Adolescents' response and Parents' response towards impact of 'Parental Involvement' on 'Academic Achievement'.

The Null Hypothesis was tested using Independent t-Test.

Table 79 shows the relationship of mean scores of Adolescents' response and Parents' response towards impact of PI on AA.

Table 79 : Adolescents' & Parents' Response Towards Impact of PI on AA

Group	N	Mean	Std. Deviation	P Value Sig. (2-Tailed)	Result
Adolescents	250	3.28	0.483	0.893	Significant
Parents	40	3.26	0.600		

Since the P value (0.893) is more than 0.05, it can be concluded that relationship between mean scores of Adolescents and Parents is ***'Significant'*** with respect to impact of PI on AA, ***hence the Null Hypothesis is rejected*** and it is concluded that there is a 'Significant' relationship between the mean scores of Adolescents' response and Parents' response towards impact of 'Parental Involvement' on 'Academic Achievement'.

Based upon the mean values, it can be further concluded that both Adolescents (3.28) and Parents (3.26) have opined impact of PI on AA as ***'Moderate'***.

Interpretation of Result

For the total adolescents and parents sample it was observed that they have similar responses for impact of 'Parental Involvement' (PI) on 'Academic Achievement' (AA), as can be seen from above analysis (Table 79).

As observed from the above analysis, perceived impact of PI on AA by both Parents and Adolescents was '***Moderate***', which may be due to similar expectations and perceptions of Parents and Adolescents for the following items, as reflected in the questionnaire (Appx A and Appx B) :-

1. May be the parents motivate adolescents to do their best in academics.

2. Parents may be taking out time to teach their children and help them in assignments.

3. Adolescents might be getting appreciated for their hard work by parents.

4. Parents may be in continuous communication with teachers, which in turn might be motivating adolescents to perform better.

Thus it can be inferred that both parents and adolescents perception to PI affecting AA is at similar level. Adolescents concur with parents that their involvement moderately helps them in 'Academic Achievement'. This is probably due to their acceptance of whatever time parents' are able to take out from their busy schedule; or maybe they are content with the guidance from parents in spite of their limitations. Furthermore, maybe the parents perceive that they are able to moderately contribute to the Academic growth of their child but not as much as they would want, due to their busy schedules or inability to help their child in school activities and assignments.

5.15 Testing of Hypothesis 10

H10₀ : There is no significant relationship between the mean scores of Adolescents' response and Parents' response towards impact of 'Parental Involvement' on 'Behaviour Adjustment'.

The Null Hypothesis was tested using Independent t-Test.

Table 80 shows the relationship of mean scores of Adolescents' response and Parents' response towards impact of PI on BA.

Table 80 : Adolescents' & Parents' Response Towards impact of PI on BA

Group	N	Mean	Std. Deviation	P Value Sig. (2-tailed)	Result
Adolescents	250	3.07	0.359	0.000	Not Significant
Parents	40	2.76	0.374		

Since the P value (0.000) is less than 0.05, it can be concluded that relationship between mean scores of Adolescents and Parents is ***'Not Significant'*** with respect to impact of PI on BA, ***hence the Null Hypothesis is accepted*** and it is concluded that there is no 'Significant' relationship between the mean scores of Adolescents' response and Parents' response towards impact of 'Parental Involvement' on 'Behaviour Adjustment'.

Interpretation of Result

For the total Adolescents and Parents' sample it was observed that they have different responses for impact of 'Parental Involvement' (PI) on 'Behaviour Adjustment' (BA), as can be seen from above analysis (Table 80).

As observed from the above analysis, the relationship perceived by adolescents is higher than that of parents between PI and BA.

Different responses of adolescents and parents might be due to different perception and expectations for following items, as reflected in the questionnaire (Appx A and Appx B) :-

1. Adolescents taking parents reprimand / counselling positively and changing their Behaviour accordingly.

2. Adolescents comfort at discussing their personal problems with their parents.

3. Parents observe their child to get irritated and doing the exact opposite when they try to suggest their choices of clothes, friends and food to them.

4. Parents observe that discussion with their child lead to arguments followed by him / her getting upset and walking away.

Thus it can be inferred that adolescence is a phase where children go through a personality conflict, wherein their self belief of being an adult or grown up may lead to their judgment of parents' expectations or counselling for their Behaviour to be overbearing or too strict, leading them to their perception of relationship between PI & BA. Parents' perception that their expectations for their child's Behaviour might not be getting fulfilled, maybe due to digital distraction or peer pressure on Adolescents. Furthermore, parents' busy routine might be making them think that they are not able to spend constructive time with adolescents, so as to help them in 'Behaviour Adjustment', resulting in different perception of relationship between PI and BA.

5.16 Testing of Hypothesis 11

$H11_0$: There is no significant relationship between the mean scores of Adolescents' response and teacher's response towards impact of Teacher's Involvement on 'Academic Achievement'.

The Null Hypothesis was tested using Independent T Test.

Table 81 shows the relationship of mean scores of Adolescents' response and Teacher's response towards impact of TI on AA.

Table 81 : Adolescents' & Teacher's Response Towards impact of TI on AA

Group	N	Mean	Std. Deviation	P Value Sig. (2-Tailed)	Result
Adolescents	250	3.21	0.513	0.676	Significant
Teachers	40	3.18	0.447		

Since the P value (0.676) is more than 0.05, it can be concluded that relationship between mean scores of Adolescents and Teachers is ***'Significant'*** with respect to impact of TI on AA, ***hence the Null Hypothesis is rejected*** and it is concluded that there is a 'Significant' relationship between the mean scores of Adolescents' response and Teacher's response towards impact of Teacher's Involvement on 'Academic Achievement'.

Based upon the mean values, it can be further concluded that both Adolescents (3.21) and Teachers (3.18) have opined impact of TI on AA as ***'Moderate'***.

Interpretation of Result

For the total adolescent and teacher sample it was observed that they have similar responses for impact of 'Teacher's Involvement' (TI) on 'Academic Achievement' (AA), as can be seen from above analysis (Table 81).

As observed from the above analysis, perceived impact of TI on AA by both parents and adolescents was 'Moderate', which may be due to similar expectation and perception by Parents and Adolescents for following items, as reflected in the questionnaire (Appx A and Appx C) :-

1. Class teacher encourages students to ask doubts and questions in class.

2. Class teacher uses teaching aids and innovative techniques while teaching.

3. The teacher finds the students to complete homework and assignments on time with her / his constant monitoring.

4. The teacher finds students approach him / her regarding the difficulties they face in any subject.

Thus it can be inferred that adolescents trust on teacher's knowledge prowess, sincerity and ways of teaching might be the reasons for perceived positive relationship between TI and AA, while they sometimes might be getting flustered by teacher's continuous watchfulness leading to '***Moderate***' rating. On the other hand, teachers may be content with their efforts and ways of teaching to guide their students academically, which may be the reason for their perception of positive relationship between TI and AA of adolescents, while their observation of adolescents getting stressed out sometimes due to constant vigilance on studies may be the reason for their assessment as '***Moderate***'.

5.17 Testing of Hypothesis 12

$H12_0$: There is no significant relationship between the mean scores of Adolescents' response and teacher's response towards impact of Teacher's Involvement on 'Behaviour Adjustment'.

The Null Hypothesis was tested using Independent t-Test.

Table 82 shows the relationship of mean scores of Adolescents' response and Teacher's response towards impact of TI on BA.

Table 82 : Adolescents' & Teacher's Response Towards impact of TI on BA

Group	N	Mean	Std. Deviation	P Value Sig. (2-Tailed)	Result
Adolescents	250	3.15	0.537	0.000	Non Significant
Teachers	40	3.86	0.542		

Since the P value (0.000) is less than 0.05, it can be concluded that relationship between mean scores of Adolescents and Teachers is '***Non Significant'*** with respect to impact of TI on BA, ***hence the Null Hypothesis is accepted*** and it is concluded that there is no 'Significant' relationship between the mean scores of Adolescents' response and Teacher's response towards impact of Teacher's Involvement on 'Behaviour Adjustment'.

Interpretation of Result

Adolescents and teachers were observed to have different responses for impact of 'Teacher's Involvement' (TI) on 'Behaviour Adjustment' (BA), as can be seen from above analysis (Table 82).

As observed from the above analysis, the relationship perceived by teachers is higher than that of adolescents between TI and BA.

Different responses of Adolescents and Teachers might be due to different perceptions and expectations for following items, as reflected in the questionnaire (Appx A and Appx C) :-

1. Discussion by class teacher about likes and interests of students.

2. Class teacher involving all children in all class activities.

3. Adolescents perception for teacher's instructions about the rules and its importance to mould their Behaviour positively.

4. Adolescents comfort in discussing their personal problems.

Thus it can be inferred that reasons for adolescents' lower perception may be their unease to share personal problems with teachers which may not be letting them connect to teachers emotionally, their reluctance to follow rules and their perception of counselling to be strict or unnecessary. Reason for teacher's higher rating for impact of TI on BA may be their perceived satisfaction in their efforts to counsel adolescents about rules to help them mould their Behaviour, as also their observation in improvement of adolescents' Behaviour post counselling.

5.18 Testing of Hypothesis 13

H13₀ : There is no significant gender difference in the following variables :-

1. Parental Involvement (PI).
2. Impact of Parental Involvement (PI) on Academic Achievement (AA).
3. Impact of Parental Involvement' (PI) on Behaviour Adjustment (BA).
4. Teacher's Involvement (TI).
5. Impact of Teacher's Involvement (TI) on Academic Achievement (AA).
6. Impact of 'Teacher's Involvement (TI) on Behaviour Adjustment (BA).

The Null Hypothesis was tested using Independent t-Test.

Table 83 shows the gender differences in variables.

Table 83 : Gender Differences in Variables

Ser	Variables	Group	N	Mean	Std. Deviation	P Value Sig. (2-Tailed)	Result
1.	PI	Boys	160	3.36	0.378	0.012	Not Significant
		Girls	90	3.24	0.350		
2.	Impact of PI on AA	Boys	160	3.17	0.465	0.000	Not Significant
		Girls	90	3.47	0.453		
3.	Impact of PI on BA	Boys	160	3.10	0.379	0.051	Significant
		Girls	90	3.00	0.312		
4.	TI	Boys	160	3.08	0.368	0.398	Significant
		Girls	90	3.04	0.340		
5.	Impact of TI on AA	Boys	160	3.13	0.497	0.000	Not Significant
		Girls	90	3.36	0.508		
6.	Impact of TI on BA	Boys	160	3.11	0.529	0.152	Significant
		Girls	90	3.21	0.552		

Interpretation of Result

1. Since the P value (0.012) is less than 0.05, it can be concluded that gender difference of boys and girls is ***'Not Significant'*** with respect 'Parental Involvement' (PI), ***hence the Null Hypothesis is accepted*** and it is concluded that there is no 'Significant' gender difference in the mean scores of PI. Based upon the mean values, it can be further concluded that Boys (3.24) and Girls (3.36) opined 'Parental Involvement' (PI) as ***'Moderate'***.

2. Since the P value (0.000) is less than 0.05, it can be concluded gender difference of boys and girls is ***'Not Significant'*** with respect to impact of PI on AA, ***hence the Null Hypothesis is accepted*** and it is concluded that there is no 'Significant' gender difference in the mean scores of impact of PI on AA. Based upon the mean values, it can be further concluded that Boys (3.17) and Girls (3.47) opined impact of PI on AA as ***'Moderate'***.

3. Since the P value (0.040) is more than 0.05, it can be concluded that gender difference of boys and girls is ***'Significant'*** with respect to impact of PI on BA, ***hence the Null Hypothesis is rejected*** and it is concluded that there is 'Significant' gender difference in the mean scores of impact of PI on BA. As can be observed from the mean score, perception of boys for PI on BA is slightly more than that of girls. In evolving Indian society the expectations of adolescent girls are also changing where they expect equal rights and rules as exist for boys. The aberration of rules might be the reason for girls to perceive restrictions and involvement by parents as excessive or overbearing resulting in their lower perception.

4. Since the P value (0.398) is more than 0.05, it can be concluded that gender difference of boys and girls is ***'Significant'*** with respect to 'Teacher's Involvement' (TI), ***hence the Null Hypothesis is rejected*** and it is concluded that there is a 'Significant' gender difference in the mean scores of TI. As can be observed from the mean score, perception of boys for Teacher's Involvement is slightly more than that of girls. The reason for this difference may be either boys have fewer expectations from teachers than girls or their expectations are being met. Girls on the other hand are more sensitive so maybe they expect more involvement from teachers or their expectations are partially or fully are not being met, leading to their lower perception.

5. Since the P value (0.000) is less than 0.05, it can be concluded that gender difference of boys and girls is ***'Not Significant'*** with respect to impact of TI on AA, ***hence the Null Hypothesis is accepted*** and it is concluded that there is no 'Significant' gender difference in the mean scores of impact of TI on AA. Based upon the mean values, it can be further concluded that Boys (3.13) and Girls (3.36) opined impact of TI on AA as ***'Moderate'***.

6. Since the P value (0.398) is more than 0.05, it can be concluded that gender difference of boys and girls is ***'Significant'*** with respect to impact of TI on BA, ***hence the Null Hypothesis is rejected*** and it is concluded that there is a 'Significant' gender difference in the mean scores of impact of TI on BA. As can be observed from the mean score, perception of girls (3.21) for impact of Teacher's Involvement on 'Behaviour Adjustment' is slightly more than that of boys (3.11). The reason for this difference may be that girls might be finding counselling by teachers impacting, in understanding rules and its importance, and thereby guiding them to mould their Behaviour accordingly, while the boys' perception might be different for the same.

5.19 Testing of Hypothesis 14

H14₀ : There is no significant impact of following constructs of PI on AA from Adolescents' response :-

1. Emotional.
2. Aspiration.
3. Structure.
4. School & Studies.
5. Friends.

The Null Hypothesis was tested using the Path Coefficients of the model.

Table 84 : Path Coefficients with Regression Weights & P Values For AA

Independent Variable	Regression Weights	S.e.	C.r.	P	Result
Emotional	0.115	0.079	1.457	0.145	Not Significant
Aspiration	0.122	0.062	1.972	0.049	Significant
Structure	0.113	0.049	2.29	0.022	Significant
school & Studies	0.127	0.062	2.042	0.041	Significant
Friends	- 0.072	0.062	-1.165	0.244	Not Significant

Interpretation of Result

1. Since the P value (0.145) is more than 0.05, it can be concluded that relationship between 'Emotional Involvement' with 'Academic Achievement' (AA) as perceived by adolescents is '**Not Significant**', ***hence the Null Hypothesis is accepted*** and it is concluded that there is no 'Significant' relationship between 'Emotional Involvement' as a construct of PI with AA of adolescents.

2. Since the P value (0.049) is less than 0.05, it can be concluded that relationship between 'Aspiration of Parents' with 'Academic Achievement' (AA) as perceived by adolescents is '**Significant**', ***hence the Null Hypothesis is rejected*** and it is concluded that there is a 'Significant' relationship between 'Aspiration of Parents' as a construct of PI with AA of adolescents.

3. Since the P value (0.022) is less than 0.05, it can be concluded that relationship between 'Structure by Parents' with 'Academic Achievement' (AA) as perceived by adolescents is '**Significant'**, ***hence the Null Hypothesis is rejected*** and it is concluded that there is a 'Significant' relationship between 'Structure by Parents' as a construct of PI with AA of adolescents.

4. Since the P value (0.041) is less than 0.05, it can be concluded that relationship between 'Involvement in school & Studies' with 'Academic Achievement' (AA) as perceived by adolescents is '**Significant'**, ***hence the Null Hypothesis is rejected*** and it is concluded that there is a 'Significant' relationship between 'Parental Involvement' in school & Studies" as a construct of PI with AA of adolescents.

5. Since the P value (0.244) is more than 0.05, it can be concluded that relationship between 'Involvement with Friends' with 'Academic Achievement' (AA) as perceived by adolescents is '**Not Significant'**, ***hence the Null Hypothesis is accepted*** and it is concluded that there is no 'Significant' relationship between 'Involvement with Friends' as a construct of PI with AA of adolescents.

It can be inferred from above analysis that "Parents' Aspiration", "Structure by Parents" and "Involvement in school & Studies" were the constructs which were observed to have positive impact on 'Academic Achievement' of adolescents, while "Involvement with Friends" and "Emotional Involvement" were not found to have any 'Significant' relationship with 'Academic Achievement' of adolescents.

Reasons for positive impact of parents' 'Aspiration', 'Structuring', 'Involvement in school & Studies' as constructs of 'Parental Involvement' on 'Academic Achievement' may be due to adolescents' perception for following :-

(a) 'Parents' Aspiration' that includes discussions by parents about their Aspiration for their child's future, their effort to know their child's goals along with regular motivation from parents to achieve these goals. These activities probably might be helpful in building the children's confidence and willingness to work towards their goal, inspiring them to work harder.

(b) 'Structure by Parents' involves keeping tab of TV and internet usage, timetable at home, ensuring completion of homework and assignments. Structuring may be helping adolescents to plan their day giving him / her more time for studies which probably might be helping them in improving their 'Academic Achievement'.

(c) 'Involvement with school & Studies' includes parents helping their children in completing projects and homework, parents keeping track of marks and exams, attending school events and PTMs. 'Parental Involvement' in studies and school might be making children realise the importance of studies thereby encouraging them to study harder. Furthermore, with parents' offering to assist children in studies, children may feel encouraged to seek assistance.

'Emotional Involvement' and 'Involvement with Friends' as constructs of 'Parental Involvement' were not found to impact 'Academic Achievement' as perceived by adolescents. Following might be the reason for the same :-

(a) 'Emotional Involvement', which includes talking about school events, discussing personal problems and appreciation for their good work. May be adolescents' perceived emotional involvement as inadequate as per their expectations or may not be motivating for improving Academic performance.

(b) 'Involvement with Friends' includes parents inviting their child's friends at home, involving in activities with friends like movies, picnic, etc. Children relate to their friends the most during adolescence. Either parents might be judging their friends or comparing with them in academics, leading to adolescents' perception of 'Parental Involvement' with friends not impacting their 'Academic Achievement'.

5.20 Testing of Hypothesis 15

$H15_0$: There is no significant impact of following constructs of PI on BA from Adolescents' response :-

1. Emotional.
2. Aspiration.
3. Structure.
4. School & Studies.
5. Friends.

The Null Hypothesis was tested using the Path Coefficients of the model.

Table 85 : Path Coefficients with Regression Weights & P Values

Independent Variable	Regression Weights	S.e.	C.r.	P	Result
Emotional	0.14	0.067	2.106	0.035	Significant
Aspiration	0.015	0.053	0.285	0.776	Not Significant
Structure	0.024	0.058	0.409	0.682	Not Significant
school & Studies	0.046	0.073	0.634	0.526	Not Significant
Friends	0.155	0.052	2.996	0.003	Significant

Interpretation of Result

1. Since the P value (0.035) is less than 0.05, it can be concluded that relationship between 'Emotional Involvement' with 'Behaviour Adjustment' (BA) as perceived by adolescents is **'Significant'**, ***hence the Null Hypothesis is rejected*** and it is concluded that there is a 'Significant' relationship between 'Emotional Involvement' as a construct of PI with BA of adolescents.

2. Since the P value (0.776) is more than 0.05, it can be concluded that relationship between 'Aspiration of Parents' with 'Behaviour Adjustment' (BA) as perceived by adolescents is **'Not Significant'**, ***hence the Null Hypothesis is accepted*** and it is concluded that there is no 'Significant' relationship between 'Aspiration of Parents' as a construct of PI with BA of adolescents.

3. Since the P value (0.682) is more than 0.05, it can be concluded that relationship between 'Structure by Parents' with 'Behaviour Adjustment' (BA) as perceived by adolescents is '**No Significant'**, ***hence the Null Hypothesis is accepted*** and it is concluded that there is no 'Significant' relationship between 'Structure by Parents' as a construct of PI with BA of adolescents.

4. Since the P value (0.526) is more than 0.05, it can be concluded that relationship between 'Involvement in school & Studies' with 'Behaviour Adjustment' (BA) as perceived by adolescents is '**Not Significant'**, ***hence the Null Hypothesis is accepted*** and it is concluded that there is no 'Significant' relationship between "'Parental Involvement' in school & Studies" as a construct of PI with BA of adolescents.

5. Since the P value (0.003) is less than 0.05, it can be concluded that relationship between 'Involvement with Friends' with 'Behaviour Adjustment' (BA) as perceived by adolescents is '**Significant'**, ***hence the Null Hypothesis is rejected*** and it is concluded that there is a 'Significant' relationship between 'Involvement with Friends' as a construct of PI with BA of adolescents.

It can be inferred from the above analysis that "Parents' Emotional Involvement" and "Parental Involvement' with Friends" were the constructs which were observed to have positive impact on 'Behaviour Adjustment' of adolescents while "Parents' Aspiration", "Structure by Parents" and "Involvement in school & Studies" were not found to have any 'Significant' relationship with 'Behaviour Adjustment' of adolescents.

'Emotional Involvement' and 'Involvement with Friends' as constructs of 'Parental Involvement' were found to impact 'Behaviour Adjustment', as perceived by adolescents. Following may be the reason for the same :-

(a) 'Emotional Involvement' includes talking about school events, discussing personal problems and appreciation for their good work. May be when parents appreciate children or help them in solving their personal problems, children feel relaxed and stress free, which makes them want to put effort in behaving as per parents' expectation.

(b) 'Involvement with Friends' includes parents inviting their child's friends at home, involving in activities with friends like movies, picnic, etc. Adolescents relate to their friends the most and when parents get involved in activities with their friend or make an effort to know their friends, they might feel their choices are being accepted and respected, which in turn motivates them to behave in a manner agreeable by their parents.

'Parents' Aspiration', 'Structuring' and 'Involvement in school & Studies' were found to have no impact on 'Behaviour Adjustment' as perceived by adolescents. Following may be the reason for the same :-

(a) 'Parents Aspiration' includes discussions by parents about their Aspiration for their child's future, their effort to know their child's goals along with regular motivation from parents to achieve these goals. These activities probably focus more on academics and probably parents might not be focusing on their Aspiration related to Behaviour.

(b) 'Structure by Parents' involves keeping tab of TV and internet usage, timetable at home, ensuring completion of homework and assignments. Children might feel that their life is being controlled, causing stress or making them revolt and behave in an unruly manner.

(c) 'Involvement in school & Studies' includes parents helping their children in completing their projects and homework, parents keeping track of marks and exams, attending school events and PTMs. 'Parental Involvement' in the studies and school might be making children strained or they might feel the monitoring too overbearing.

5.21 Testing of Hypothesis 16

H16₀ : There is no significant impact of following constructs of TI on AA from Adolescents' response :-

1. Emotional.
2. Interaction with Parents.
3. Instrumental.
4. Structure.

The Null Hypothesis was tested using the Path Coefficients of the model.

Table 86 : Path Coefficients with Regression Weights & P Values

Independent Variable	Regression Weights	S.e.	C.r.	P	Result
Emotional	0.229	0.092	2.495	0.013	Significant
Interaction with Parents	-0.099	0.07	-1.421	0.155	Not Significant
Instrumental	0.306	0.062	4.915	0.023	Significant
Structure	0.089	0.054	1.641	0.101	Not Significant

Interpretation of Result

1. Since the P value (0.013) is less than 0.05, it can be concluded that relationship between 'Emotional Involvement' with 'Academic Achievement' (AA) as perceived by adolescents is '**Significant**', ***hence the Null Hypothesis is rejected*** and it is concluded that there is a 'Significant' relationship between 'Emotional Involvement' as a construct of TI with AA of adolescents.

2. Since the P value (0.155) is more than 0.05, it can be concluded that relationship between 'Interaction with Parents' with 'Academic Achievement' (AA) as perceived by adolescents is '**Not Significant**', ***hence the Null Hypothesis is accepted*** and it is concluded that there is no 'Significant' relationship between 'Interaction with Parents' as a construct of TI with AA of adolescents.

3. Since the P value (0.023) is less than 0.05, it can be concluded that relationship between 'Instrumental Support' with 'Academic Achievement' (AA) as perceived by adolescents is '**Significant**', ***hence the Null Hypothesis is rejected*** and it is concluded

that there is a 'Significant' relationship between 'Instrumental Support by Teacher's as a construct of TI with AA of adolescents.

4. Since the P value (0.101) is more than 0.05, it can be concluded that relationship between 'Structure by Teacher's with 'Academic Achievement' (AA) as perceived by adolescents is '**Not Significant**', ***hence the Null Hypothesis is accepted*** and it is concluded that there is no 'Significant' relationship between 'Structure by Teacher' as a construct of TI with AA of adolescents.

It can be inferred from the above analysis that "Teacher's Emotional Involvement" and "Teacher's Instrumental Support" were the constructs which were observed to have positive impact on 'Academic Achievement' of adolescents while "Teacher's Interaction with Parents" and "Structure by Teachers" were not found to have any 'Significant' relationship with 'Academic Achievement' of adolescents.

'Emotional Involvement' and 'Instrumental Support', as constructs of Teacher's Involvement, were found to impact 'Academic Achievement', as perceived by adolescents. Following might be the reason for the same :-

(a) 'Emotional Involvement' by teachers includes personal attention to each child, discussion of likes and dislikes of children, involvement in class activities. When teachers make an effort to know their students and involve them in class activities, maybe the children feel connected to teachers, increasing their trust on teachers and their teaching or make them more attentive during teaching sessions, helping improve their Academic performance.

(b) 'Instrumental Support 'includes using innovating teaching methods, encouraging asking doubts, checking homework and assignments. When teachers use interesting and innovative teaching techniques, it is quite possible that students' attention span, interest in the subject or their understanding improves. Teacher's effort to teach the subject could also be making children respect them and thus inspiring them to put more efforts in studying better.

'Academic Achievement' of adolescents was found to have no relationship with 'Interaction with Parents' and 'Structure by Teacher's as constructs of Teacher's Involvement, as perceived by adolescents. Following may the reasons for the same :-

(a) 'Interaction with Parents' includes teachers updating parents about child's performance, informing parents if the child seems upset or disturbed. The constant interaction might be irking students, making them feel stressed, which might be affecting their concentration or fading their will to study.

(b) 'Structuring by Teacher's includes planning fun activities, appreciating children for good work and Behaviour, explaining rules and ensuring everyone follows it. Adolescence is the age where children do not like rules in general and probably repetition of rules and its importance by teachers or too tight schedule in class cause their attention to distract from studies.

5.22 Testing of Hypothesis 17

$H17_0$: There is no significant impact of following constructs of TI on BA from Adolescents' response :-

1. Emotional.
2. Interaction with Parents.
3. Instrumental.
4. Structure.

The Null Hypothesis was tested using the Path Coefficients of the model.

Table 87: Path Coefficients with Regression Weights & P Values

Independent Variable	Regression Weights	S.e.	C.r.	P	Result
Emotional	0.288	0.072	3.987	0.011	Significant
Interaction with Parents	0.136	0.058	2.352	0.019	Significant
Instrumental	- 0.075	0.079	0.954	0.34	Not Significant
Structure	0.049	0.045	1.091	0.275	Not Significant

Interpretation of Result

1. Since the P value (0.011) is less than 0.05, it can be concluded that relationship between 'Emotional Involvement' with 'Behaviour Adjustment' (BA) as perceived by adolescents is '**Significant**', ***hence the Null Hypothesis is rejected*** and it is concluded that there is a 'Significant' relationship between 'Emotional Involvement' as a construct of TI with BA of adolescents.

2. Since the P value (0.19) is less than 0.05, it can be concluded that relationship between 'Interaction with Parents' with 'Behaviour Adjustment' (BA) as perceived by adolescents is '**Significant**', ***hence the Null Hypothesis is rejected*** and it is concluded that there is a 'Significant' relationship between 'Interaction with Parents' as a construct of TI with BA of adolescents.

3. Since the P value (0.34) is more than 0.05, it can be concluded that relationship between 'Instrumental Support' with 'Behaviour Adjustment' (BA) as perceived by adolescents is '**Not Significant**', ***hence the Null Hypothesis is accepted***

and it is concluded that there is no 'Significant' relationship between 'Instrumental Support by Teacher's as a construct of TI with BA of adolescents.

4. Since the P value (0.275) is more than 0.05, it can be concluded that relationship between 'Structure by Teacher's with 'Behaviour Adjustment' (BA) as perceived by adolescents is '**Not Significant**', ***hence the Null Hypothesis is accepted*** and it is concluded that there is no 'Significant' relationship between 'Structure by Teacher's as a construct of TI with BA of adolescents.

It can be inferred from the above analysis that "Teacher's Emotional Involvement" and "Teacher's Interaction with Parents" were the constructs which were observed to have positive impact on 'Behaviour Adjustment' of adolescents while "Structure by Teachers" and "Instrumental Support by Teachers" were not found to have any 'Significant' relationship with 'Behaviour Adjustment' of adolescents.

'Behaviour Adjustment' of adolescents was found to have positive relationship with 'Emotional Involvement' and 'Interaction with Parents' as constructs of Teacher's Involvement, as perceived by adolescents. Following may the reasons for the same :-

(a) 'Emotional Involvement by Teacher's includes personal attention to each child, discussion of likes and dislikes of children, involvement in class activities. Teacher's effort to know their students and to involve them in class activities may be creating a stronger bond between Teacher and students, reducing their stress and making them behave in accordance of teacher's liking.

(b) 'Interaction with Parents' includes teachers updating parents about child's performance, informing parents if the child seems upset or disturbed. The interaction between parents and teachers might be helping them to understand the reasons of the child's mental state allowing them to help him / her come out of the situation from both sides impacting his / her 'Behaviour Adjustment'.

'Behaviour Adjustment' of adolescents was found to have no relationship with 'Structure by Teacher's and 'Instrumental Support' as constructs of Teacher's Involvement, as perceived by adolescents. Following may the reasons for the same :-

(a) 'Structuring by Teacher's includes planning fun activities, appreciating children for good work and Behaviour, explaining rules and ensuring everyone follows it. Adolescence is the age where children do not like rules in general and probably repetition of rules and its importance by teachers or too tight schedule in class maybe the reason for their rowdy Behaviour.

(b) 'Instrumental Support' includes using innovating teaching methods, encouraging asking doubts, checking homework and assignments. Teacher's usage of interesting and innovative teaching techniques might be helping them academically but probably it does not inspire them to improve their Behaviour.

CHAPTER 6

CONCLUSION AND RECOMMENDATION

6.1 Background

Adolescents are the future of the human society. To achieve positive progression and development of the society at large, all round development and mental stability of adults during their adolescence is a quintessential prerequisite and should thus receive utmost priority from the adults (parents, teachers and peers) who may be directly or indirectly related to adolescents parents, educators and members of our society unequivocally acknowledge that adolescence is a critical period for physical, emotional and mental development that will ultimately provide adult life contentment and a sense of achievement. Researchers across the world have reiterated that 13-19 years of age are the most fascinating years of growth when children experience not only physical transformation but also undergo hormonal changes. These changes lead adolescents to adopt both positive and negative outlook / decision making when they come at the crossroads in life.

Parents, educators and psychologists around the world have been found to show keen interest in identifying various factors which might positively affect Adolescents' 'Academic Achievement' and 'Behaviour Adjustment'. This research aims to determine how and to what extent, Parental and Teacher's Involvement influences the achievements and 'Behaviour Adjustment' of teenagers. Comprehensive knowledge of this subject may not only help to recommend 'Parenting Practices' but also 'Policies, Practices and Activities of Educational Institutions', with both working in tandem towards the common goal. It may also facilitate teachers in devising a roadmap for their involvement, while aiming for improved Academic results and 'Behaviour Adjustment' in teenagers. The research may help in designing and developing a concrete plan for Parental and Teacher's Involvement, including constructs that eventually may get identified which have most positive and powerful impact in adolescents. Epstein et al. (2002), through their work, harmonised that "When parents, teachers, students, and others view one another as partners in education, a caring community forms around students and begins its work". The partnership activities ought to facilitate them to guide, connect and motivate adolescents to achieve triumph not just academically but also behaviourally.

6.1.1 Adolescents and their Characteristics

WHO (2015) defines 'Adolescents' as "Individuals in the 10-19 year age group". In India, Adolescent age is defined as children in the range of 10-19 years. American Psychological Association (APA, 2002) further adds that "During the adolescence period, major changes occur at varying rates in physical characteristics, sexual characteristics and sexual interest, resulting in 'Significant' impacts on body image, self-concept and self-esteem. Major cognitive and social developments take place as well". Kasomo (2006) in his research said "Adolescence is a stage in human life when rapid changes take place during which an individual grows physically, mentally and socially while his personality develops new dimensions".

According to Hall (1904) "Adolescence is a period of 'storm' and 'stress' where major physical changes takes place causing major psychological changes. It is crucial period of life filled with changes, difficulties and special problems, 'turbulent' and 'unstable', a time of self discovery and self assertion". Casey et al.(2008) states that reasons for these are mainly the biological changes which cause mood swings, along with the fact that their minds are however still developing to comprehend the same.

6.2 Need of the Study

The researcher being from the field of education has experienced first-hand the dilemma of parents to get involvement in the adolescents' life. Having travelled the length and breadth of the country in the capacity of an army officer's wife, the researcher has observed the struggle of parents closely. The researcher in her duties as the principal and a teacher in various aided and unaided schools have gained diverse experience on the subject which has been the field of her core competence. Throughout the journey, as a principal and teacher, it has been the researcher's observation that some parents outdo other parents when it comes to involvement in their child's school activities, while in certain other instances parents were observed to be indifferent about their child's activities, whether academically or socially. The researcher observed that some teachers were more forthcoming in helping adolescents in their difficult times, whether emotionally or academically, while few others were complacent with only completing their task. Some teachers took initiative in making their class more interesting through various aids, teaching methodology, etc. and also helped children in coping with their adolescent quandary and stress management.

During the literature review it became evident that one of the most intriguing topics of interest for researchers and educators across the globe has been the relationship of adolescents with parents as well as teachers. Over the years, various researchers from different countries have tried to understand and examine the Impact of Parental' and Teacher's Involvement on Adolescents' life, with focus on their wellbeing, Academic excellence, happiness quotient and motivation to name a few.

Literature review has revealed on the one hand that children's Behaviour, as observed both in and outside school, is closely related to the family dynamics and the home environment, while on the other hand it has also recognised that teacher's role in adolescents' life is multidimensional and has high potential to influence emotional wellbeing and mental health of adolescents.

When all the stakeholders namely parents, teachers, students and others view each other as partners in education, they form a kind community around the students for their synchronised betterment. Students were also observed to behave better when they perceived teachers as caring and responsive, along with support and motivation from parents to perform well in school.

The need of this study arises as the researcher found very few studies related to the involvement of both parents and teachers and their individual / combined impact on Adolescents' 'Academic Achievement' as well as 'Behaviour Adjustment' / emotional wellbeing. During the literature review, there were rarely any studies which took into consideration views of all stakeholders, specifically adolescents, parents and teachers and presented results after comparison of data. Some studies just focused on teacher's Involvement and its impact on either Adolescents' 'Academic Achievement' or emotional wellbeing or both while some studied the impact of Parental' involvement on these aspects. There were hardly any research studies which deliberated the impact of both Parental and Teacher's Involvement on Adolescents' 'Academic Achievement' and / or 'Behaviour Adjustment', which gave an impetus to the researcher for choosing this inadequately addressed topic for her study.

In contemporary times, in many cases both parents are working and their busy working schedules might not offer them opportunity to spend adequate time with their children, thus leading to considerable decline in their adolescents' mental wellbeing, loss of focus, inhibited problem solving ability and declining Academic results. On the other hand, with a diverse teaching faculty, skewed teacher-Student ratio and excessive syllabus in school, teachers might not get to know each Student individually, thereby making adolescents feel awkward to approach their teachers for seeking help in solving their problems in academics or in personal life. Another viable reason for difference in opinion, expectation and acceptable behaviour of adolescents with the adults in their life i.e parents and teachers is generation gap. Things which the adolescents feel and accept as normal behaviour may not be acceptable for their parents or teachers causing them to feel frustrated or misunderstood. This feeling of being unimportant or uncared, both by parents and teachers, can lead to adolescents feeling alienated from studies, school and peers and may lead them to depression. The state of poor mental wellbeing, inadequate Academic performance and resulting hopelessness for a reasonable future may lead them to seek solace in easier but high risk pitfalls like drugs, violence, sexual misconduct, etc. They could either become a recluse or a rebel; they might either start spending more time with peers or take respite in the virtual world of friends and games. Spending too much time with peers might alienate adolescents further from their parents deepening the gap while time on internet can cause them to fall prey to internet evils like pornography, frauds, addiction to games, etc. The 'Blue Whale Challenge' amongst others has been lately in news for targeting such susceptible adolescents and manipulating them to take their own lives. Events of such nature compel us to rethink the significance of parents and teacher's role in adolescents' life. There is a need to re-evaluate and revise the roles of parents and teachers according to changing times and requirement. Involvement of parents and teachers need a scrutiny and fresher perspective. Conscious efforts are required to understand the evolving needs of adolescents so as to facilitate parents and teachers to make necessary changes in their involvement for helping and guiding adolescents in a better way with the aim of achieving overall development.All above aspects led the researcher to the need for finding the impact of parental and teacher involvement on behavioural adjustment and academic achievement of adolescent students.

6.3 Statement of Aim

The aim of the current study is to analyse data from the viewpoint of adolescents, teachers and parents to find the impact of involvement by both parents and teachers on 'Behaviour Adjustment' and 'Academic Achievement' of adolescents so as to identify constructs that positively facilitate in improving both the aspects of adolescents. These constructs would not only act as a guide to parents and teachers in assisting the adolescents to improve their 'Behaviour Adjustment' as well as 'Academic Achievement' but also be a valuable addition to the body of knowledge for researchers worldwide.

"Impact of Parental & Teacher Involvement on Behaviour Adjustment and Academic Achievement in Adolescent students."

6.4 Definition of Key Terms

6.4.1 Conceptual Definition of Key Terms

6.4.1.1 Parental Involvement.

According to Brito & Waller (1994) parent's involvement includes various activities ranging from an impersonal once a year visit to school to regular parent-teacher meetings and active participation in school governorship. Tomlinson (1991) upholds that parental involvement in schools might take one of four forms namely exchange of information; personal involvement in educational matters; formal involvement in school governing; and informal involvement in administrative matters through the parent association. Fullan (1982) on the other hand also identified four forms of parent involvement such as instruction at home, instruction at school, school governance, and community service.

6.4.1.2 Teacher Involvement.

According to Vieno et al. (2005) teacher support is a measurement of school connectedness and bonding. It is related to student's sense of belongingness, being accepted and receiving help when required within the school. Furman (1996) and Furman & Buhrmester (1985) identified elements of teacher support as bonding, social support, instrumental support and shared activities.

6.4.1.3 Behaviour Adjustment.

Behavioural performance or adjustment, as described by Carey (2009) deals with the following six BASICS elements namely Behavioural competence (Relation with others), Achievement (school work and play), Self- relation (Self assured or troubled), internal status (thoughts & feelings), coping (adaptive) and symptoms (dysfunction).

6.4.1.4 **Academic Achievement.**

According to APA Dictionary of psychology, Academic achievement in educational psychology is "A level of proficiency in scholastic work in general or in a specific skill, such as arithmetic or reading. Evidence of future academic achievement is usually based on the results of standardized ability tests and assessment of performance by a teacher or other supervisor".

6.4.2 Operational Definitions

6.4.2.1 **Parental Involvement.**

In the present research study 'Parental Involvement' includes looking after, or monitoring a child's activities at home and in school during Adolescent years. Following constructs of 'Parental Involvement' have been used in the present study :-

1. Emotional Involvement (helping in personal problems, counselling, etc.).
2. Aspiration (discussing future goals, motivation to achieve them, etc.).
3. Structure (keeping a tab on TV/internet usage, making timetable for studies, etc.).
4. School & Studies (helping in assignments, track progress in Academic).
5. Involvement with friends (inviting friends at home, getting to know friends, etc).

6.4.2.2 **Teacher Involvement.**

In the present research study 'Teacher Involvement' includes motivating, monitoring and influencing a child's activities in school during adolescent years. Following constructs of 'Teacher Involvement' have been used in the present study :-

1. Emotional (to know likes/dislikes of students, help in personal problems, etc.).
2. Interaction with parents (PTM, updating on important issues, etc.).
3. Instrumental (Innovative teaching, use of aids, etc.).
4. Structure (deciding rules of the class and explaining its importance, maintaining discipline, etc.).

6.4.2.3 **Impact on Academic Achievement.**

In the present research study 'Impact on Academic Achievement' is the extent to which students achieve their short or long term educational goals. Grades of previous exam along with responses from questionnaire given to adolescents, parents and teachers were taken into consideration to measure impact on academic achievement.

6.4.2.4 **Impact on Behaviour Adjustment.**

In the present research study 'Impact on Behaviour Adjustment' is the extent in which the adolescents are able to cope up to ever changing environment at home, outside and in school. Responses from questionnaire given to adolescents, parents and teachers were taken into consideration to measure impact on behaviour adjustment.

6.5 Objectives of the Study

The objectives of the current study are :-

1. To study the impact of Parental Involvement on Academic Achievement of the students in their Adolescent years.
2. To study the impact of Parental Involvement on Behaviour Adjustment of the students in their Adolescent years.
3. To study the impact of Teacher's Involvement on Academic Achievement of the students in their Adolescent years.
4. To study the impact of Teacher's Involvement on Behaviour Adjustment of the students in their Adolescent years.
5. To compare responses from adolescents, parents and teachers.
6. To ascertain gender difference of adolescents in the following variables :-

(a) Parental Involvement.

(b) Impact of Parental Involvement on Academic Achievement.

(c) Impact of Parental Involvement on Behaviour Adjustment.

(d) Teachers Involvement.

(e) Impact of Teacher's Involvement on Academic Achievement.

(f) Impact of Teacher's Involvement on Behaviour Adjustment.

7. To ascertain which constructs of Parental Involvement impact Behaviour Adjustment of the students in their adolescent years.
8. To ascertain which constructs of Parental Involvement impact Academic Achievement of the students in their adolescent years.
9. To ascertain which constructs of Teacher's Involvement impact Behaviour Adjustment of the students in their adolescent years.
10. To ascertain which constructs of Teacher's Involvement impact Academic Achievement of the students in their adolescent years.

6.6 Hypothesis

Following 'Null Hypotheses' have been considered for the research :-

1. There is no significant impact of Parental Involvement on Academic Achievement for total adolescent sample.
2. There is no significant impact of Parental Involvement on Behaviour Adjustment for total adolescent sample.
3. There is no significant impact of Teacher's Involvement on Academic Achievement' for total adolescent Sample.
4. There is no significant impact of Teacher's Involvement on Behaviour Adjustment' for total adolescent sample.
5. There is no significant relationship in the mean scores of adolescents' response and parents' response towards Parental Involvement.
6. There is no significant relationship in the mean scores of adolescents' and teachers' response towards Teacher's Involvement.
7. There is no significant relationship in the mean scores of parents' response and teachers' response towards Parental Involvement.
8. There is no significant relationship in the mean scores of parents' response and teachers' response towards Teacher's Involvement.
9. There is no significant relationship between the mean scores of adolescents' response and parents' response towards impact of Parental Involvement on Academic Achievement.
10. There is no significant relationship between the mean scores of adolescents' response and parents' response towards impact of Parental Involvement on Behaviour Adjustment.
11. There is no significant relationship between the mean scores of adolescents' response and teachers' response towards impact of Teacher's Involvement on Academic Achievement.
12. There is no significant relationship between the mean scores of adolescents' response and teacher's response towards impact of Teacher's Involvement on Behaviour Adjustment.

13. There is no significant gender difference of adolescents in the following variables :-

(a) Parental Involvement (PI).

(b) Impact of PI on Behaviour Adjustment (BA).

(c) Impact of PI on Academic Achievement (AA).

(d) Teacher's Involvement (TI).

(e) Impact of TI on Behaviour Adjustment (BA).

(f) Impact of TI on Academic Achievement (AA).

14. There is no significant impact of following constructs of PI on BA as perceived by adolescents :-

(a) Emotional.

(b) Aspiration.

(c) Structure.

(d) School & Studies.

(e) Friends.

15. There is no significant impact of following constructs of PI on AA as perceived by adolescents :-

(a) Emotional.

(b) Aspiration.

(c) Structure.

(d) School & Studies.

(e) Friends.

16. There is no significant impact of following constructs of TI on BA as perceived by adolescents :-

(a) Emotional.

(b) Interaction with parents.

(c) Instrumental.

(d) Structure.

17. There is no significant impact of following constructs of TI on AA as perceived by adolescents :-

(a) Emotional.

(b) Interaction with parents.

(c) Instrumental.

(d) Structure.

6.7 Limitations & Scope of the Study

The impact of Parental and Teacher Involvement was limited to adolescents' 'Academic Achievement' and Behaviour Adjustment only. The other variables like self concept, self esteem, creativity, study habits, stress, family dynamics and school type, etc. were not included This research was restricted to the students of standard 9th and did not include those studying at any other level of education in school or college. The present research study involved only the students studying through the CBSE Board and not ICSE, SSC, IGCSE or IE.

The variable 'Academic Achievement' was studied with respect to adolescents' 'Academic Achievement' in their previous exam along with responses from participants (parents, teachers and adolescents) related to increased interest / keenness to work towards 'Academic Achievement'. The 'Academic Achievement' under other existing cognitive domains was not under the scope of this study.

The variable 'Behaviour Adjustment' was studied with respect to adolescents' ability to adjust to their environment at home and school only, which could be confirmed by them or their parents and teachers. The Behaviour Adjustment included constructs as listed in the research definitions only. The unobserved 'Behaviour Adjustment', as well those that happened at places other than home and school were not under the scope of the present research study.

The sample included students from public and private schools of the CBSE Board. Schools situated in Greater Mumbai were only included for the present research study. The schools coming under the jurisdiction of Navi Mumbai and Thane were not included. The present research study was conducted in English medium schools and it excluded schools with other mediums of instruction such as Marathi, Hindi.

The present research study includes gender difference of adolescents response with respect to parents' and teacher's involvement and its' impact. No other constrains like financial status, parents' education level, parental style, home environment, social stress of the students, gender difference of parents & teachers, etc. were considered for the present study. It focused only on impact of parental and teacher's involvement on 'Behaviour Adjustment' and 'Academic Achievement' of adolescents. It purposefully did not include involvement by others and their impact, nor did it include variables other than 'Academic Achievement' and 'Behaviour Adjustment' which may have also got affected by Parental and Teacher's Involvement.

6.8 Significance of the Study

Adolescents are the bearers of humanity for the future generations of the free world. With such onerous responsibility lined up for their delicate shoulders, it becomes vital that they are raised as healthy, happy individuals and to achieve this it is imperative they get appropriate support from parents and teachers.

Over time, parental involvement and teacher involvement have proved very pertinent, keeping both practitioners and theoreticians in the field of education busy. The researcher observed that many national and international literature claimed that everyone concerned – students, parents, teachers, schools, society as a whole – will benefit if parents and teachers are convinced to get involved in their children's education.

The present research study advocates that, in spite of the popularity of the concept, parental involvement and teacher involvement concepts are still vague, and their impact is rather unclear. This research study shall prove beneficial in understanding the scope of parental involvement and teacher involvement and also their impact on behaviour adjustment and academic achievement in adolescents. Parents are willing to give their support to their adolescent child at home and at school too but are often apprehensive or clueless as to how they could participate in their child's life. This research study helps them to not only understand their role but also how to guide their adolescent child to gain maximum benefit.

The research study also provides teachers with a framework to aid their students to improve their academic performance and interpersonal interactions. The significance of the present study is to facilitate all round development of adolescents with focus on 'Behaviour Adjustment' and 'Academic Achievement'. The researcher emphasises that parents and teachers should shoulder responsibility to show adolescents the right direction to improve themselves and this research helps in the same.

The present research study focuses on parental and teacher's involvement on adolescents studying in class 9th and its impact on adolescents' 'Behaviour Adjustment' as well as 'Academic Achievement'. Since scarcely any studies have been done in the past on this topic and it is the gap in the existing body of knowledge, the present research study is beneficial in filling these gaps.

The present research study is helpful to the schools, parents, teachers and students as it gives an understanding about how exactly the parental and teacher involvement in adolescent years can help in quantifiably improving the 'Academic Achievement' and 'Behaviour Adjustment'.

This research study throws light upon various constructs of parental and teacher involvement which facilitates in recommending parental and teachers involvement procedures beneficial for the 'Academic Performance' and 'Behaviour Adjustment' of adolescents, with collaboration of all stakeholders in the field of education like students, parents, teachers and school.

The present research study is especially significant in bringing to the fore the relatively lesser addressed inter-dependent variables, and in turn the multiple constructs, which cumulatively have a cascading effect in the shaping of adolescents as robust and capable citizens of the future world.

6.9 Research Design

The researcher designed models to measure parental and teacher involvement and its impact on behaviour adjustment and academic achievement. These models helped the researcher in conducting the study in a planned manner.

6.9.1 Model 1

For Measuring Impact of Parental Involvement

A model is an abstract way of schematising a process, so that the strategy can be generalised to solve similar problems in other fields. This model is inspired by PI Constructs' in Keith et al. and is aimed at finding the relationship between 'Parental Involvement' and 'Behaviour Adjustment', 'Parental Involvement' and 'Academic Achievement'.'Parental Involvement' is further divided into five constructs namely 'Emotional Involvement', 'Aspiration of Parents', 'Structure by Parents', and 'school & Studies Involvement'.

'Emotional Involvement' is the support parents give to their child to help him / her emotionally during adolescent years, 'Aspiration of Parents' refers to how the parents convey their future aspirations for their child so as to inspire and motivate them. 'Structuring by parents' takes account of the daily routine and timetable parents make to organise their child's life. 'School & Studies Involvement' consists of the activities parents participate with respect to their child's school and studies. 'Involvement with

Friends' comprises the extent to which the parents involve themselves with their child's friends.

The model tries to establish impact of 'Parental Involvement' with the help of above constructs on 'Behaviour Adjustment' as well as 'Academic Achievement' in adolescent students. Figure 44 shows the proposed model for measuring impact of 'Parental Involvement' on 'Behaviour Adjustment' and 'Academic Achievement'.

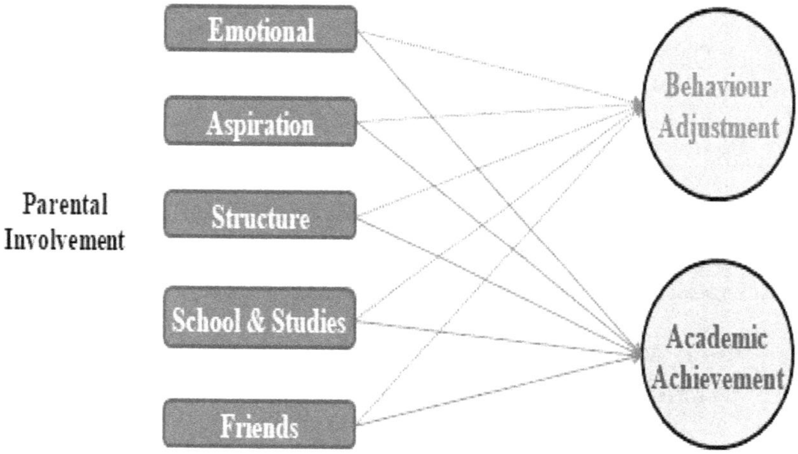

Figure 44 : Model Measuring impact of 'Parental Involvement' on 'Behaviour Adjustment' & 'Academic Achievement'

6.9.2 **Model 2**

For Measuring Impact of Teacher's Involvement

Figure 45 illustrates 'Model for Measuring impact of 'Teacher's Involvement' on 'Behaviour Adjustment' and 'Academic Achievement' and is inspired by the theoretical model of Affective Teacher-Student Relationships (TSR) and students' school Outcomes by Roorda D. L et al.

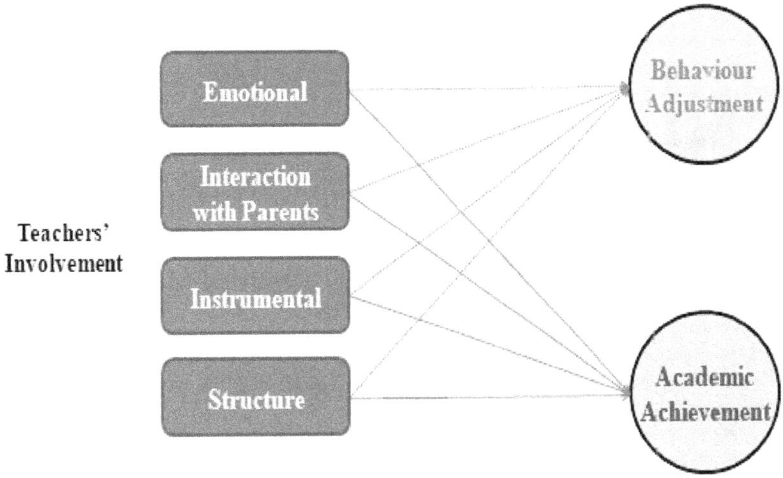

Figure 45 : Model Measuring impact of 'Teacher's Involvement' on 'Behaviour Adjustment' & 'Academic Achievement'

6.9.3 Model 3

For Measuring Impact of Parental & Teacher Involvement

The model is inspired by Development Indicators of Adolescents from Sinbad A.M. PI Constructs' in Keith et al. and theoretical model of Affective Teacher-Student Relationships (TSR) and students' school Outcomes by Roorda D. L et al. The endeavour of the model is to find relationship between Parental and Teacher's Involvement with 'Academic Achievement' and 'Behaviour Adjustment'. Figure 46 illustrates 'Model for measuring impact of Parental and Teacher Involvement on 'Behaviour Adjustment' and 'Academic Achievement'.

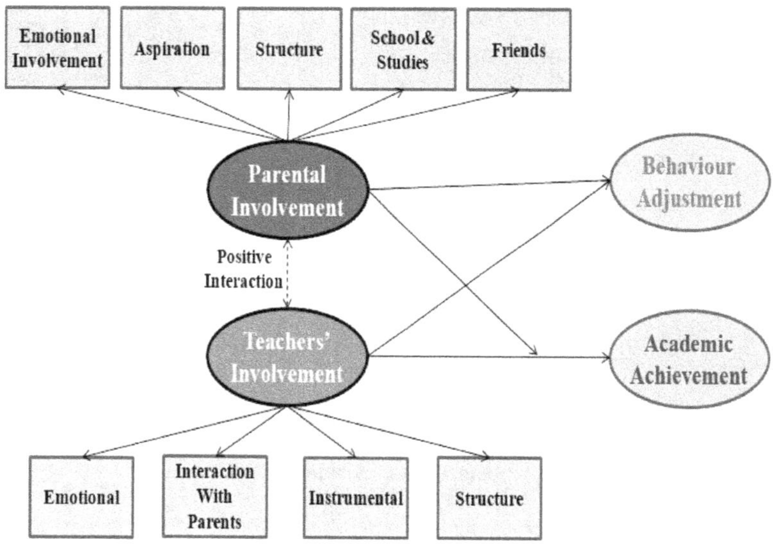

Figure 46 : Model Measuring impact of Parental & Teacher Involvement on 'Behaviour Adjustment' & 'Academic Achievement'

6.9.3.1 **'Parental Involvement'**

In the present research study, the researcher has considered 'Parental Involvement' as activities including looking after or monitoring a child's activities at home and in school during adolescent years. She further classified 'Parental Involvement' into following constructs :-

1. **Emotional Involvement.** Emotional Involvement includes emotional wellbeing of adolescents through expressing love, care and understanding to their child so that he / she feel confident to share his / her problems and emotional needs with them. Their availability of time, interest and emotional support is reflected in adolescents' perception for their Parents' emotional involvement which was measured through questions like "My parents take out time and sit with me whenever I have faltered", etc.

2. **Aspiration.** This involves parents' discussing about their as well as their child's ambitions and aims in life. Parents guiding and explaining different options that can be pursued by their child which will help him / her to choose a goal and decide his / her aspirations. Perception of adolescents with relation to Aspiration of Parents as an indicator of 'Parental Involvement' was measured through questions such as "My parents discuss with me my career options", etc.

3. **Structure.** This involves parents' monitoring and Structuring their child's daily activity or routine for studies, sports, screen time, etc. Stating clear expectations and rules; maintaining discipline via mechanisms as taking out time and explaining the mistake and motivating him / her to correct and using punishment as a last resort can be termed as Structuring by Parents. Adolescents were asked to rate their 'Parental Involvement' for Structuring at home through questions like "My parents keep a tab on my daily usage of TV / internet", etc.

4. **School & Studies.** It includes 'Parental Involvement' in their child's studies and school activities, their organised and unorganised interaction with teachers and guidance at home for studies. Adolescents rated parents for their help and guidance to improve their grades and accomplishments in school activities through questions such as "My parents take out time to teach me and help me in my assignments", etc.

5. **Friends.** Friends being a very crucial element of being an adolescent can't be ignored. Adolescents tend to get affected by how their parents treat their friends. Involvement of Parents in The present research study includes parents' interaction with their child's friends, organising events and activities with them, knowing them personally or guiding their child about whom to be friends with. Adolescents perceived

their 'Parental Involvement' with their friends through questions like "My parents get involved in all the activities with my friends like movie, picnic, etc", etc.

6.9.3.2 **Impact of Parental Involvement on 'Behaviour Adjustment'**

Adjustment can be described as the process by which living organisms maintain a balance between the needs and the circumstances Shaffer L.F(1961). Kulshrestha S.P. (1979) explained that the Adjustment process is a way for individuals to deal with tensions, stress, conflicts, etc., that come along the way to meet his or her needs. In this process, the individual also attempts to maintain a harmonious relationship with the environment. UNICEF (2011) report estimated that around 20 percent of the world's adolescents have mental health or behaviour problems. To understand 'Behaviour adjustment' in adolescents, problem behaviour and social competence are important criteria. Social competence can be measured in school through participation in class discussions, cooperation with classmates, completion of work, etc. while at home the parameters could be spending time with family, discussing personal issues and following instructions, etc. Problem Behaviour in class can be assessed though analysing items such as anxiety, disruption in class and difficulty following directions. Similarly, at home, lack of socialising, tantrums and aloofness can be signs of problem Behaviour.
In the present research study, 'Behaviour Adjustment' has been considered as the extent to which the adolescents are able to cope up to ever changing environment at home, outside and school.
Adolescents' perception of Parental' Involvement and its impact on Behaviour was observed through constructs like supportive emotional environment at home that made adolescents comfortable to ask questions or share their personal problems, improvement in Behaviour due to parents' intervention, discipline and rules for life.
Perceived impact on 'Behaviour Adjustment' was measured through questions like "My problems get solved whenever I approach my parents", etc.

6.9.3.3 **Impact of Parental Involvement on 'Academic Achievement'**

'Academic Achievement' has been explained as measured performance of a present level of Student knowledge through a series of standardised educational tests held in school. More frequently the term is used to depict performance in the curriculum subjects. 'Academic Achievement' or performance can be described as the degree to which a Student, teacher or the institution has accomplished their short or long-term

educational goals. It is also an indicator of mental wellness of an adolescent and unexpected fall in the performance could be a precursor of mental stress owing to some external factors. Numerous methods are useful in measuring the Academic performance including standardised Achievement test scores, report cards, grades and teacher ratings. In the present research study, the researcher has considered 'Academic Achievement' as the extent to which students achieve their short or long term educational goals. Cumulative marks or grades are also representative of 'Academic Achievement'.
students' descriptions of Parental' involvement and maintaining a supportive environment, that help and guide them to perform better academically and / or help them achieve their short term and long term goals for 'Academic Achievement', were used to measure impact of Parental' involvement on 'Academic Achievement'. Perceived impact on 'Academic Achievement' was measured through grades in previous exams along with questions like "My parents monitoring of my grades motivates me to perform better academically", etc.

6.9.3.4 **Process of Analysis of Questionnaires**

Adolescents' Questionnaire

The response set for all the questions utilised a 5-Point Likert Type Scale in order to match the previous items and be easier for students to use with choices ranging from 'Never' to 'Very Often'. The negatively worded items were reverse coded for scoring purposes.

The items in the section of the adolescents' questionnaire asked adolescents to react to various statements regarding 'My parents' wherein they were instructed to consider about either of the Parent or both, as applicable, for individual questions before they started marking the answers.

Parents' Questionnaire

Parents' questionnaire carried same questions but worded from parents' point of view to compare the perception of parents and adolescents for 'Parental Involvement' in all sub groups namely emotional, aspiration, structure, school & studies and friends.

6.9.3.5 **'Teacher's Involvement'**

In the present research study, the researcher has considered 'Teacher's Involvement' as activities including motivating, monitoring and influencing a child's activities in school during adolescent years. She further classified Teacher's Involvement into following constructs :-

1. **Emotional Involvement.** 'Emotional Involvement' involves teacher's support and interest in students' wellbeing along with their Academic progress. Teachers spending time, showing interest in students' life, their sense of caring and emotional support are some parameters which exceeds the 'required' teaching Behaviours and is reflected in students' perception of teacher's attempts to connect on an emotional level. Students were requested to rate their teacher's care for their wellbeing via questions like "My class teacher gives personal attention to every Student in the class", etc.
2. **Interaction with Parents.** 'Interaction with Parents' includes communication of teachers with parents in the form of feedbacks, counselling session, PTMs, etc. It also includes whether the teacher is able to recognise students' Academic and / or emotional distress. Students' perception about the interaction was measured using questions like "My class teacher keeps my parents updated about my performance in school", etc.
3. **Instrumental Support.** 'Instrumental Support' involves teaching practices which teachers incorporate to impart Academic concepts to the entire class and individual students, using diverse strategies (e.g. smart boards, group discussions, etc.) to provide additional learning experience. Students rated teachers for their help and guidance to improve their classroom grades and accomplishments through questions like "My class teacher uses teaching aids and innovative techniques (e.g. smart board, quiz, crossword, etc.) while teaching in class", etc.
4. **Structure Support.** 'Structure by Teacher's involves stating clear expectations, providing rewards, fair treatment and consequences, feedback for mistakes and ways for improvement, maintain discipline via mechanisms as taking out time and explaining the wrongdoer his / her mistake and motivate him / her to correct it and using punishment only as a last resort. Questions were asked to measure the perceived Structure support by Teachers as "My class teacher separately counsels me when I make any mistake", etc.

6.9.3.6 Impact of Teacher's Involvement on 'Behaviour Adjustment'

In the present research study, the researcher has considered as 'Behaviour Adjustment' as the extent to which the adolescents are able to cope up to ever changing environment at home, outside and school.

students' descriptions of Teacher's Involvement and creation of supportive emotional environment that made them comfortable to share their personal problems, ask questions, adjust their Behaviour as per rules, lead disciplined life, etc. were used to measure the impact of Teacher's Involvement on Behavioural Adjustment as perceived by adolescents. Perceived impact on Behavioural Adjustment was measured through questions like "I find my Teacher's instructions about the rules and its importance helpful to mould my Behaviour positively", etc.

6.9.3.7 **Impact of Teacher's Involvement on 'Academic Achievement'**

In the present research study, the researcher has considered 'Academic Achievement' as the extent to which students achieve their short or long term educational goals. Cumulative marks or grades are also representative of 'Academic Achievement'.
students' descriptions of Teacher's Involvement and creation of supportive environment, that help and guide them to perform better academically and / or help them achieve their short term and long term goals for 'Academic Achievement', were used to measure impact of Teacher's Involvement on 'Academic Achievement'. Perceived impact on 'Academic Achievement' was measured through grades in previous exams along with questions like "With constant monitoring of homework and assignment by my class teacher, I complete my homework and improve my assignments on time", etc.

6.9.3.8 **Process of Analysis of Questionnaires**

Adolescents' Questionnaire

The response set for all of the items utilised a 5-Point Likert Type Scale in order to match the previous items and be easier for students to use with choices ranging from 'Never' to 'Very Often'. The negatively worded items were reverse coded for scoring purposes. The questions in the section of the adolescents' questionnaire asked adolescents to react to various statements regarding "My teacher". However, since multiple teachers through the day taught participants, students assumed 'Class Teacher' as that teacher for marking the answers to avoid any confusion.

Teacher's Questionnaire

Teacher's questionnaire had same questions but worded from teacher's point of view to compare the perception of teachers and adolescent for Teacher's Involvement in all sub groups namely emotional, Interaction with Parents, Instrumental and structural support.

6.10 Procedure

For the present research study, theoretical models were developed by the researcher on the basis of extensive study conducted on the related existing body of knowledge. Further, a set of questionnaire was formulated by the researcher and vetted by seven renowned experts for adolescents, parents and teachers each. The data was then collected from adolescents, their parents and teachers of class 9th from CBSE schools of Mumbai city. Once the data was collected, it was analysed by the researcher using various descriptive and inferential analysis techniques and hypothesis was tested. The final stage involved documenting the results and inferences of the research. Figure 47 shows detailed procedure followed in the present research study.

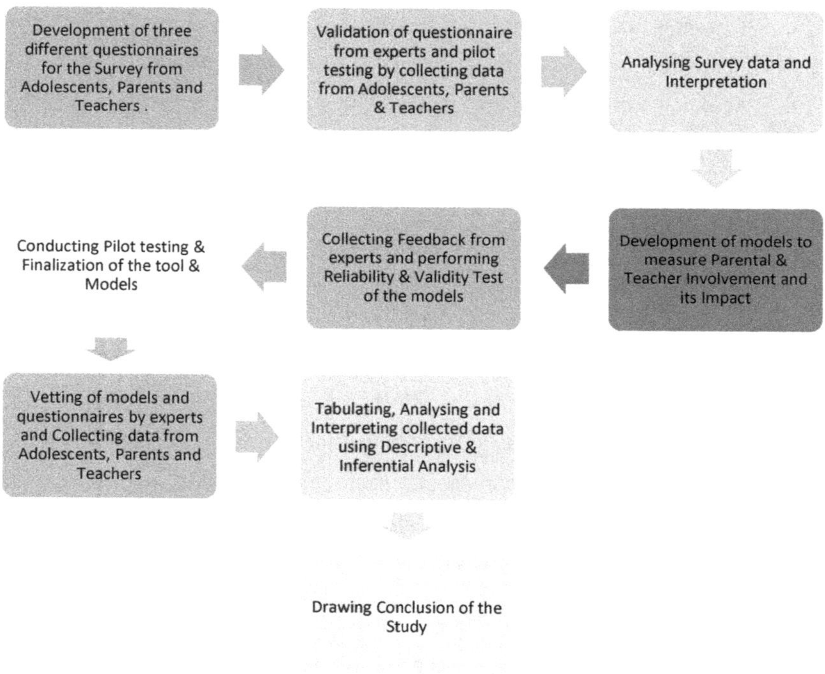

Figure 47 : Procedure Followed in the Present Research Study

6.11 Testing of Hypotheses

Testing of Hypothesis 1

($H1_0$) : There is no significant impact of 'Parental Involvement' on 'Academic Achievement' for total adolescent sample.

Conclusion

For the total Adolescent sample, it was observed that they perceived positive impact of 'Parental Involvement' (PI) on 'Academic Achievement' (AA). H***ence the Null Hypothesis is rejected*** and it is concluded that there is a 'Significant' relationship between PI and AA as perceived by adolescents.

Discussion

The relationship perceived by adolescents is positive and ***'Moderate'*** Perceptions and expectations of adolescents as reflected in the questionnaire (Appx A), might be the reasons for the same :-

1. Parents discuss about career options.
2. With parents help adolescents able to perform better.
3. Regular interaction of parents and teachers guide adolescents to improve academically.
4. Structuring access to T.V/internet, adolescents have more time to focus on studies.

Thus, it may be inferred from the above analysis that the adolescents might be comfortable with whatever time and help their parents are able to provide them to improve their Academic performance, leading them to their positive perception of impact of PI on AA. However, reasons for impact to be '***Moderate'*** may be due to a) Difference in expectations or expectations being met partially, b) Parents' limited or lack of understanding for the novel education system, c) their level of education or stream of qualification, d) Different expectation and perception of individual adolescent.

Testing of Hypothesis 2

H2₀ : There is no significant impact of 'Parental Involvement' on 'Behaviour Adjustment' of total Adolescent sample.

Conclusion

For the total Adolescent sample, it was observed that that they perceived positive impact of 'Parental Involvement' (PI) on 'Behaviour Adjustment' (BA). ***Hence the Null Hypothesis is rejected*** and it is concluded that there is a 'Significant' relationship between PI and BA as perceived by adolescents.

Discussion

The relationship perceived by adolescents is positive but '***Low***'. Perceptions and expectations of adolescents for the following items, as reflected in the questionnaire (Appx A), might be the reason for the same :-

1. Parents reprimanding or ridiculing when they falter.
2. Parents deciding on the clothes/food choices.
3. Parents constantly compare with other boys and girls.
4. Adolescents maybe finding parents preaching unnecessary and tend to ignore.

Thus, it can be inferred that adolescents' acceptance of their parents' intention for their betterment leads them for positive impact of PI on BA. However, reasons for impact to be '***Low***' may be due to a) involvement perceived to be overbearing or excessive, b) Parents' busy routine might not be allowing them to spend constructive time with adolescents so as to help them in 'Behaviour Adjustment', c) the difference in opinion and expectations due to generation gap, d) Different expectation and perception of individual adolescent.

Testing of Hypothesis 3

$H3_0$: There is no significant impact of Teacher's Involvement on 'Academic Achievement' of total Adolescent sample.

Conclusion

For the total Adolescent sample, it was observed that they perceived positive impact of 'Teacher's Involvement' (TI) on 'Academic Achievement' (AA). ***Hence the Null Hypothesis is rejected*** and it is concluded that there is a 'Significant' relationship between TI and AA as perceived by adolescents.

Discussion

The impact perceived by adolescents is positive but '***Moderate***'. Perceptions and expectations of adolescents for the following items, as reflected in the questionnaire (Appx A), might be the reason for the same :-

1. Class teacher gives personal attention to every Student in the class.

2. Class teacher share adolescents' achievements with their parents.

3. Class teacher arranges for remedial classes for the subjects adolescents are weak in, which help them in coping up.

4. Class teacher uses teaching aids and innovative techniques (e.g. Smart board, quiz, crossword, etc.) while teaching in class.

Thus it can be inferred that adolescents spend lot of time with teachers and look up to them for Academic guidance. Teacher's knowledge prowess, sincerity and ways of teaching might be the reasons for perceived positive relationship between TI and AA by adolescents. However, reasons for impact to be '***Moderate***' may be due to a) Lack of time adolescents spend with the class teacher, b) Excessive syllabus and busy timetable, c) Inability of teachers to explain few topics or solve doubts, d) Different expectation and perception of individual adolescent.

Testing of Hypothesis 4

$H4_0$: There is no significant impact of Teacher's Involvement on 'Behaviour Adjustment' of total Adolescent sample.

Conclusion

For the total Adolescent sample, it was observed that both boys and girls perceived positive impact of 'Teacher's Involvement' (TI) on 'Behaviour Adjustment' (BA). ***Hence the Null Hypothesis is rejected*** and it is concluded that there is a 'Significant' relationship between TI and BA as perceived by adolescents.

Discussion

The relationship perceived by adolescents is positive and ***'Moderate'***. Perception of adolescents for following items, as reflected in the questionnaire (Appx A), might be the reasons for the same :-

1. Class teacher discusses about their likes and interests.

2. Class teacher involves all children in all class activities.

3. Adolescents find teacher's instructions about the rules and its importance helpful to mould their Behaviour positively.

4. Adolescents comfortably discuss their personal problems with their class teacher.

Thus it can be inferred that teacher's counselling to make adolescents understand rules and their importance, explanation of virtues to become a perfect individual and / or friendly Behaviour might be the reasons for perceived positive relationship between TI and BA by both adolescent boys and girls. School being a second home to adolescents offers them many lessons of life, while teachers are adults whom adolescents idolise and look up for inspiration. However, reasons for impact to be ***'Moderate'*** may be due to a) Lack of time adolescents spend with the class teacher, b) Limited trust , c) Apprehension of adolescents to discuss personal problems, d) Different point of view for accepted Behaviour.

Testing of Hypothesis 5

$H5_0$: There is no significant relationship in the mean scores of Adolescents' response and parents' response towards 'Parental Involvement'.

Conclusion

The relationship between mean scores of Adolescents and Parents is ***'Significant'*** with respect to PI, ***hence the Null Hypothesis is rejected*** and it is concluded that there is a 'Significant' relationship between the mean scores of adolescents' response and parents' response towards 'Parental Involvement'.

Discussion

The level of 'Parental Involvement' is perceived to be same by adolescents and parents, The reason might be similar perception of following items, as reflected in the questionnaire (Appx A & B) :-

1. Parents discuss with their children to know about their inclination for future career Aspiration.

2. Parents ensure to spend one evening together, either going out or playing a board game.

3. Parents keep themselves available to help solve their child's difficulties in studies and help in assignments / projects.

4. Parents inviting their child's friends at home.

Thus it can be inferred that adolescence is a difficult stage for both parents and adolescents as there is rapid change in the adolescents' life where an individual grows physically, mentally and socially. Parents' sensitive and thoughtful Behaviour might be the reason for adolescents' positive perception of PI, while parents' contentment for their efforts to get positively involved with their child may possibly be the reason for their positive perception. However, reasons for PI to be ***'Moderate'*** may be due to a) limited time spent together, b) difference in opinion and perception.

Testing of Hypothesis 6

$H6_0$: There is no significant relationship in the mean scores of Adolescents' and Teacher's response towards Teacher's Involvement.

Conclusion

The relationship between mean scores of Adolescents and Teachers is ***'Non Significant'*** with respect to TI, ***hence the Null Hypothesis is accepted*** and it is concluded that there is no 'Significant' relationship in the mean scores of Adolescents' and Teacher's response towards Teacher's Involvement.

Discussion

The level of perception of 'Teacher's Involvement' is different for teachers and adolescents, The reason might be different perceptions and expectations of teachers and adolescents on following items, as reflected in the questionnaire (Appx A & C) :-

1. Class teacher discussing about likes and interests of the students.

2. Class teacher sharing achievements with parents.

3. Class teacher encourage for asking questions/doubts.

4. Appreciation by the class teacher when the students perform well in curricular and / or co-curricular activities.

Thus it can be inferred that there is a great change in teachers and adolescents' Behaviour from a primary grade to being in middle school due to many reasons like a) Increase in syllabus, b) Lack of time, c) Change in temperament of adolescents. Adolescents' expectations not being met by their teachers due to above changes might be the reason for their lower perception of TI. On the other hand, Teacher's satisfaction about their effort to get positively involved with their students may be the reason for teacher's higher level of perception of TI.

Testing of Hypothesis 7

$H7_0$: There is no significant relationship in the mean scores of parents' response and Teacher's response towards 'Parental Involvement'.

Conclusion

The relationship between mean scores of Parents and Teachers is '***Not Significant'*** with respect to 'Parental Involvement', ***hence the Null Hypothesis is accepted*** and it is concluded that there is no 'Significant' relationship in the mean scores of parents' and Teacher's response towards 'Parental Involvement'.

Discussion

The level of 'Parental Involvement' is perceived to be different by parents and teachers, The reason may be different perceptions of parents and teachers on following items, as reflected in the questionnaire (Appx B & C) :-

1. Parents' willingness to attend all scheduled events and their readiness for interaction with teachers.

2. Parents' approach / frequency for "Parents Teacher's Interactive Session".

3. Parents' participation in activities and projects of their child in school.

4. Parents' interest in child's performance in studies/ co-curricular activities.

Thus it can be inferred that teacher's have certain expectations from parents for their involvement in adolescents' school and studies related activities, like attending PTMs, regular interaction with teachers, participation in school activities, etc. The reason for teacher's perception maybe due to the above expectations not getting met either partially or fully. On the other hand, as the total parents' population is from an urban metropolitan city where parents have a busy lifestyle, which might cause them to miss few events in school, it could lead to different opinions by parents and teachers with regards to PI.

Testing of Hypothesis 8

H8₀ : There is no significant relationship in the mean scores of parents' response and Teacher's response towards Teacher's Involvement.

Conclusion

The relationship between mean scores of parents and teachers is ***'Significant'*** with respect to TI, ***hence the Null Hypothesis is rejected*** and it is concluded that there is a 'Significant' relationship in the mean scores of parents' response and teacher's response towards Teacher's Involvement.

Discussion

The level of 'Teacher's Involvement' is perceived to be same (***'High'***) by parents and teachers, similar perception of parents and teachers on following items, as reflected in the questionnaire (Appx B & Appx C) maybe the reason :-

1. Teacher's support helps in Academic improvement of adolescents.

2. Interaction with teachers helps parents in understanding their child.

3. Class teacher discusses about child's performance or Behaviour with their parents.

4. Positive changes observed by parents in their child's Behaviour with teacher's support.

Thus it can be inferred that teachers are a pillar of support to adolescents in their growing years and parents too feel comforted when their child is in care of supporting and caring teachers. Parents' confidence on their child's teacher for guiding their child to achieve his / her best in academics and Behaviour aspects might be the reason of their positive assessment of TI. They might have also observed positive changes attributing to teacher's counselling and guidance, strengthening their perception. Furthermore, teacher's satisfaction with their efforts of constructively helping their students in academics and Behaviour aspects along with observed affirmative changes in their students' Behaviour may be the reason for their positive perception.

Testing of Hypothesis 9

$H9_0$: There is no significant relationship between the mean scores of Adolescents' response and parents' response towards impact of 'Parental Involvement' on 'Academic Achievement'.

Conclusion

The relationship between mean scores of adolescents and parents is ***'Significant'*** with respect to impact of PI on AA, ***hence the Null Hypothesis is rejected*** and it is concluded that there is a 'Significant' relationship between the mean scores of adolescents' response and parents' response towards impact of 'Parental Involvement' on 'Academic Achievement'.

Discussion

The level of impact of PI on AA is perceived to be same (***'Moderate'***) by parents and adolescents, which may be due to similar expectations and perceptions of parents and adolescents for the following items, as reflected in the questionnaire (Appx A and Appx B) :-

1. Parents motivating adolescents to do their best in academics.

2. Parents taking out time to teach their children and help them in assignments.

3. Adolescents getting appreciated for their hard work by parents.

4. Parents continuous communication with teachers motivating adolescents to perform better.

Thus it can be inferred that both parents and adolescents perception to PI affecting AA is at similar level. Adolescents concur with parents that their involvement moderately helps them in 'Academic Achievement'. This is probably due to their acceptance of whatever time parents' are able to take out from their busy schedule; or maybe they are content with the guidance from parents in spite of their limitations. Furthermore, maybe the parents perceive that they are able to moderately contribute to the academic growth of their child but not as much as they would want, due to their busy schedules or inability to help their child in school activities and assignments.

Testing of Hypothesis 10

$H10_0$: There is no significant relationship between the mean scores of Adolescents' response and parents' response towards impact of 'Parental Involvement' on 'Behaviour Adjustment'.

Conclusion

The relationship between mean scores of Adolescents and Parents is ***'Not Significant'*** with respect to impact of PI on BA, ***hence the Null Hypothesis is 'Accepted'*** and it is concluded that there is no 'Significant' relationship between the mean scores of adolescents' response and parents' response towards impact of 'Parental Involvement' on 'Behaviour Adjustment'.

Discussion

The level of impact of PI on BA is perceived to be different by adolescents and parents, Different responses of adolescents and parents might be due to different perception and expectations for following items, as reflected in the questionnaire (Appx A and Appx B) :-

1. Adolescents taking parents reprimand / counselling positively and changing their Behaviour accordingly.

2. Adolescents comfort at discussing their personal problems with their parents.

3. Parents observe their child to get irritated and doing the exact opposite when they try to suggest their choices of clothes, friends and food to them.

4. Parents observe that discussion with their child lead to arguments followed by him / her getting upset and walking away.

Thus it can be inferred that adolescence is a phase where children go through a personality conflict, wherein their self belief of being an adult or grown up may lead to their judgment of parents' expectations or counselling for their Behaviour to be overbearing or too strict, leading them to their perception of relationship between PI & BA. Parents' perception that their expectations for their child's Behaviour might not be getting fulfilled, maybe due to digital distraction or peer pressure on adolescents. Furthermore, parents' busy routine might be making them think that they are not able to spend constructive time with adolescents, so as to help them in 'Behaviour Adjustment', resulting in different perception of relationship between PI and BA.

Testing of Hypothesis 11

$H11_0$: There is no significant relationship between the mean scores of Adolescents' response and Teacher's response towards impact of Teacher's Involvement on 'Academic Achievement'.

Conclusion

The relationship between mean scores of Adolescents and Teachers is ***'Significant'*** with respect to impact of TI on AA, ***hence the Null Hypothesis is rejected*** and it is concluded that there is a 'Significant' relationship between the mean scores of adolescents' response and teacher's response towards impact of Teacher's Involvement on 'Academic Achievement'.

Discussion

The level of impact of TI on AA is perceived to be same (***'Moderate'***) by adolescents and teachers, which may be due to similar expectation and perception by parents and adolescents for following items, as reflected in the questionnaire (Appx A and Appx C) :-

1. Class teacher encourages students to ask doubts and questions in class.

2. Class teacher uses teaching aids and innovative techniques while teaching.

3. The teacher finds the students to complete homework and assignments on time with her / his constant monitoring.

4. The teacher finds students approach him / her regarding the difficulties they face in any subject.

Thus it can be inferred that adolescents trust on teacher's knowledge prowess, sincerity and ways of teaching might be the reasons for perceived positive relationship between TI and AA, while they sometimes might be getting flustered by teacher's continuous watchfulness leading to '***Moderate***' rating. On the other hand, teachers may be content with their efforts and ways of teaching to guide their students academically, which may be the reason for their perception of positive relationship between TI and AA of adolescents, while their observation of adolescents getting stressed out sometimes due to constant vigilance on studies may be the reason for their assessment as '***Moderate***'.

Testing of Hypothesis 12

$H12_0$: There is no significant relationship between the mean scores of Adolescents' response and teacher's response towards impact of Teacher's Involvement on 'Behaviour Adjustment'.

Conclusion

The relationship between mean scores of adolescents and teachers is '***Non Significant***' with respect to impact of TI on BA, ***hence the Null Hypothesis is accepted*** and it is concluded that there is no 'Significant' relationship between the mean scores of Adolescents' response and Teacher's response towards impact of Teacher's Involvement on 'Behaviour Adjustment'.

Discussion

The level of impact of TI on BA is perceived to be different by adolescents and teachers. Different responses of adolescents and teachers might be due to different perceptions and expectations for following items, as reflected in the questionnaire (Appx A and Appx C) :-

1. Discussion by class teacher about likes and interests of students.

2. Class teacher involving all children in all class activities.

3. Adolescents perception for teacher's instructions about the rules and its importance to mould their Behaviour positively.

4. Adolescents comfort in discussing their personal problems.

Thus it can be inferred that adolescents' unease to share their personal problems with teachers, might not be letting them connect to teachers emotionally, leading to their perception. Furthermore, their reluctance to follow rules and / or perception of counselling to be strict or unnecessary might be further a reason for their lower perception. While teacher's satisfaction in their efforts to counsel adolescents about rules, as also its importance to help them mould their Behaviour, might be the reasons for their higher rating for impact of TI on BA. Also their observation in improvement of adolescents' Behaviour post counselling might be another reason.

Testing of Hypothesis 13

H13₀ : There is no significant gender difference in the following variables :-

1. Parental Involvement (PI).
2. Impact of Parental Involvement' (PI) on Academic Achievement (AA).
3. Impact of Parental Involvement' (PI) on Behaviour Adjustment (BA).
4. Teacher's Involvement (TI).
5. Impact of Teacher's Involvement (TI) on Academic Achievement (AA).
6. Impact of Teacher's Involvement (TI) on Behaviour Adjustment (BA).

Conclusion

It was observed that that there was ***'No Significant' Difference'*** with respect to gender in the mean scores of 'Parental Involvement' (PI), impact of PI on AA, and impact of TI on AA. While ***'Significant' Difference'*** was observed with respect to gender in the mean scores of impact of PI on BA , 'Teacher's Involvement'(TI) and impact of TI on BA.

Discussion

The gender difference in the mean score for impact of PI on BA may be due to higher perception of impact of PI on BA by boys as compared to girls. In evolving Indian society the expectations of adolescent girls are also changing where they expect equal rights and rules as exist for boys. The aberration of rules might be the reason for girls to perceive restrictions and involvement by parents as excessive or overbearing resulting in their lower perception.

The gender difference in the mean score for Teacher's Involvement (TI) may be due to higher perception of TI by boys as compared to girls. The reason for this difference in perception may be either due to boys having fewer expectations from teachers than girls or their expectations are being met. Girls on the other hand being more sensitive may have greater expectations from teachers or their expectations are partially or fully are not being met could be the reasons for their lower perception.

The gender difference in the mean score for impact of TI on BA may be due to higher perception of impact of TI on BA by girls as compared to boys. The reason for this difference in perception may be either that girls might be finding counselling by teachers affective in understanding rules and its importance and thereby guiding them to mould their Behaviour accordingly while the perception of boys might not be same.

Testing of Hypothesis 14

$H14_0$: There is no significant impact of following constructs of PI on AA from Adolescents' response :-

1. Emotional.
2. Aspiration.
3. Structure.
4. School & Studies.
5. Friends.

Conclusion

It can be observed that "Parents' Aspiration", "Structure by Parents" and "Involvement in school & Studies" were the constructs which were observed to have positive impact on 'Academic Achievement' of adolescents, while "Involvement with Friends" and "Emotional Involvement" were not found to have any 'Significant' relationship with 'Academic Achievement' of adolescents.

Discussion

The reason for positive impact of 'Parents' Aspiration', 'Parents' Structuring', 'Involvement in school & Studies' as constructs of 'Parental Involvement' on 'Academic Achievement' may be due to perception of Adolescents for following constructs :-

(a) 'Parents' Aspiration' that includes discussions by parents about their Aspiration for their child's future, their effort to know their child's goals along with regular motivation from parents to achieve these goals. These activities probably might be helpful in building the children's confidence and willingness to work towards their goal, inspiring them to work harder.

(b) 'Structure by Parents' involves keeping tab of TV and internet usage, timetable at home, ensuring completion of homework and assignments. Structuring may be helping adolescents to plan their day giving him / her more time for studies which probably might be helping them in improving their 'Academic Achievement'.

(c) 'Involvement with school & Studies' includes parents helping their children in completing their projects and homework, parents keeping track of marks and exams, attending school events and PTMs. 'Parental Involvement' in the studies and school might be making children realise the importance of studies thereby encouraging them to study harder. Furthermore, with parents' offering to assist their children in studies, children might feel encouraged to seek their assistance.

'Emotional Involvement' and 'Involvement with Friends' as constructs of 'Parental Involvement' were not found to impact 'Academic Achievement' as perceived by Adolescents. Following might be the reason for the same :-

(a) 'Emotional Involvement' which includes talking about school events, discussing personal problems and appreciation for their good work. May be the adolescents' perceived emotional involvement as inadequate as per their expectations or might not be motivating them for improving their Academic performance.

(b) 'Involvement with Friends' includes parents inviting their child's friends at home, involving in activities with friends like movies, picnic, etc. Children relate to their friends the most during adolescence. Either parents might be judging their friends or comparing with them in academics, leading to adolescents' perception of 'Parental Involvement' with friends not impacting their 'Academic Achievement'.

Testing of Hypothesis 15

H15$_0$: There is no significant impact of following constructs of PI on BA from adolescents' response :-

1. Emotional.
2. Aspiration.
3. Structure.
4. School & Studies.
5. Friends.

Conclusion

It can be observed that that "Parents' Emotional Involvement" and "Parents' Involvement' with Friends" were the constructs which were observed to have positive impact on 'Behaviour Adjustment' of adolescents while "Parents' Aspiration", "Structure by Parents" and "Involvement in school & Studies" were not found to have any 'Significant' relationship with 'Behaviour Adjustment' of adolescents.

Discussion

'Emotional Involvement' and 'Involvement with Friends' as constructs of 'Parental Involvement' were found to impact 'Behaviour Adjustment', as perceived by adolescents. Following may be the reason for the same :-

(a) 'Emotional Involvement' includes talking about school events, discussing personal problems and appreciation for their good work. May be when parents appreciate children or help them in solving their personal problems, children feel relaxed and stress free, which makes them want to put effort in behaving as per parents' expectation.

(b) 'Involvement with Friends' includes parents inviting their child's friends at home, involving in activities with friends like movies, picnic, etc. Adolescents relate to their friends the most and when parents get involved in activities with their friend or make an effort to know their friends, they might feel their choices are being accepted and respected, which in turn motivates them to behave in a manner agreeable by their parents.

'Parents' Aspiration', 'Structuring' and 'Involvement in school & Studies' were found to have no impact on 'Behaviour Adjustment' as perceived by adolescents. Following may be the reason for the same :-

(a) 'Parents Aspiration' includes discussions by parents about their Aspiration for their child's future, their effort to know their child's goals along with regular motivation from parents to achieve these goals. These activities probably focus more on academics and probably parents might not be focusing on their Aspiration related to Behaviour.

(b) 'Structure by Parents' involves keeping tab of TV and internet usage, timetable at home, ensuring completion of homework and assignments. Children might feel that their life is being controlled, causing stress or making them revolt and behave in an unruly manner.

(c) 'Involvement in school & Studies' includes parents helping their children in completing their projects and homework, parents keeping track of marks and exams, attending school events and PTMs. 'Parental Involvement' in the studies and school might be making children strained or they might feel the monitoring too overbearing.

Testing of Hypothesis 16

$H16_0$: There is no significant impact of following constructs of TI on AA from adolescents' response :-

1. Emotional.
2. Interaction with Parents.
3. Instrumental.
4. Structure.

Conclusion

It can be observed that "Teacher's Emotional Involvement" and "Teacher's Instrumental Support" were the constructs which were observed to have positive impact on 'Academic Achievement' of adolescents while "Teacher's Interaction with Parents" and "Structure by Teachers" were not found to have any 'Significant' relationship with 'Academic Achievement' of adolescents.

Discussion

'Emotional Involvement' and 'Instrumental Support', as constructs of Teacher's Involvement, were found to impact 'Academic Achievement', as perceived by adolescents. Following might be the reason for the same :-

(a) 'Emotional Involvement' by Teachers includes personal attention to each child, discussion of likes and dislikes of children, involvement in class activities. When teachers make an effort to know their students and involve them in class activities, maybe the children feel connected to teachers, increasing their trust on teachers and their teaching or make them more attentive during teaching sessions, helping improve their Academic performance.

(b) 'Instrumental Support 'includes using innovating teaching methods, encouraging asking doubts, checking homework and assignments. When teachers use interesting and innovative teaching techniques, it is quite possible that students' attention span, interest in the subject or their understanding improves. Teacher's effort to teach the subject could also be making children respect them and thus inspiring them to put more efforts in studying better.

'Academic Achievement' of adolescents was found to have no relationship with 'Interaction with Parents' and 'Structure by Teacher's as constructs of Teacher's Involvement, as perceived by adolescents. Following may the reasons for the same :-

(a) 'Interaction with Parents' includes teachers updating parents about child's performance, informing parents if the child seems upset or disturbed. The constant interaction might be irking students, making them feel stressed, which might be affecting their concentration or fading their will to study.

(b) 'Structuring by Teacher's includes planning fun activities, appreciating children for good work and Behaviour, explaining rules and ensuring everyone follows it. Adolescence is the age where children do not like rules in general and probably repetition of rules and its importance by teachers or too tight schedule in class cause their attention to distract from studies.

Testing of Hypothesis 17

$H17_0$: There is no significant impact of following constructs of TI on BA from adolescents' response :-

1. Emotional.
2. Interaction with Parents.
3. Instrumental.
4. Structure.

Conclusion

It can be observed that "Teacher's Emotional Involvement" and "Teacher's Interaction with Parents" were the constructs which were observed to have positive impact on 'Behaviour Adjustment' of adolescents while "Structure by Teachers" and "Instrumental Support by Teachers" were not found to have any 'Significant' relationship with 'Behaviour Adjustment' of adolescents.

Discussion

'Behaviour Adjustment' of adolescents was found to have positive relationship with 'Emotional Involvement' and 'Interaction with Parents' as constructs of Teacher's Involvement, as perceived by adolescents. Following may the reasons for the same :-

(a) 'Emotional Involvement by Teacher's includes personal attention to each child, discussion of likes and dislikes of children, involvement in class activities. Teacher's effort to know their students and to involve them in class activities may be creating a stronger bond between teacher and students, reducing their stress and making them behave in accordance of teacher's liking.

(b) 'Interaction with Parents' includes teachers updating parents about child's performance, informing parents if the child seems upset or disturbed. The interaction between parents and teachers might be helping them to understand the reasons of the child's mental state allowing them to help him / her come out of the situation from both sides impacting his / her 'Behaviour Adjustment'.

'Behaviour Adjustment' of adolescents was found to have no relationship with 'Structure by Teacher's and 'Instrumental Support' as constructs of Teacher's Involvement, as perceived by adolescents. Following may the reasons for the same :-

(a) 'Structuring by Teacher's includes planning fun activities, appreciating children for good work and Behaviour, explaining rules and ensuring everyone follows it. Adolescence is the age where children do not like rules in general and probably repetition of rules and its importance by teachers or too tight schedule in class maybe the reason for their rowdy Behaviour.

(b) 'Instrumental Support' includes using innovating teaching methods, encouraging asking doubts, checking homework and assignments. Teacher's usage of interesting and innovative teaching techniques might be helping them academically but probably it does not inspire them to improve their Behaviour.

6.12 Conclusion & Findings of the Study

6.12.1 Impact of 'Parental Involvement' on Adolescents

Parents are an integral part of adolescents' life and a facilitator for easier transition of adolescents from childhood to adulthood. The present research study persevered to understand relationship of parents with their adolescents and its impact on their 'Behaviour Adjustment' and 'Academic Achievement'. After descriptive and inferential analysis, the research demonstrated positive influence of family factors on adolescents' education and also found evidence that 'Parental Involvement' was positively correlated with adolescents' 'Academic Achievement', which was in line with previous studies done by Epstein et al.(1992); Fan et al. (1999); Singh & Gera (2016); Talluri & Esther (2017), Bhavna & Kaur (2015). Children whose parents get involved in their formal education tend to do better in school and thus 'Parental Involvement' can be termed as a powerful influence on the learning of middle school students (Keith et al, 1993). Parents have a 'Significant' role in student's 'Academic Achievement' Smith (2011).

Most of the adolescents perceived PI as 'Moderate', which was in line with Vijayalakshmi & Muniappan (2016); Abdirahman et al. (2012). The rating of adolescents and parents converged for PI and impact of PI on AA, while it varied for impact of PI on BA. Mean score of impact of PI on AA was found to have no gender difference in our study, which was unlike findings of Talluri & Esther (2017) where girls perceived impact of 'Parental Involvement' on 'Academic Achievement' to be greater as compared to boys. Mean scores of impact of PI on BA indicated boys to perceive greater impact on their Behaviour through PI as compared to girls, as was revealed by Nilsson (2006) where girls reported to have more conflicts with parents as they felt closely monitored and felt suffocated. Junger et al. (2004) and Svensson (2004) also in their research found parents to be more worried about their daughters than about their son, thus leading girls to be more controlled by parents. Further, it was seen that parents and teacher's view on PI and its impact was of contrast view, where parents' perception was higher than that of teachers.

The current study found 'Aspiration of Parents', 'Involvement in school & Studies', 'Structuring by Parents' as positive parameters of 'Parental Involvement' (PI) to impact 'Academic Achievement' (AA) of adolescents. When parents discuss about their Aspiration with kids and encourage them to work towards their goals, they tend to work hard and improve their Academic performance, as was found in studies by Kumar & Lal (2014), Shute et al. (2009); Chowa et al. (2013); Ghysens (2009) and Fan et al. (1999). When parents' helped their children in completing their assignments and got involved in school activities, it was observed as a 'Significant' factor in improving 'Academic Achievement', which was in concurrence with studies done by Vijayalakshmi & Muniappan (2016); Shute Valerie J et al. (2009); Wang & Sheikh (2014). However, Bora & Ahmed (2008) in their study found that helping in homework and communication with school / teachers did not affect Academic performance of adolescents. Structuring by parents, that included parents keeping tab on internet / TV viewing at home and monitoring homework completion, was revealed as a positive contributor in improving 'Academic Achievement', as was found in previous studies by Vijayalakshmi & Muniappan (2016); Chowa et al. (2013) and Keith et al. (1993), while Fan et al. (1999) found that home supervision played lesser role in students' Achievement.

The positive findings of 'Parental Involvement' harmonise with widely held belief that it plays an important role not only in promoting their own child's Academic performance, but more broadly in closing existing gaps and shortcomings by assisting in improving performance.

Involvement with school & Studies was found to be a 'Non Significant' factor as also found in Bora & Ahmed (2008) and also in Chowa et al. (2013), where adolescents were observed to get stressed due to 'Parental Involvement' in school and regular interaction with teachers. However, it did not match with Desforges & Abouchaar (2003), who observed that helping in school work and participating in school activities influenced child's level of success. Emotional Involvement was found to be 'Non Significant', unlike in Ghysens (2009), Kumar & Lal (2014), Desforges & Abouchaar (2003) who found that a secure and emotionally stable atmosphere helped adolescents to build confidence and attain better 'Academic Achievement'. 'Parental Involvement' with friends was observed to be a 'Non Significant' parameter for improving the 'Academic Achievement' of adolescents.

Furthermore, it was established by the study that a happy home rears happy children. 'Parental Involvement' was found to positively link 'Behaviour Adjustment' of the adolescents, which resonated with the findings of Arulsubila & Subasree (2019), where positive Parenting was recommended to rear happy and confident children along with psychological wellbeing. Pengpid & Peltzer (2018) in their research had also identified 'Parental Involvement' to be effective in improving mental health, helping adolescents in learning how to cope with stress and increased perceived personal mastery and control, thereby improving mental health and Behaviour. The current study revealed emotional involvement and involvement with friends had positive impact on 'Behaviour Adjustment' of adolescents, while involvement in school & Studies, Structuring by Parents and Aspiration of Parents was not found to impact 'Behaviour Adjustment' in adolescents.

Emotional Involvement was found to be significantly linked to 'Behaviour Adjustment', as was in the study conducted by Sharma & Sandhu (2006) and Wang & Sheikh (2014). Parent-Child relationships affected adolescents' Behaviour (Sandha & Kaur, 2012) and when adolescents perceived their parents to be more understanding, they had lower probability of mental health problems (Abdirahman et al., 2012). Parental acceptance was found to help in wellbeing of adolescents, while it was seen to be negatively affected with Parental avoidance Bhatia (2012). The effect on mental wellbeing seems to get stronger with increasing levels of 'Parental Involvement' (Pengpid & Peltzer, 2018). Perceived 'Parental Involvement' and Parent–Adolescent conflict intervened in adolescent problem Behaviour (Dmitrieva et al, 2004). When adolescents experienced their parents as accepting and supportive, they were found less prone to depression (Bean et al, 2006). The present research study also revealed that when parents got involved with their children's friends, it positively affected 'Behaviour Adjustment' of adolescents as it strengthened their bond with parents. It also assured them that parents are interested in their life and approve of their friends and choices in general, which in turn motivated them to positively mould their Behaviour according to their parents' desire.

Aspiration as a parameter of 'Parental Involvement' was observed to be a 'Non Significant' factor impacting adolescents' 'Behaviour Adjustment', unlike the findings of Sharma & Sandhu (2006) who revealed that when parents emphasised 'Expected Behaviour' to their children, it was noted to be linked with low levels of Behavioural problems. When parents got involved in school activities and also in studies at home, it did not significantly impact adolescents' 'Behaviour Adjustment' but the researcher did not find any study which looked into this parameter as a construct of 'Parental Involvement' to rebut or confirm the result. Similarly, Structuring by Parents was also observed as a 'Non Significant' factor, unlike the results of Sharma & Sandhu (2006), where close monitoring was noted to be linked with low levels of Behavioural problems and Abdirahman et al. (2012) who found that when parents monitored free time activities of adolescents, they reported fewer mental health issues.

6.12.2 **Impact of 'Teacher's Involvement' on Adolescents**

Teacher-Student relationship has been established as a parameter to forecast problems and successes in a child's life by many researchers in their study. The present study also found evidence that linked 'Academic Achievement' of adolescents with Teacher's Involvement, which was consistent with many studies done earlier by Archambault et al. (2012); Kosir & Tement (2014); Gurganious (2017). Environment in class that supports effective teaching along with facilitating learning is bound to affect the Academic performance positively (Sharma, 2016). Kumar (2019) in his research established that poor Teacher-Student relationship had a noteworthy negative influence on students' performance in Maths. Fredriksen & Rhodes (2004) highlighted that Teacher-Student relationship facilitates learning and 'Academic Achievement' of students. Supportive teachers could motivate students to learn and perform well even in subjects they like the least. The current study observed Emotional Involvement of Teachers and Instrumental Support by Teachers to have positive impact on 'Academic Achievement' of adolescents, while Structure by Teachers and parents' interaction were 'Non Significant' factors for 'Academic Achievement'.

Level of perceived TI by adolescents was found to have no gender difference in the present research study as both boys and girls perceived it as 'Moderate' and at similar level. Boys and girls agreed on impact of TI on BA to be 'Moderate', which was in concurrence with the finding of Rajeswari & Eljo (2013), which also found no significant difference in gender with relation to school Adjustment. However, perception of boys and girls deviated for impact of TI on AA, where girls perceived to have greater impact than boys unlike by Konishi et al. (2010), where boys were observed to have better effect of Teacher-Student relationship on Academic performance as compared to girls. Response of adolescents and teachers did not converge except for impact of TI on AA, which was perceived as 'Moderate' by both. Teacher's were observed to rate TI and impact of TI on AA higher, than by adolescents. However, it was seen that parents were in concurrence in teachers for TI and its impact, as both perceived it to be quite 'High'.

Emotional Involvement by Teachers was found to be a 'Significant' factor in improving 'Academic Achievement' of adolescents. Teacher's Behaviour was found to be highly and positively 'Significant' to the 'Academic Achievement' of students Shah (2009). When teacher's involved children in classroom activities or gave personal attention to children, the students found themselves to connect better with teachers, which in turn helped them score better in academics. When teachers motivated children in class, they ought to work hard and perform well, Chetri (2014). Konishi et al. (2010) also resonated in their study that positive relationship existed between Teacher-Student connectedness and Academic performance. When students perceived higher level of teacher's acceptance and support, their academic level increased.(Kosir & Tement, 2014). Instrumental Support by Teachers was observed to have a positive relationship with 'Academic Achievement', as was also revealed by Shashidhar et al. (2009) who highlighted the importance of implementing newer strategies by teachers for better Achievement in academics. It was discovered that when teacher's used different motivational techniques for teaching, students were observed to be satisfied and connected better with their teachers. (Shah, 2009; Sharma, 2016; Gurganious, 2017).

Structure by Teachers was not found to be 'Significant' factor to impact 'Academic Achievement', unlike in the study by Shashidhar et al. (2009) who revealed that focusing on strict study patterns and creating conducive school environment is a positive parameter to achieve better scholastic performances. Shah (2009) had also established in his study that appreciation of teachers, when they 'performed well', and 'fair marking' were positive contributor to 'Academic Achievement' of students. Interaction with Parents was observed to be 'Non Significant' factor in affecting adolescents' 'Behaviour Adjustment' in the present research study. It was found that when teachers interacted with Parents about their child's progress or gave feedback about their results, there was no change observed in the Academic performance of adolescents.

Effective teacher's Involvement was observed to have a 'High' impact on the long term wellbeing of students, acting not only on their 'Academic Achievement' and how far they will study, but also their mental wellbeing and 'Behaviour Adjustment'. It is evident that classroom social Adjustment is influenced by Teacher-Student relationships (Pianta, 1999). The present study too found evidence of teacher's support and its' impact on students' wellbeing and Adjustment. Teachers were observed to have a multidimensional role in adolescents' life and to have higher potential of influencing emotional wellbeing and mental health of adolescents (Cattley, 2004; Fredriksen & Rhodes, 2004). Jayalekshmi et al. (2011) in her study detailed that when teachers listened to and assisted early adolescents in learning, they could provide them with critical skills that would not only prevent and reduce violence but also other Behaviour problems classified as internalising and externalising. Rajeswari & Eljo (2013) also reiterated in their study that teachers could enable adolescents to cope with their emotional challenges and develop adjustability, which would further lead to positive development and mental health. Vranda (2015) concluded in her study that teachers as an existing resource have capabilities to effectively deliver mental health promotion interventions in schools. Emotional Involvement and Interaction with Parents were noted as positive parameters to impact 'Behaviour Adjustment', while Instrumental Support and Structure by Teachers were found to have no 'Significant' impact on 'Behaviour Adjustment'.

Emotional Involvement was revealed as a positive parameter for 'Behaviour Adjustment' of adolescents, as was observed in Suldo et al. (2009) and Blazar & Kraft (2017). Jayalekshmi et al. (2011) had found that teachers who listened to problems of adolescents were able to help in reducing and preventing Behaviour problems. Furthermore, Khanna & Singh (2015) also concluded in their research that teachers helped in improving wellbeing of students through building confidence, explaining importance of education, giving them real world exposure and imparting value education. Gregory & Ripski (2008) had also concluded that association between adolescents' perceptions of their teachers as trustworthy authority positively affected their Behaviour. Wang, Brinkworth & Eccles (2013) reaffirmed that warmth and trust of teachers moderated the negative influences of adolescents' misconduct and helped at-risk adolescents in emotional and 'Behaviour Adjustment'. Interaction with Parents also was observed as positive indicator of 'Behaviour Adjustment' of adolescents. When teacher's observed and shared with parents about distress or misbehaviour of their child, it was found that children behaved better. With counselling from both sides, adolescents altered their Behaviour positively.

Instrumental Support was instituted as a 'Non Significant' factor to impact 'Behaviour Adjustment' of adolescents in The present research study, which was contradictory to Bharath & Kumar (2010), where learning methods involving games, role plays, debates and group discussion by teachers helped the adolescents to be better adjusted in classroom. Furthermore, Suldo et al. (2009) and Jayalekshmi et al. (2011) also found teaching subjects by more interesting methods and participatory activities to be effective in improving Behavioural performance along with academics. Structure by Teachers was also found to be a 'Non Significant' factor in impacting 'Behaviour Adjustment' of adolescents, contradictory to the findings of Blazar &

Kraft (2017) and Jayalekshmi et al. (2011), which emphasised self discipline to be valuable in improving Behavioural performance of adolescents.

6.13 Result of Descriptive Analysis

6.13.1 Analysis of Adolescents' Response

250 adolescents comprising of 160 boys and 90 girls were subjected to the questionnaire (Appx A) in which majority of the students had scores between 60-70%. Through a set of questions, adolescents were asked to rate mother, father, teachers and friends in terms of 'Closeness'. The result revealed that most of the adolescents (3.68%) were found to be close to their mothers, followed by their friends (27.6%). Most of the adolescents felt comfortable in sharing their personal problems with their friends, while they confided in their mothers if they scored less marks and sought help from teachers in Academic related problems. It was worth noting that most adolescents felt that they got the most appreciation for school performance from their fathers.

In the present study, 'Parental Involvement' (PI) was divided into following five constructs for better understanding :-

1. Emotional Involvement (helping in personal problems, counsels, etc.).
2. Aspiration (discussing about future goals, motivation to achieve them, etc).
3. Structure (keeping a tab on TV / internet usage, making timetable, etc.).
4. Schools & Studies (helping in assignments, keeping track of progress).
5. Involvement with friends (inviting friends, planning activities with them).

The analysis of the questionnaires (Appx A) collected from adolescents included 4-5 items related to each construct. Adolescents perception for Emotional Involvement, Structure by Parents, 'school & Studies Involvement' and 'Involvement with Friends' as construct of PI were perceived as 'Moderate', while 'Aspiration of Parents' was perceived to be 'High'. It can be inferred that while most of the constructs of PI were considered to be at average level, however Aspiration of Parents, which included discussion about future of adolescents and motivation to achieve these goals, were perceived to be more frequent. Adolescence is the age where children need to choose their stream of studies and make choice of their profession. However, there are lot of distractions in their life, peer pressure, attraction to opposite sex, gadgets, to name a few, making parents anxious and providing constant monitoring and motivation, thus resulting in adolescents' perception.

In the present study, 'Teacher's Involvement' (TI) was divided into following four constructs for better understanding :-

1. Emotional (trying to know likes and dislikes, solving their personal problems).
2. Interaction with Parents (PTM, updating Parents on important issues, etc.).
3. Instrumental (innovative teaching, use of aids, etc.).
4. Structure (deciding rules of the class, maintaining discipline, etc).

Teacher's Involvement as perceived by adolescents, were also measured through the questionnaire (Appx A). All constructs i.e. Emotional Involvement, Interaction with Parents, Instrumental and Structure by Teachers were perceived by adolescents to be as 'Moderate'. Teachers being an integral part of growing up of adolescents' life, have ability to guide and motivate students. It can be inferred that increase in syllabus, busy schedule, different teachers for different, less interaction of adolescents and teachers along with adolescents change in personality, resistance for rules and mood swings could be presumed reasons for adolescents' perception for teacher's Involvement.

6.13.2 **Analysis of Parents' Response**

40 parents, comprising of 20 mothers and 20 fathers, were subjected to the questionnaire (Appx B) which included similar questions as those asked to adolescents, worded differently, to understand their perception regarding their involvement and its impact towards 'Academic Achievement' and 'Behaviour Adjustment' of their adolescent child. It was observed that most of the parents felt that adolescents were close to their mothers more than to their fathers. They also agreed that their child was friendlier with his / her mother and also confided about his / her personal problems with her along with their friends. On the other hand, most parents thought that fathers were more involved in their child' academics at home and their child were fearful of his / her father.

PI constructs were same for parents too i.e. Emotional Involvement, Aspiration, school & Studies Involvement, Structure and Involvement with Friends. Emotional Involvement, Aspiration of Parents, school & Studies Involvement were perceived to be 'Moderate' while Structure was perceived to be 'High'. Adolescence is an age where children like to spend more time with friends and in current times digital platforms, social media and gadgets have taken a prominent place in their life. Parents might feel that their children are wasting lot of important time in all these distractions hence the need to Structure their time may have taken precedence over other aspects of involvement. Structuring by Parents include keeping tab of usage of T.V / internet, fixing time for studies, overseeing that they complete their assignments, etc. It can be inferred that as adolescence is a crucial phase for children with respect to their future plans, as also parents' concern for adolescents' time getting wasted, might have propelled them to increase Structure at home.

Parents rated 'Teacher's Involvement' (TI) and its impact on their children to be 'High' (Mean = 3.66). It can be inferred that parents seem to be content with the Teacher's Involvement in their child's life and the impact it had on the 'Academic Achievement' and 'Behaviour Adjustment'. Parents might have noticed improvement in performance and Behaviour of their child through teacher's motivation and guidance.

6.13.3 **Analysis of Teachers' Response**

40 teachers comprising of 28 female and 12 male teachers were subjected to the questionnaire (Appx C) which included similar questions as those asked to adolescents worded differently to understand their perception regarding their involvement and its impact towards 'Academic Achievement' and 'Behaviour Adjustment' of their adolescent students. Teacher's perception about traits of adolescents revealed that they perceived girls to be better performer in academics, more forthcoming in sharing their problems and also more talkative while boys were assessed to be more physically active and also restless & destructive in nature.

TI constructs were same for teachers too i.e. Emotional Involvement, Interaction with Parents, Instrumental and Structure. Teacher's perception for Interaction with Parents, Instrumental Support were perceived to be 'Moderate' while Emotional Involvement and Structure by Teachers were perceived to be 'High' by most of the teachers. While teachers might be pleased with their Instrumental Support and involvement with parents but they seem to be more content with emotional involvement and Structuring in class. As adolescence is an age of stress and emotional instability, teachers might be focussing more on connecting with the students at an emotional level. Hence the effort to make students comfortable in sharing personal problems with him/her and to improve happiness quotient through friendly gestures could be more. In addition, adolescents often become rowdy and do not want to follow any rules making it a priority of teachers to make children understand class rules, explain its importance and encourage them to follow these rules. It can be inferred that above reasons might have lead to higher perception for emotional involvement and Structuring by Teachers. PI and its impact were perceived to be low (Mean=2.48) by teachers. It can be inferred that teachers were not content with 'Parental Involvement' in school activities like attending PTM, personal interaction with teachers, help in homework and assignments, monitoring of grades.

6.14 Suggestions for Teachers and Parents

Teachers and parents are those adults who are an 'Integral' as also 'Imperative' part of adolescents' life. Being most frequent to interact, they have a natural opportunity to facilitate adolescents in all domains. They can provide guidance for handling problems and assist in 'Behaviour Adjustment' as per societal norms. They are equally capable of motivating adolescents for better Academic performance and cope with stress. With strong and supportive relationships with parents and teachers, adolescents feel safer and more secure, which facilitates them to develop positive connections with peers, achieve greater Academic progress, increase their happiness quotient and promote amicable behaviour. Conversely, conflict with parents and / or teachers may leave them susceptible to failures in coping academically and socially.

The current study recommends collaborative functioning between parents and teachers to achieve their common goal of facilitating adolescents in 'Academic Achievement' and 'Behaviour Adjustment', based on their appreciative understanding of the direct correlation between all activities, both at home and at school.

The findings also resonate with earlier studies where results suggested that collaboration with parents through 'Parent Intervention Programs' could ensure social competence and Academic excellence in early adolescents (Wentzel, 2002). Parents' and Educators' support could make a positive learning environment for betterment of the students (Jayalekshmi et al., 2011). Sanders (1998) in his study had established that with simultaneous support from all three sources i.e. Family, school and Community, the effect on their attitude about self and Academics increases manifolds. Similarly Hill and Craft (2003) in their study found that teachers observed improvement in children's school performance, with Parental dedication to education and increased 'Parental Involvement' at home and at school.

Adolescents' 'Behaviour Adjustment' and 'Academic Achievement' are affected by three key elements – the Adolescent, the Home and the school. While adolescents' and parents' resilience, preparedness and timely adaption to the environmental changes play a key role, the most 'Significant' influencing factor in school is the 'Teacher'. While a talented child from a caring home environment can, in solitary, go only so far, but with suitable Teacher's support 'Sky is the Limit'.

The current study revealed the following as per adolescents' perception :-

1. Constructs of 'Parental Involvement' that impacted 'Academic Achievement' were "Parents' Aspiration", 'Structure by Parents' and 'Involvement in school & Studies'.
2. Constructs of 'Behaviour Adjustment' were 'Emotional Involvement' and 'Involvement with Friends'.
3. Constructs of 'Teacher's Involvement' that adolescents found to positively impact academically were "Teacher's Emotional Involvement" and "Teacher's Instrumental Support".
4. 'Behaviour Adjustment' was observed to get impacted positively by 'Emotional Involvement' and 'Involvement with Parents'.

Keeping in mind the above observations, following are some specific suggestions for teachers :-

- Teachers need to divide their attention equally among students.
- Teacher need to try and get to know his / her students to create a rapport, which enables students to ask their doubts without any hitch.
- Teachers need to use innovative and interesting teaching techniques.
- Teachers need to create a stimulating environment and encourage students to ask questions.
- Teachers need to encourage & provide emotional support.
- Teachers need to counsel with reasoning when students falter.
- Teachers need to have regular interaction with parents.
- Teachers need to update parents on important issues or when they find any abnormality in Behaviour of students.

A teacher's impact is limited by the students 'Degree of Acceptance' as also by the home factors. This impact can however be alleviated through parents complementing the teachers by supporting the students at home. Following are some specific suggestions for parents :-

- ❖ Parents need to gauge child's aspirations and balance them with his / her existing capabilities or create an environment to develop required skills.
- ❖ In addition to child's aspirations, parents need to also discuss about own aspirations from child and motivate him/her in choosing better of the two.
- ❖ Parents need to help in making a timetable for their child to divide his / her time constructively between studies and other activities.
- ❖ Parents need to keep a tab on internet / TV usage of their child.
- ❖ Parents need to help and guide in school assignments and homework.
- ❖ Parents need to connect with teachers and follow their child's progress.
- ❖ Parents need to be available and forthcoming to share child's problems.
- ❖ Parents need to remain receptive to child's point of view.
- ❖ Counselling by parents need to be done patiently.
- ❖ Parents need to make efforts to know well their child's friends and create conducive environment for making themselves approachable.
- ❖ Parents need to plan activities with their child to identify and develop skills which interest him / her.

Parents often are conscious and unaware of their role in getting involved in their adolescent child's activities therefore the researcher recommends the school and teachers to encourage and guide parents so as to get maximum involvement from them at both home and school related activities. Furthermore, training for teachers is quintessential to understand psychological needs of adolescents, so as to facilitate them in handling students in an appropriate manner along with Parental support, with the aim of bringing out the best results for Adolescent students, both academically and behaviourally.

6.15 Recommendation for Further Studies

The research has been helpful in revealing unanswered questions pertaining to the impact of Parental and Teacher's Involvement but there is scope for further research. As observed, constructs that were found to have 'Significant' impact on 'Academic

Achievement' and 'Behaviour Adjustment' in the present study were not consistent to few other studies. Likely explanation for the differing conclusions may be due to diverse definitions, dimensions, constructs and measurements of Parental and Teacher's Involvement used in different studies. Parent and Teacher's Involvement are both very vast concepts, covering domains from Styles, Aspiration, Structure, Interactions, Attitudes and Ideals for various direct and indirect methods of involvement.

To comprehend the mechanism behind Parental and Teacher's Involvement to improve 'Academic Achievement' and 'Behaviour Adjustment', more research is called for testing the model formulated in the current study with population from different strata and cities of the country, to quantify and evaluate the underlying construct of Parental and Teacher's Involvement. At other level, "Parents' Education Level" might be considered as an intervening variable. "Gender Difference of Parents and Teachers" might also be studied with respect to their involvement and impact.

CPSIA information can be obtained
at www.ICGtesting.com
Printed in the USA
LVHW041121090223
739019LV00017B/1398

9 781805 459453